They Were
There on the
Western Front
1914–1918

They Were There on the Western Front 1914–1918

100 Eye Witnesses

Alan Weeks

The Book Guild Ltd

First published in Great Britain in 2017 by
The Book Guild Ltd
9 Priory Business Park
Wistow Road, Kibworth
Leicestershire, LE8 0RX
Freephone: 0800 999 2982
www.bookguild.co.uk
Email: info@bookguild.co.uk
Twitter: @bookguild

Typeset in Aldine 401 BT

Printed and bound in Great Britain by CPI Group (UK) Ltd, Croydon, CR0 4YY

ISBN 978 1912083 718

British Library Cataloguing in Publication Data.
A catalogue record for this book is available from the British Library.

To Pam – the love of my life

MAPS

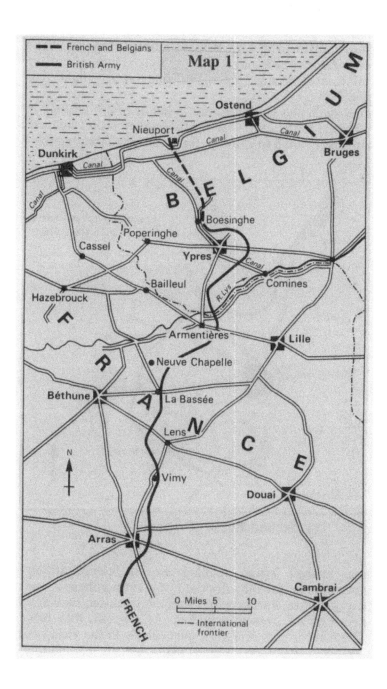

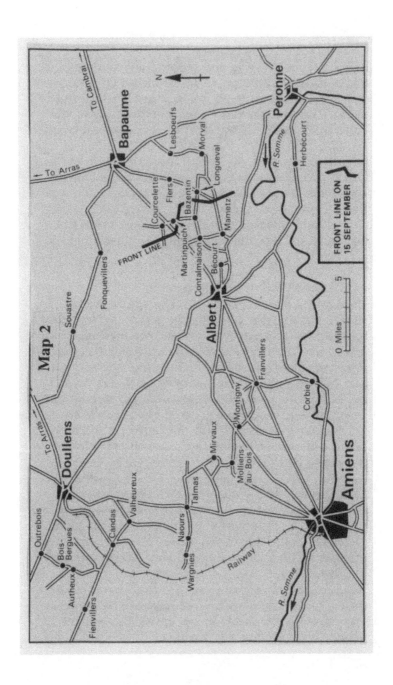

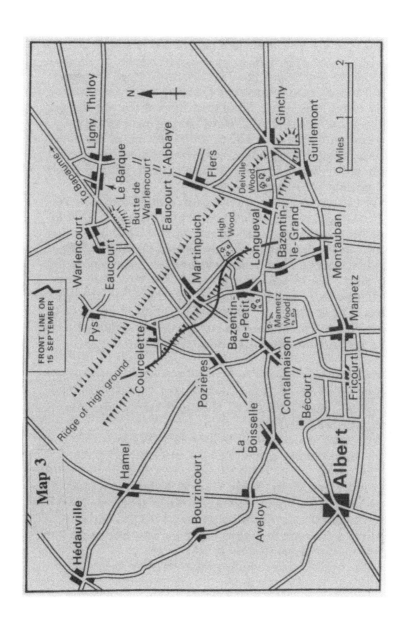

Map 3

FRONT LINE ON
15 SEPTEMBER

Ridge of high ground

N

0 Miles 1 2

Hédauville

Bouzincourt

Hamel

Aveloy

La
Boisselle

Albert

Bécourt

Contalmaison

Fricourt

Mametz

Mametz
Wood

Bazentin-
le-Petit

Poziéres

Courcelette

Pys

Warlencourt

Eaucourt

To Bapaume

Ligny Thilloy

Le Barque

Butte de
Warlencourt

Eaucourt L'Abbaye

Martinpuich

High
Wood

Bazentin-
le-Grand

Longueval

Montauban

Delville
Wood

Flers

Ginchy

Guillemont

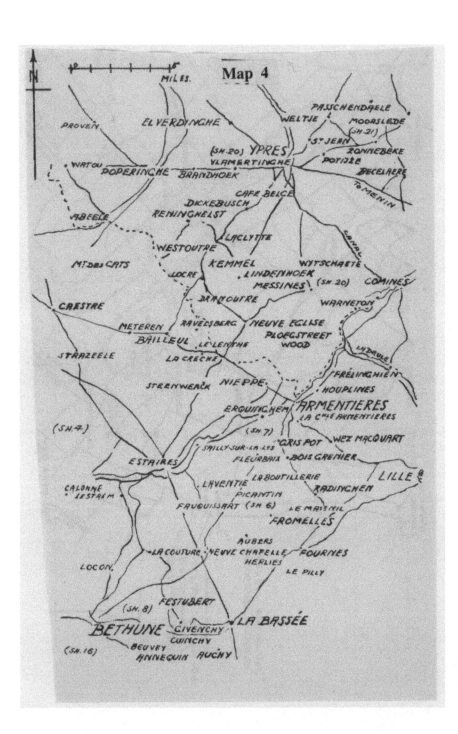

Map 4

INTRODUCTION

Why did they write diaries, memoirs and letters?

Captain Charlie May, a New Zealander in the Manchester Pals' Battalion, thought that his diary had become 'a tyrant that would ere long rule me, and I am reduced to impotence unable to refuse the call'.

Why was the urge to record his war experiences on the Western Front so compelling? Harry Drinkwater, of the Birmingham Pals, also felt this compulsion to scribble notes on scraps of paper in a half water-filled hole in the ground under the flickering light of a single candle.

'Here I am,' he recorded on May 24, 1916, 'back in my billet, writing like the dickens – 2 a.m.'. His sense of duty perhaps emanated from his Methodist upbringing. There must be a grain of truth in the idea that it was 'muscular Christianity' that sustained many of these men through very dark days, and induced a few of them to record them for posterity, although we must also remember Dr D. C. Dunn's contention that it was the good things that stuck in the memory longest.

Private Len Smith of the 7th City of London Battalion, wondered whether he would have a 'tomorrow' but 'today' he had a duty to maintain his diary. Even though he desperately needed sleep the writing had to come first. Why?

I think that each of these quite ordinary men reckoned that they were embroiled in an extraordinary historical event, and they had to record their part in it. 'This is the most colossal battle both in magnitude and importance that the world has ever known', wrote 2nd Lieutenant Walter Giffard. The Western Front was momentous in that it witnessed the first large-scale deployment of powerful weapons of destruction. These promptly halted any prospect of prolonged advance thus driving the adversaries into hundreds of miles of trench lines.

Charlie May found it all 'peculiar' – a seemingly never-ending war of attrition against an almost invisible enemy who might destroy or maim him or his comrades at any second.

Such men had been suddenly thrust from an Edwardian peace into this cauldron of fire. The impact it wrought stayed with these participants: many who did not write during the war later felt impelled to do so afterwards as perhaps the fear of forgetting overwhelmed them. Charles Gibbs of the Sussex Regiment set down his account in the 1930s. 'As I write of these far-away events I wonder whether they happened in another existence. I can't really believe they happened to me'.

My own father thought about the Western Front in 1917 and 1918 (and Germany in 1919) for the rest of his life, to the extent that he decided to write down what he could remember of the war when he was more than 70 years of age, 50 years after the war ended. To the men who had fought in France and Flanders this was the most significant event of their lives. They would never forget it (nor forget their comrades who lost their lives in it).

Very few diarists or composers of memoirs were professional writers. They had no idea that anyone would want to publish their accounts: they wrote for family and friends. Some were insistent that it was for their grandchildren so that later generations would understand what these soldiers endured.

In this way at least three generations would know of the personal details.

This was the case with 'Dick' Read of the Leicestershire Regiment. On the first page of his book 'A Narrative 1914-1919' remembered and illustrated by I. L. Read... for my grandchildren.' Cecil Slack of the East Yorkshire Regiment dedicated his memoir to his children and grandchildren. These later generations generally appreciated the privilege of such first-hand accounts. Cecil's family added explanatory notes for the book of his memories.

Other reasons for writing are also evident: Matthew Cooper claimed it was simply for his own 'amusement' – just to have a detailed record of the amazing things that happened to him. He thus kept the diary a close secret and his family only found it 70 years later. Alexander Stewart also referred to 'his own amusement'. Perhaps this does not do justice to a soldier who was prepared to keep his diary up-to-date in a shell hole in no man's land in the hell-hole that was High Wood on the Somme (July 29, 1916)? He did add that his record was also for his family – who later published it.

Robert Graves made the surprising claim that he wrote 'Goodbye to all that' in order to forget about the war – lay it to rest (he had a rough time in the front line). But on his own admission he failed to forget. Edmund Blunder knew he would never forget.

The publication of a memoir must often have convinced other veterans that they should write down their own account, in some cases with a view to publication. My dad, George, left his memories in a box file (written immaculately on pieces of cut-up wallpaper). On top of this was a 1930 copy of 'War is War' written by Ex-Private X (who was in fact Alfred McLelland Burrage). George had come across this in a book sale and obviously thought to himself, "Well, I was there in 1917 and 1918 so why can't I write about it, as well?" He did not do it to get a published book. He might have intended his children to find it. He certainly would have been highly delighted to find himself in print ('Dangerous Work: The Memoir of Private George Weeks of the Labour Corps 1917 – 1919', The History Press, 2014).

A few soldiers wrote home to family or friends on most days, and published collections of these featuring many hundreds of letters – notably those from Edward Hernon, who sent around 600 letters to his wife before his death in 1917. Other prolific letter-writers were William Whittaker, Aubrey Smith, Rowland Feilding, Pat Leonard, Paul Jones and Graham Greenwell.

Diarists

To attempt to keep up a daily diary was extremely difficult for soldiers on the Western Front, particularly in the case of other ranks. Officers in the trenches could usually count on a few hours of relative safety and shelter in dug-outs. Yet even they, including senior officers such as James Jack, were often thwarted by calls of duty or physical privations such as bad weather, wounds and sickness (John Glubb is another good example of this). Both Harry Drinkwater and Len Smith mentioned frozen fingers as a reason for missing entries.

There are some short-lived daily diaries which are almost complete. Elmer Sherwood an American gunner, had a complete daily diary from February 21, 1918 till the end of the war (and beyond) The diary of the Unknown Soldier 2 lasts only a few weeks but some days had to be missed out. Lieutenant Jack Giffard had an entry for every day between August 16 and September 17, 1914, when he arrived back in England badly wounded. His brother, Eddie, wrote almost daily for 3 years apart from times when he was on leave. However, the great bulk of these entries were only between 1 and 6 lines in length and in short note form.

Captain F. C. Hitchcock was another daily diarist between 1916 and 1918 but had two long spells away from the Western Front. When he was there he did write every single day except for three occasions when he coupled two days together and in October 1918 when he blocked together large chunks of that month.

Periods of comparative rest in camps or billets usually provided more opportunities for all to maintain a daily record or to catch up on missed days (sometimes grouped together). Signallers, stretcher-bearers, sappers and gunners on the whole had more opportunities to write in comfort.

Every diary has a story, a history of its own. Some started out as scribbled notes on pieces of paper whilst in the front line. Harry Drinkwater and Len Smith always carried around scraps of paper in their tunic pockets. James Jack composed cryptic notes in a tiny notebook: only he knew what they meant – perhaps in view of the fact that diaries were forbidden by the Army in case they fell into enemy hands Every now and again he sent his diary home with a trusted friend for safekeeping (so did Major Ralph Hamilton, RHA). A senior officer found breaking regulations would be in serious trouble. Captain Hitchcock also used a notebook. Dr J. C. Dunn wrote in cryptic form. Billie Nevill used a code consisting of series of dots, and also other devices. For instance, 'Albert' was 'one of Mrs. Bull's sons. Not Fred.'

Jim Maultshead had a small black notebook and sketch pads. When he was wounded on the first day of the Somme his platoon officer, Lieutenant Monach, went searching for these in Martinsart and found them in a rucksack, much to Jim's delight.

But perhaps the most remarkable 'diary' is that of Patrick MacGill, who had established himself as a very popular author before the war. His was a 'super diary' – a full-blown account of the Battle of Loos whilst he was still fighting it. This book stands out as a unique achievement: writing in a fine literary style whilst in trenches and billets beggars belief.

When the diarist had more time to himself, say, at stand-down at dusk, back in camp or billet or in hospital, the notes could be written up more fully perhaps with additional material. Harry Drinkwater actually found time to do this in a mine tunnel in the gaps of a few minutes between filling up sandbags (Arras, 1916). Stretcher-bearers like Frank Dunham and signallers such as Walter Williamson had a little more time to themselves. Norman Tennant, a gunner, was often in forward observation posts, with time to write as well as to watch between shifts.

If they survived the war many diarists were keen to improve and perhaps augment their diaries with extra material – review and embellishment. A few wanted to put it all in an impressive book, perhaps a lovingly-crafted artefact. The one produced by Harry Drinkwater was leather-bound with an embossed cover title – 'War Diary'.

Len Smith's book was also bound in leather and entitled 'My War Diary of the Great Adventure'. Actually he did not change his original account much because he wanted it to 'ring true', to be in words written soon after the heat of battle. It is thus a rather rambling narrative yet fascinating and vivid.

John Jackson wrote up his daily diary in 1926 in a beautifully handwritten document. His niece, in much later years, copied it on to a computer, and with the support of Professor Huw Strachan it became a published book – 'Private 12768'.

Lieutenant John Glubb kept an almost daily diary except when he was wounded. This diary rested in a drawer for more than 60 years and he almost forgot about it. When he retrieved it the pencilled script was very faded but he painstakingly re-wrote it word for word, adding explanatory notes.

It is possible that some would-be diarists did not write or stopped writing in fear of the consequences of breaking Army regulations. There are some cases where diarist and censoring officers clashed: Jack Martin was frequently at loggerheads with his C.O. over his writing. After the war he kept it a secret and his grandson, to his complete surprise, found it over 80 years later.

Charlie May's diary, consisting of seven wallet-sized pocket books, was discovered about 1980 in a suitcase in an attic. His great nephew edited a published book – but not until 2015. Charlie was killed during the war.

Also in an attic for more than 50 years lay Lieutenant Jack Giffard's diary – but not his original one. He had brought it home from France when he was wounded in the first month of the war. His sister, Maud, copied the diary and it was this version which was preserved, along with Eddie Giffard's diary.

Another great nephew, David Mason, found Len Smith's fabulous book hidden away in a box. Len had failed to get it published in the 1970s. Charles Meeres's son, Frank, got his father's work published in 2013. The spate of published diaries and memoirs which emerged at this time had much to do with the advent of the centenary of the Great War.

John Lucy destroyed his diary on purpose on November 1, 1914 after the disasters of Mons and Le Cateau and the loss of so many Regular Army pals. He was later able to recover some lost information because as Battalion clerk (1915) he was able to collect together earlier Battalion messages.

Private John Brough (Royal Marine Light Infantry) lost the diary he kept from 1914 to October 1917, when he was taken prisoner at Passchendaele. The diary which his son found in the Royal Marine Museum in Southsea covers John's period of captivity until April 1918 when he stopped writing.

Other diaries, such as Edie Appleton's, have whole sections missing for some unknown reason. Part of Billy Congreve's diary was lost in a fire. Elmer Sherwood lost his first diary (April 1917 to February 1918).

Many diarists did not aspire to a daily record but were content to write something possibly every few days, perhaps with some days grouped together under one heading. Norman Gladden wrote every few days. Neil Weir wrote periodic reviews, possibly while he was in hospital in 1916, with some specific dates. If there was some delay in writing, although the war was still on, it was really a memoir rather than a diary – for example, Bernard Adams in 1917. There might be dates but no attempt to claim that it was a diary (they might have actually written one). Bruce Bairnsfather's 'Bullets and Billets' was published in 1916 but in no way was this was a diary.

A few hitherto prolific diarists suddenly stopped writing, notably Billy Congreve, Henry Clapham and Edwin Vaughan. In Congreve's case this was possibly due to his promotion to staff officer: he was probably too busy, and a staff officer breaking regulations was an unwise situation.

Some diarists only referred to them in later memoirs, such as John Reith, Stuart Dolden and George Coppard. Other diaries may have existed but were not mentioned later. Sydney Rogerson wrote his memoir '12 Days on the Somme' in 1933 but although it was crammed with detail there is no indication of a diary. Perhaps there is a clue in W.H.A. Groom's mention of 'my original notes' (rather than a full diary). However, in Chapter 8 he actually copied out diary entries for August 13–17, 1917.

What distinguishes the diaries (and memoirs) in this book is that they have been published. When the current work on the many thousands which have not been published progresses this will throw even more light on the history of these written records.

Letters

Soldiers writing many letters faced the attentions of censors – their own officers and more senior ones at HQ. Because of that, place names were commonly omitted. William Whittaker tried using a code but he found this too risky. Pat Leonard tried code at times – 'Blank to Dash' meant the Menin Road. Aubrey Smith added place names to his 'Four Years on the Western Front', published in 1922, as these were not allowed in his letters, and so did Rowland Feilding.

When these collections were edited into a published book the family to whom the letters had been bequeathed usually took this initiative – for instance, Harry Jones for his son Paul in 1918 (Paul was killed in 1917) and for William Whittaker and Pat Leonard in 2014, possibly prompted by the onset of the Great War centenary. Graham Greenwell edited his own selection of his letters to his mother in 1935. In several letters he referred to the constant difficulty of finding enough paper on which to write so much (many diarists had the same complaint). Graham often had to use official message or telegraph forms.

Edward Hernon's grand daughter, Anne Nason, published his 600-odd letters in 2009. Extracts from the letters of Harry Blackburne (a padre like Pat Leonard) were substantiated with explanatory information, but it was divided into years rather than days.

Hugh Quigley's 'Passchendaele and the Somme', published in 1928, is something of a puzzle. He wrote the entries with date and place and sent them home. Some of them appear to be addressed to an unknown specific person but he obviously intended to use them later as the basis of a book.

As with diaries many thousands of letters await transcription at the Imperial War Museum.

Memoirs

Memoirs basically differ from diaries in that they were written a considerable time after the events they cover (although many are based on diaries, perhaps very full ones like those of Stuart Dolden and Thomas Floyd, and the letters of the latter's, too). In the case of a war this would normally mean that the account was written after it had ended, but some Great War memoirs were composed before the end of 1918 – Bernard Adams, Bruce Bairnsfather – and also Robert Graves, who started on 'Goodbye to all That' in 1916. W. H. L. Watson published his 'Adventures of a Despatch Rider' in 1915, based on his letters sent home. Charles Arnold composed a memoir for his wife during 1918.

C. E. M. Joad published the first edition of 'Diary of a Dead Officer' (the papers of Arthur Graeme West) in 1918–1919.

The work continued just after the Armistice – Matthew Cooper used a 1917 diary to write his memoir, and William Cull produced 'At all Costs' in 1919. He had been a prisoner of war and he was writing at a time when there were ongoing enquiries about the treatment of prisoners. Of the '100' accounts in this book 8 were published before the end of 1920.

George Ashurst developed his memoir in the 1920s from some form of diary, and Edward Lynch was busy with his pencil and exercise books (20 of them) setting out the experiences later to feature in the book 'Somme Mud'. Arthur Behrend produced 'Nine Days' in 1921, from a file of gunnery messages of March 1918. The account developed by Alexander Stewart in 1927 and 1928 was based on brief war diaries. However, memory was now playing a dominant part in the reconstructions, clearly the case with Alfred Burrage's 'War is War' (published 1930) and Edmund Blunden's book (1924), and even more so with Charles Durie's 'The Weary Road' (1929). Of the '100' in this book 8 were published in the 1920s.

John Reith and Sydey Rogerson published in the early 1930s, along with Stormont Gibbs and Dick Richards. Ernest Parker also wrote 'Into Battle' at this time but did not publish until 30 years later – strange because he actually worked in a publishing house. John Lucy wrote his memoir in 1936. Of the '100' in this book 10 were published in the 1930s.

The Great War as a topic for books naturally faded in the 1940s and 1950s, although Henry Ogle did write in this period. Richard Talbot Kelly put together his memoir around 1950, based on his diary and letters and Arthur Behrend composed 'As From Kemmel Hill', elaborating on his earlier 'Nine Days'. Stronger interest in Great War memoirs surfaced again in the late 1960s and in the 1970s (14 publications of the '100' in this book).

Horton published 'Stretcher Bearer' in 1970, about the time Arthur Sambrook was assembling his memories for his father to elaborate into a published book, and my father was filling up his pieces of wallpaper. P. J. Campbell was writing about the same time, Frederick Hodges in the 1990s. Of the '100' in this book 18 were published in the 1980s and 1990s – 42 of them in this century.

Some memoirs have been produced after recorded interviews with historians (notably Richard Van Emden for Ben Clouting, Norman Collins and Harry Patch), family members or friends.

'The War the Infantry Knew' was compiled anonymously by Dr J. C. Dunn in 1938 and is possibly unique in being a Battalion memoir, not to be confused with official Battalion or other accounts. He used his diary and letters but also invited in contributions from others who had served with the 2nd Battalion of the Royal Welch Regiment.

Forgetting

A basic problem with memoirs is the failure of memory over time. Many of these writers admit freely to the possibility that their chronology of events could be inaccurate. My father, for instance, put down the year of the formation of the Labour Corps as 1918 when the correct year for this was 1917. Research of records shows up factual mistakes: Dad had the number of his Labour Company completely wrong because the one he recorded was actually a Chinese Labour Company! Yet his recall of place names and some precise dates is remarkable when you consider that he was trying to think back over 50 years (as far as I know he had nothing written down).

Even men who had maintained some sort of diary during the war had trouble with place names and dates. Perhaps they thought that the narrative was of prime importance and that precise names and dates were secondary to the tale they had to tell. Cecil Slack's memoir has a marked absence of when and where. Even his 'Postwar notes' did not have many although for 1918 he did make use of his diary to include many place names and dates. George Ashurst kept a diary and wrote his memoir in the 1920s yet he also had few place names and dates. As Henry Ogle observed putting dates and places together was very difficult, and July 13, 1915 was 'one of my very few dates combined with place'. More than one soldier pointed out that no gave the poor bloody infantry maps and there were no sign posts (Ginger Byrne, for instance). In direct contrast, Major Ralph Hamilton had a heading for each day stating where he was.

Anthony French has few place names and just one date but this narrative is such a brilliant piece of writing it hardly seems to matter.

Sometimes the names of comrades and others are forgotten, and fictional names are used. In other records made-up names are used for no stated reason. Alfred McLelland Burrage claimed that he used made-up names in order not to court personal controversy.

There were periods of which memoir writers could remember almost nothing. Charles Gibbs arrived on the Somme in August 1916 and yet September is a complete blank. He remembered being promoted to Adjutant but then recall utterly fails him (perhaps he was too busy?). He can only pick up his story in the Spring of 1917.

Richard Talbot Kelly kept a diary of 1915 to 1917 yet the very brief entries at the end of 1916 and the beginning of 1917 were but 'faint ghosts' in his mind. Even daily diarists such as John Jackson (who called his book a 'memoir') had trouble with dates and places – the same for Charles Meeres.

William Cull said that his problems with memory were exacerbated by his wounds and poor treatment whilst he was a prisoner of war. Charles Durie and Dr Dunn thought that men easily forgot painful memories, especially when close pals were lost (some actions do not feature prominently in historical accounts but still resulted in terrible casualty rates).

Richard Talbot Kelly has interesting comments on how memory 'plays tricks'. Some long-ago events could be recalled as though they had happened yesterday: but other memories were vague, 'as if in a dream'. When you can remember it is either as if you were a character in a story: more rarely it is real as though these things were occurring again. Sights, sounds or even smells can suddenly trigger vivid recall. Working with sandbags in 1939 Richard was back in a trench at Festubert in June, 1915.

'To this day if I hear the sounds of footsteps on wooden boards or a plank bridge I see the awful landscape of Courcelette' (Henry Ogle). 'Haunting memories come unbidden' into Frederick Hodges's mind as he put the kettle on 70 years after the war.

Editing

The editing of Frederick Kelly's 'War Diary' (a thick, leather-bound volume, plus seven pocket books) was unusual in that this work was rather savagely cut down by his erstwhile comrade, Brigadier – General Arthur Asquith (son of the Prime Minister). He thought the diary was far too long for publication and also that it contained too many criticisms of people with whom Kelly served. Rarely could the narrative of a memoir be sustained by an editor's research: the best example of this was Richard Devonald- Lewis's work on the memoir of Charles Gibbs.

Much more commonly editors tried faithfully to preserve what had been written. However, as in Kelly's case, sometimes the text was too long for publication and had to be reduced – the case with James Jack (cut down a third by John Terraine) and Edie Appleton (who had written about a quarter of a million words). The correcting of factual and chronological errors has been a major task for editors. This often entailed research into official records and other sources. Richard Holmes, in introducing George Ashurst's account, observed that all memoirs were prone to such mistakes, usually the result of forgetting. The researcher will often be a professional historian, like Holmes, Terraine and Saul David (for Neil Weir) but sometimes an ordinary family member (such as William Carr's daughter) or friend.

Research also often produces substantiation or extension for the original accounts, such as Richard Devonald Lewis for Charles Gibbs, Gerry Harrison (his grandnephew) for Charlie May and James Sambrook for his father. Introductions are usually added. Aaron Pegram not only did this for William Cull but also wrote an 'endnote' and epilogue. Explanatory historical notes are commonly added – Richard Van Emden for Ben Clouting, R. H. Haigh and P. W. Turner for Frank Dunham, R. G. Loosman for Richard Talbot Kelly and Saul David for Neil Weir.

Letter collections usually consist of simple selections from large numbers of letters but Ruth Elwin Harris's book on the letters of Billie and Amy Nevill had her own narrative around selected letters or sections of them. There is often inter-connecting material written by the editor to link letters, notably in the case of Peter Vansittart for John Masefield's letters from the front.

Writing Skills

The Education Act of 1870 provided elementary education for all. By 1914 soldiers were potentially able to write. But it was far from being a universal skill: Walter Williamson was probably placed on a signalling course because he could write his name and address quickly and clearly. The Army field postcards ('quick firers') were useful to many soldiers because they simply had to cross out words in order to let their loved ones know how they were faring. Yet many thousands of them were writing long letters home.

My father left school at 13 yet his grammar, vocabulary, spelling and handwriting were good (something had gone wrong with his punctuation!). The Unknown Soldier 1 (from Bermondsey) was equally adept. These were ordinary East End kids.

Some elementary schoolchildren did go into quite skilled jobs. Horace Bruckshaw became a draughtsman. His war diaries consisted of two bound books with 474 pages in feint rule completed in a clear, flowing hand. Although some of the entries were in note form e.g.

'Morning broke fine but stiff breeze', he could break out into finely detailed descriptions of events and environments.

Just over two fifths of these men had received only an elementary education. A further fifth had gone to secondary school (including Edie Appeton, the only woman in the 100). Another fifth had been to university and 15% to public schools (some University men had also attended public school). Harry Drinkwater studied at Stratford-on-Avon Grammar School but described himself as 'an amateur pen', in itself a phrase of some sophistication. He continued – 'can faithfully portray the conditions we were in…

Robert Graves, Edmund Blunden, John Masefield, Siegfried Sassoon and Patrick MacGill were very well-known and popular authors (Arthur Graeme West was less-well known). Frederick Kelly was a composer and concert pianist (and an Olympic champion). Mark Plowman was a poet and journalist and Alfred Burrage wrote short stories for magazines and periodicals. Hugh Quigley sent home highly prose-poetic entries (diary letters?) and concluded his book with a moving poem – 'A Death in Hospital'. Indeed, the work of some non-professional authors, such as Bernard Adams, Anthony French and Henry Clapham, compares very well with these more famous writers.

Writing Style

The vast majority of war authors were Kitchener New Army men; their language was not military. There were traces of this in the diaries of some pre-war soldiers, such as James Jack. He would use words like 'commence' rather than 'begin' and 'assist' rather than 'help'.

Charlie May was a typical New Army author – enthusiastic, jolly, full of humour, encapsulating a great flow of detail about the men with whom he served, events and environments – beautiful and ugly. He believed that a good diary should offer a wide range of information as well as an account of personal experience. William Whittaker's letters included philosophy, ethics and politics, along with simpler subjects such as food, drink and entertainment.

Edward Lynch's style is straightforward, honest, it 'put you in the Somme trenches' reckoned one commentator. Another, referring to the writing of another Australian, W. H. Downing, described his account as 'the true picture – the monument we still want for our rich dead'. Both Lynch and Downing, can also be extremely amusing. The latter's 'A Shot on the Wrong Target' was about the theft of the Brigadier's Mercedes car from outside his HQ.

Experts at the Imperial War Museum referred to George Coppard's 'emotional intensity'. Jack Martin left school at 14 yet his diary style was often elegant, often funny. After leaving school Jack taught himself law and accountancy.

When the soldier was very busy fighting and working there would be times when to get some of sort of account down he had to be content with a brief note, like the one shown above for Horace Bruckshaw.

It is thus quite incredible that Patrick MacGill wrote a book ('The Great Push') whilst enduring the ravages of the Battle of Loos.

Charles Arnold's 'The Story of My Life' was composed completely of a series of short sentences. Richard Talbot Kelly wrote on May 22, 1917 – 'Spent day at Rest Camp. Sports and footer', and on May 23 – 'Tophole day. Tea at Boulogne at Prè Catalan. V. Good concert. Passed out fit'.

Jack Giffard's very short diary (August–September 1914) was mostly written in short note form – 'August 16 Arrived S'hampton 10 a.m. with left half battery' His brother, Eddie, also wrote like that for 3 years.

But some memoirs spent many pages on general topics, for instance, Bernard Adams wrote at length on 'working parties', 'sniping' and 'wounded', William Cull on 'Psychology of Battle' and 'Men and Episodes'. Similarly, Walter Downing had sections on 'Some Characteristics', which was about the nature of the Australian infantryman. Frederick Hodges commented on British politics and the general war situation as well as specific topics such as 'a guide to the Brigadier General'. John Masefield, reporting on American voluntary medical aid, and later the Battle of the Somme, included views on the general war situation in his letters to his wife.

There was also the slightly ironic, whimsical British humour epitomised in 'The Wipers Times'. Bruce Bairnsfather wrote in this fashion and so did Dr J. C. Dunn, and also Len Smith. This is a striking illustration of the resilience and courage of these brave soldiers. Walter Giffard, the kite balloonist, also provided many a laugh: a mouse fell out of the rigging at 4,000 feet and Walter failed to catch it and give it a parachute

Letters obviously contained more personal details – references to family and friends, although Aubrey Smith dealt strictly with his war experience. The soldiers were careful to play down the dangers which they faced, not wishing to alarm their loved ones. However, as the Western Front became more and more of a desperate struggle the tone of many letters did slowly reflect growing weariness, especially for officers worn down by their never-ending responsibilities. In Edward Hernon's earlier letters he used words like 'merry' and 'laughing' but later succumbed to the strains of leadership. The missives from Norman Collins became less cheerful and much shorter, perhaps as he heard the cries of dying men in no man's land. However, in the case of Rowland Feilding, his wife expressively asked him not to spare her the ghastly details.

Captain Lancelot Spicer had a whimsical way of broaching the topic with his wife. 'You probably pictured me hurrying up the road with a large fat Hun with a very long bayonet pursuing me'. In 1935 Graham Greenwell published his selection of letters to his mother at a time when disillusionment with the Great War was rife (Lloyd George had just written his rather gloomy 'War Memoirs'). Some critics thus objected to Captain Greenwell's 'cheerfulness' in many of his missives but as you can see from my account of his book there were numerous occasions when he revealed how depressed and anxious he was. I think it was unfair to accuse him of trying to hide the horrors of the trenches from his mother.

When 'Billie The Nevill Letters 1914–1916' was published in 1991 no one objected to his constant professions of happiness and safety. Times had changed.

Some accounts are generally under-stated, almost dispassionate, a reflection of the resilience of the Tommy in the face of extreme danger and fear. This tone is apparent in the diary of the Unknown Soldier 1 fighting valiantly in the Ypres Salient in April 1917. Frank Dunham also writes somewhat flatly when you consider the perils of trying to pick up wounded men in the heat of battle.

Some diaries and memoirs are written with intense detail, almost blow-by-blow accounts, leading to entries many pages in length – anything up to 20 pages on a single day. The largely military account by Major Ralph Hamilton (1914–1918) runs to many hundreds of pages.

Where the material is on a particular aspect of army life it can represent some of the best history of that aspect – for instance, Stuart Dolden on cooks and cooking.

Edwin Vaughan had something to write about everything and everybody. Battling in front of Passchendaele on August 25, 1917 he set down this experience yard by yard. It was his very last entry in a diary which stopped abruptly. His last sentence was 'I gazed into a black and empty future'. Yet by the end of the war he had won the Military Cross and had attained the rank of Captain.

Walter Williamson wrote several pages on many days, reflecting his many interests, especially music and the theatre. The officer who had to read all this complained but Walter pointed out that there was no regulation restricting the length of letters. Thomas Floyd, in a cauldron of fire at Ypres, still showed interest in British politics and the general situation of the Great War. Indeed, his C.O. called him 'General'. Lancelot Dykes Spicer was especially concerned with British politics and the general war situation because his father (Sir A. Spicer) was an M.P.

Frank Dunham's diary could be so detailed that it read rather like an early 20th century Facebook.

He was able to include the name of every camp and village where he was. The editors producing the book on his account omitted some entries to 'avoid the very sameness and monotony of trench warfare'.

Sapper Jack Martin filled up 12 books of profuse observations: Len Smith penned volumes in order to 'ring true'. There are some good descriptions of the shattered environments of France and Flanders, for instance, the depiction of the Somme battlefields in the Spring of 1917 (the Germans were retiring to the Hindenburg Line) by P. J. Campbell and by George Weeks. Bruce Bairnsfather's account of the Christmas 'Truce' of 1914 in his sector is one of the best on this topic.

Wilfrid Ewart's rather eccentric memoir has remarkable and almost poetic descriptions of environments – the innumerable sights and sounds of a working party out in no man's land, Paris during the war etc.

The recording of actual dialogue is feasible if written down within a few days of taking part in it, as in the case of Patrick MacGill. His recorded conversations sound so authentic the reader can possibly picture the men doing the talking.

Remembering dialogue for a memoir is obviously more difficult but Bernard Adams was writing while the war was still in progress (he was able to put down the actual words he used in advising snipers and recalling conversations with officers; servants). Edward Lynch wrote in 1921, Aubrey Smith in 1922. Of course, if the dialogue was significant enough it would stick in the memory for many years. When an officer was telling my Dad to get his hair cut in March, 1917 he said, "Get that busby seen to!"

Two WACs confronted R. A. Lloyd in Aux-le-Chateau as he was collecting fruit. "Garn," one said, "give us a bite!" in the tones of the Mile End Road.

"What the hell were those flappers doing out here?" wondered one of Lloyd's pals.

George Ashurst said to an officer in February 1917, "I have done my whack of war and if you consider this is mutiny – your revolver is handy…"

Giles Eyre of the KRRC, writing 21 years after the Battle of the Somme, had pages of precise conversations. He obviously remembered the gist of these exchanges and made up the rest. P. J. Campbell included much dialogue in his memoirs, which were written 60 years after the war. It is as though he is referring to a diary. When William Cull's daughter was interviewing him in the 1980s he could recall what he said 70 years before. But Henry Clapham was able to refer to a diary written within days of particular conversations.

A few writers were able to include maps and diagrams illustrating their involvement in and behind the front lines, such as Ralph Hamilton and John Glubb (both gunners) and Bernard Adams (who professed to be very poor in military matters but obviously very quickly learnt his trade). J. C. Dunn (a medical officer!) has 27 sheets of detailed maps to show the whereabouts of his Battalion over 5 years of war.

Captain Hitchcock has very clear and detailed sketch maps of front line landscapes and other military illustrations.

Artists at Work

A handful of diarists and memoir authors were also gifted artists. Len Smith and Jim Maultshead have the most colourful of these publications, both books crammed with hundreds and hundreds of appealing and amusing illustrations. Len was eventually employed by the Army to illustrate the front line. Jim's work was cut short on the first day of the Somme but he returned in 1917 – to the Chinese Labour Corps.

Richard Talbot Kelly also painted official panoramas – shown in his book along with many of his sketches. Paul Maze, a French post-impressionist painter, worked for the British Army throughout the war sketching front lines, as well as working with Generals such as Gough obtaining and passing on information about the front line situations in all the major battles. After the war he became one of France's most famous artists.

Dick Read's book had a delightful and evocative collection of line and wash sketches to illustrate the people and places he saw, especially behind the front line.

Norman Tennant was persuaded by his pals to start writing a diary in 1916 to accompany his constant drawing. Arthur Sambrook included sketches in his 1970s memoir (later used by his son in a book). Charles Meers has very talented sketches and paintings in his book.

Henry Buckle's 'A Tommy's Sketchbook' has numerous water colour paintings of the time he served in 1915, including a vivid record of the Sailly-au-Bois neighbourhood.

Bruce Bairnsfather was probably the most famous war artist of the Western Front. His 1916 publication 'Bullets and Billets' contains many of his brilliant, whimsical cartoons – such as 'Where did that one go?'

They Were There on the Western Front 1914–1918

100 Eye Witnesses

ADAMS, BERNARD (1890–1917)
Nothing of Importance
A Record of Eight Months at the front-line
October, 1915–June, 1916
The Strong Oak Press with Tom Donovan Publishing, 1988

The book was first published in 1917. This edition represents the complete original text but there is a new introduction and added notes. Bernard (or 'Bill' as fellow officers called him) was wounded in the arm in June 1916 and wrote this account whilst convalescing in England. He died in March 1917.

He served as a Lieutenant in the 1st Battalion of the Royal Welch Fusiliers – along with two famous writers, Siegfried Sassoon and Robert Graves. What marks out his story is the intense detail of trench and billet existence by a highly literate writer (he was educated at Cambridge University). The period described is relatively brief but the text is long. He would tell a Tommy with freezing feet to stamp them, knowing full well that he would stop as soon as his officer was out of sight. There was banter with equally unhappy German sentries.

The expansive text allowed for separate chapters on topics such as 'working parties' (perhaps providing a 'cushy' time). Precise dates came from his numerous letters to home. Then there was 'rest', preceded by a long, weary march to Montagne. The main joy of rest was nightly sleep in a bed. But there were also field days, lectures and courses, yet also football matches.

Adams admitted to a 'terrible ignorance' of his profession – perhaps common amongst officers of the New Army. There was a nice break in Amiens (Map 2) over Christmas

Marching to a new front – from Givenchy to Bois Francois (Map 4) to near Morlancourt (south of Albert – Map 2) could be daunting for someone leading a company in case he lost his way. The account of this is full of maps, diagrams and other technicalities which demonstrated that his knowledge of his profession improved. The battalion was there from February to June, 1916. He provided precise diaries of a day's activities in amazing detail. This is the book to read for a blow-by-blow account of what Tommy and officers did on a 'quiet' front.

There is a chapter on 'sniping'. The snipers worked in pairs and believed that Lieutenant Adams had a 'supernatural' knowledge of the German trenches but it was simply down to compass-bearings and air photography. He pointed out to one sniper that shooting at a dummy head held up by a German sentry would reveal his own position to the enemy. There are detailed diagrams, including one of a sniper's post. Detailed dialogue with snipers is instructive about how officers managed them – 'cunning hunters' with steady hands and unwavering eyes.

'On Patrol' reads like an adventure story. No officer in the battalion had been wounded since it arrived but 'Whom the Gods Love' had the detail of the first death of a fellow officer. The dialogue makes the account very real – as real as a trench mock-up in a museum.

'Officers' Servants' again demonstrates through dialogue the way officers operated with the men helping them personally. There is detail of mining operations in no man's land and morning, afternoon and evening in billets (end of May 1916). Bernard Adams wrote this material soon after the events it described so these exact conversations are probably authentic. It is like reading a novel.

In 'Wounded' a Lance Corporal was killed on Tuesday, June 6, 1916. 'Bill' Adams felt 'on edge' all day and eventually he was hit in the arm whilst out in no-man's land with a barbed wire repair patrol. He gave a day-to-day account of what happened to him after this: it was a 'Blighty One'. He returned to the front in January 1917 but was mortally wounded in February, dying in March.

APPLETON, EDITH (1877–1958)
The Great War Diaries of Sister Edith Appleton
Edited by Ruth Cowen
Simon & Schuster, 2013

Edith (or 'Edie') Appleton joined the Queen Alexandra Imperial Military Nursing Service in April, 1914 and arrived at No. 10 Stationary Hospital, St Omer early in September, 1914. She had previously been a civilian nurse for many years.

Edie wrote up her diary on most days but unfortunately much of it is missing although it was kept in drawers by her family. Volume 1 (the only part Edie managed to type up) thus starts on page 112 (April 5, 1915). Other sections are also not available, most critically that covering November, 1916 to June, 1918. In all, it left Ruth Cowen about 400 pages, in excess of 100,000 words, and this had to be shortened so the present book is about 70,000 words in length. Edie must have originally written more than a quarter of a million!

In April, 1915 Edie was in the No. 3 casualty clearing station (CCS) in Poperinghe (Maps 1 & 4). 'Men who came in today were in a terrible state of nervous collapse…' (April 8). The Germans were attempting to take the Ypres Salient; on April 18 over 600 wounded came into the CCS, with many amputations. Edie worked from 7 a.m. to 10 p.m. on the 20th ('… hundreds of things to be done at once…').

Poperinghe itself was badly shelled at the end of April and the CCS had to be moved to Bailleul (Maps 1 & 4). Here, the CCS began to take in soldiers who had been gassed – '… about 150 in all calling out for drinks and mouthwashes…' (May 12). There were only 4 nurses, looking after anything up to 200 men each.

Some of the wounded were in terrible pain for days, and many spoke to the nurses about their mothers – '… it would drive her mad (to see me)'. Death could come dreadfully slowly – '… cheerful, brave things… They loved to be given a clean handkerchief'.

On May 25 the station was overflowing with gassed men (Edie had 163 in her ward, designed for 60). She just hoped a convoy would take most of them to a stationary hospital before the next batch came in. Some days could by quiet – just 15 on July 29. But there were days when nearly 2,000 would arrive.

The nurses were supported by male orderlies, many of them Irish. They had a whole range of jobs, and the nurses prayed for reliable, hard-working volunteers. For instance, they had to bury the dead ('… men is 'ammered, officers is screwed…' complained one orderly not always sure if a corpse was an ex-officer or not). Very sadly, their mess tent was hit by a shell during August and 4 were killed, 2 wounded. The CCS frequently had to move because of enemy shelling and bombing; for instance No. 3 evacuated to St Omer in August, and then came back to Bailleul on the 10th.

Edie always enjoyed her few hours off work – she loved walking, going to concerts, meeting nurses from other stations and hospitals. She even took up the local craft of lace-making. In September the Matron in Chief of Alexandra nurses decided that Edie should move on to another CCS ('… I wish she would mind her own business…' complained Edie, who liked Bailleul).

One man was detained in the CCS with a self-inflicted bullet wound in his big toe – perhaps not accidental (November 3). He had given three different versions of how this happened. The usual reason for detaining men was because they were expected to die within a few hours. In cases where they managed to hang on to life they could be there for days.

Later in the month Edie did transfer – to Hospital No. 1 at Etrétat, on the coast near Havre. The patients helped to decorate it for Christmas celebrations, and they had a nice day with extra special food, drink and entertainment and a party. 1916 arrived – '… the convoys kept coming and going…'

Edie liked to draw little sketches in her diary, adding amusing notes on them. One showed a nurse in a gale with her skirts blown above her head. It was often stormy along this coast, holding up Blighty-bound patients desperate to get home (some found it painful to be moved but would have gone 'strapped to the roof' rather than be delayed). They were thwarted by mines and submarines in the English Channel, too. Edie called them the 'English' patients.

She sometimes thought that the senior officer running the hospital was too ready to say 'yes' to another convoy when there were already too many patients in the hospital, whereas other hospitals had more space. An extra 400 could bring serious overfilling. On May 2, 1916 Edie was expected to look after 190 wounded men – 140 being her customary capacity. Amazingly, she still found time to talk at length to individuals when she could.

The first waves of Somme casualties arrived on July 4, when it took more than 24 hours to dress their wounds, wash and feed them. By the 6th the hospital had managed to set up 1,300 beds using other venues in the town – a large restaurant, the orderlies' barracks, an ambulance garage, a Casino and part of the officers' mess.

Using primitive periscopes and mirrors British soldiers observe
the 'Hun' lines from below the firing line.

Over July and August Edie was looking after 'an ill boy' called Lennox who took 42 days in hospital to die. Of nearly 400 patients in on September 11 over 300 were shell-shocked – '… they dither like palsied old men and talk all the time about their mates who were blown to bits or… were wounded and not brought in…'

Another large Somme convoy came in on September 19, including many German prisoners. She hated the enemy but gave these men her full care and attention. She also disliked 'Austr – I –ians'.

Volume 3 of the diaries ended on November 15, 1916 and Volume 4 only resumed on June 21, 1918. At that latter date she had just returned from leave and was sent to No. 3 Hospital at Le Treport, also on the French coast. At this late stage of the war, when the Allies was starting a real 'Great Push' the wounded still poured in. On August 16 Edie had a room full of men dying from gas-gangrene and fractured spines, '… the ward was a shambles of men with broken skulls, legs off and spines broken'. There was '… no breathing between trains…' (August 30). There were also many visiting fathers, mothers, brothers and aunts.

Edith Appleton was awarded the OBE, the Royal Red Cross and the Belgian Queen Elizabeth medals,

ARNOLD, CHARLES (1893–1941)
From Mons to Messines and Beyond
The Great War Experience of Sergeant Charles Arnold
Edited by Stephen Royle
K.A.F. Brewin Books, 1985

This publication is based mainly on the contents of a small black notebook called 'The Story of My Life', written by Charles Arnold between June and September 1918 for his wife, Mary. Stephen Royle was his grandson.

Mr. Royle collected together documents left by Charles and which had only been discovered in 1980. Apart from the notebook there were two exercise books full of clippings, poems, jokes, stories etc. One was put together between July and November 1915 and the second book had material collected from 1919 to 1922, when Charles had left the army.

Sergeant Arnold fought in the first engagements of the Western Front at Mons and Le Cateau, where he was shot in the foot and badly wounded in the abdomen. He was also wounded in the Battle of the Somme in 1916 and gassed in the Ypres Salient in 1917.

'The Story of My Life' was a factual and understated account composed mainly of a series of short sentences. The editor added relevant notes and some material from Charles's exercise books and information garnered from some of his old comrades. Charles made the odd chronological mistake, which his grandson corrected by researching Battalion records. Mr. Royle was also able to provide details of time and place to augment the account.

Charles Arnold went to France in August 1914 with the 1st Battalion of the East Surrey Regiment. Despite being hit in the left foot he volunteered to go back into the desperate struggle to hold back a rampant enemy. Then one of the bullets from a shrapnel shell went straight through his body and he only just escaped capture by being driven away on a gun limber.

He was taken to hospital in Beauvais (south of Amiens – Map 2) from where a kind French nurse wrote home to his parents. It was a nasty wound but he was recovering quickly, she reported. He had to be fed through a tube for several weeks. He wrote very highly of the treatment and care he received from the French doctors and nurses.

Late in 1914 he was taken to a London hospital but was back ready to fight again in France in March 1915. He was in action at Loos (near Lens – Map 1) and the Ypres Salient. In November he was transferred to the 6th Battalion of the Border Regiment (he was now a Sergeant) and served in Egypt until the Summer of 1916. In July he was in the trenches near Arras (Map 1).

In September 1916 he was in the thick of the Battle of the Somme at Flers and Courcelette (Maps 2 & 3). Then came the action at Thiepval , after which Charles was one of the walking wounded and finished up in hospital in England again.

But he was back at Messines (Map 4) in June 1917 in time to feel the vibrations of what he called 'The Big Mine' (actually it was 19 mines which were exploded under the German line). By the time the Borderers were relieved Sergeant Arnold was totally exhausted and wrapped in a blanket and given half a pint of rum by Lieutenant Adams. This brave officer also won the Military Cross at Messines.

The 6th Borderers were in the Ypres Salient by July 1917. There were mistakes in Charles's account of the action of July 20–21 but there was no mistaking the fact that mustard gas gave him some nasty injuries – the gas burnt off his hair. That was the end of his war.

ASHURST, GEORGE (born 1895)
My Bit: A Lancashire Fusilier at War 1914–1918
Marlborough, 1987

George kept some form of diary during his time on the Western Front but the present account was composed in the 1920s. This included a section on his earlier years. He did very well at elementary school in Wigan.

This was a narrative with few precise dates or place names. Perhaps George did have these in his original diary but regarded them as less important than the story.

This published book was edited by Richard Holmes but he made only small changes to George's 56,000 words. For instance, he left out the archaic inverted commas and capital letters common in the writing of working class men of that period, for instance my own father (see George Weeks).

Richard Holmes did write an excellent introduction about Great War diaries and memoirs in general. He also added explanatory notes in appropriate places, including corrections to George's occasional mistakes. Holmes observed that such memoirs were prone to haphazard chronology.

George joined the Special Reserve of the 2nd Battalion of the Lancashire Fusiliers and was called up at the beginning of the war and was soon in the fray at Le Cateau (Mons). He fought in the early trench battles and participated in the Christmas 'Truce' of 1914.

But on the first day of 1915 he was on a hospital train suffering from badly swollen feet. There followed a restful and entertaining spell near Boulogne on convalescence and with riotous nights in the Rue des Bon Enfants in Armentières (Maps 1 & 4).

He was in the front line for the Second Battle of Ypres in April 1915, then promoted to corporal. But bad fortune stalked him again and he was badly gassed and sent home to England.

On recovery, George served in Gallipoli and Egypt in the 1st Battalion of the Lancashire Fusiliers. He returned to France in the Somme region in March 1916. There he was engaged in a series of high risk raids on German trenches, a stern test of his commitment and courage – and he stood up to everything he was ordered to do.

George described in great detail his part in the early stages of the Battle of the Somme, a time when his Battalion suffered hideous losses. But he survived, never struck by a bullet or blown up by a shell in all the battles he fought. But then, working 600 yards behind the front line, he was hit on the leg by a stray bullet when back on the Ypres front – and that was another 'Blighty One'.

Yet back again he came – this time in the 16th Battalion of his Regiment (the 'Salford Pals') in February 1917, now a Sergeant. George was a sturdy soul and did not take kindly to unreasonable orders from incompetent officers.

"I have done my whack of war," he told one of them, "and if you consider this is mutiny – your revolver is handy…"

He was in the Nieuport (Map 1) sector during the Third Battle of Ypres: his most notable experience there was being buried when a shell exploded next to him.

In 1918 he was despatched for officer training in England but the Armistice intervened before he could finish his course.

George Ashurst was a fine example of the typical 'Tommy' – ready to obey authority and also to complain about it to his pals, and prepared to stand up against rank injustice. He had great respect for brave officers and contempt for the nervous ones. He was no saint, enjoying a good booze-up and a bit of fun.

He did not hate 'Fritz', only the 'Heads' who had brought about the Great War. He considered that he had 'done his bit'. Malingering and even desertion did cross his mind during some of the darkest days but his sense of duty and common sense prevailed. At the end of the day he knew this war had to be won.

George Ashurst as a corporal, convalescing in Eastbourne, 1915.

BAIRNSFATHER, BRUCE (1897–1959)
Bullets and Billets
Bystander, 1916

Lieutenant Bruce Bairnsfather was posted to France with the 1st Battalion of the Royal Warwickshire Regiment in November 1914. He was wounded in the Second Battle of Ypres in April 1915 and sent home to hospital in England.

Because of his growing fame as a war cartoonist he wrote in the Foreword to 'Bullets and Billets' that he had 'by request, made a record of my time out there'. This was written in a notebook in pencil whilst back on active service on the Somme. It was published in 1916 by the Bystander magazine, which had been publishing his cartoons.

Bruce came from a military background and was educated at the United Forces College at Westward Ho! and later at Trinity College in Stratford-upon-Avon. His writing was as amusing and whimsical as his cartoons. He described his Base Camp as 'Fields grassless – 1, Tents bed – 500.'

He composed his book as a narrative with short chapters and lots of headings but with few dates. But he had down all the places where he was. Written so soon after his experience it is crammed with rich and colourful detail of trench and billet life. He was in charge of a machine gun section, first at the famous Bois de Ploegsteert ('Plugstreet' Wood – Map 4) near Ypres. 'Bullets and Billets' is embellished with some of his famous cartoons and drawings. He described the hellish conditions of trench warfare in its primitive state late in 1914 and early in 1915, made much worse by a cold and wet winter. The troops, he wrote, 'lived in a vast bog'.

He became very attached to his fellow junior officers and the men under his charge. Of a platoon commander Bairnsfather wrote 'no one in the war could have hated it more than he did, and no one could more conscientiously have done his very best' (this officer was later killed). Of his servant Bairnsfather remembered his attempt to curry a Machonochie ration. He had 'never forgiven him' for this culinary disaster. But they all laboured day and night with 'customary fed-up vigour'.

His first billet was at 'Transport Farm' near Neuve Eglise (Map 4), where he was 'fleeced by the Flemish' whilst 'wallowing in rest'. He described his experience of the Christmas 'Truce' of 1914 in fascinating detail.

On the walls of a ruined cottage in St. Yvon, in January 1915 he started to draw cartoons of trench warfare (before the war he was well-known as a cartoonist and illustrator). He sent a copy of one of the sketches – 'Where did that one go?' to Bystander, and it was accepted for publication.

Following the Battle of Neuve Chapelle (Maps 1 & 4) the Royal Warwickshires were in the front line near Messines (Map 4). By that time his drawings were in great demand for nearby trenches and billets and he obliged on farmhouse walls (anywhere really) in Indian Ink, charcoal and a 'G. S. blue and red pencil'. This was when famous cartoons such as 'My Dream of Years to Come' were born, part of the later published series 'Fragments from France'.

He spent some enjoyable evenings in Bailleul (Maps 1 & 4), some nice dinners at a hotel followed by entertainment at the music hall, which he loved. But half an hour after such fun he would be 'enveloped in the most uncomfortable, soul-destroying trench ever known'.

His battalion moved north to the Ypres Salient in April 1915 for the Second Battle of Ypres. Here, a shell fell right next to him at Wieltje (Map 4) and he was brought back to England. He described himself at the time as a 'Fragment from France'.

BAKER-CARR, CHRISTOPHER (1878–1945)
From Chauffeur to Brigadier
Founder of the Machine Gun Corps & Pioneer
of the development of the tank
C. D. Baker-Carr
Oakpost Ltd, 2014

Christopher Baker-Carr (CBC) served as a Captain in the Rifle Brigade in the Boer War but his attempt to enlist at the start of the Great War was rejected. So he became a civilian volunteer under the auspices of the RAC, taking his car to France to help wherever he could (August 1914). He did not keep a diary but this memoir was published in 1929.

He joined a convoy of fellow volunteers to Amiens (Map 2). He was sent on to Le Cateau to ferry officers to and from GHQ, dodging shells and bullets, directing lost soldiers to their units, and performed tasks for the C-in-C. At one point a British officer fired at him as he was sitting in his car.

During the Battle of the Aisne he became the driver for Major Pruce-Davis VC. He was often stopped because German spies were also driving about in cars. On one occasion they got between the French and German front lines with both sides firing at them.

CBC was in the area of Ypres when the battle started there, frequently becoming mixed up in the fighting. Eventually, he was offered a job training potential machine gunners, who were in very short supply. He had to get together instructors, machine guns and accommodation.

He managed to get two Sergeants from the School of Musketry in Hythe plus a dozen or so private soldiers likely to make efficient instructors, plus a cook and some rations. He set up shop in the Artillery Barracks in St Omer (November 20). Someone sent Captain Atkinson, who was a great right-hand assistant. But 'nobody in authority concerned himself with these weapons'.

The first class arrived – 20 officers and 80 other ranks. It was a 'happy' Machine Gun School and the divisions soon wanted it to double in size and also tactical instruction on the use of the weapon. So lectures on their use in the field developed and demand for places grew rapidly. The Artists' Rifles was a great source for instructors, plus a typist and his typewriter. The staff quickly expanded. CBC wanted to increase the number of machine guns per battalion from two to four but only units near the front line gave him any support. He did acquire more senior officers.

Major George Lindsay was one of these and he had lots of ideas about developing the use of the machine gun but CBC had to tread carefully otherwise the 'Military Mind' might just close the school. He received no help at all from GHQ which was only 400 yards away. It was actually an advantage for CBC to be a civilian because this meant that he could operate in an un-military way to get things done. One example of this was getting the Press on bis side. At last it was agreed that each battalion could have four guns.

So the idea of a separate Machine Gun Corps took shape. This was planned to bring about uniform training and agreed tactical methods. Each Brigade would have a Machine Gun Company. But it was going to be an uphill effort to get this sanctioned. Meanwhile, the school had moved into larger premises at Wisques. The school began to get important visitors, such as the king, the prime minister and Lord Kitchener.

Taking a big gamble CBC ordered 20,000 guns from an official at the Ministry of Munitions (the BEF had 300 at that time). It was the Prime Minister who came down on his side and decreed that each Battalion should have 64 guns. CBC also got his Machine Gun Corps through un-military methods. GHQ attempted to take credit for the idea but Lord Kitchener intervened and called CBC to London and personally approved of a MGC, along with 40,000 extra soldiers.

Early in 1915 Colonel Swinton had discussed with CBC how to defeat the machine gun in the static war front which was emerging, the origin of the concept of the tank. Meanwhile, the Machine Gun Corps had moved to even larger premises. These were on the coast near Étaples (but it took sanitary engineers 4 days to get rid of 'The Stink' in the ex-casino to be used as the Vickers gun school). The much larger

Lewis Gun school needed a special camp next to Le Touquet golf course to accommodate its students and tactical lessons (making the courses even more attractive).

Tanks were used at the Battle of the Somme. CBC was now able to spend time with the development of them as they became part of the MGC. He was then asked to command one of the tank Battalions. Four of these were formed around St. Pol and Hesdin (south-west of St Omer) – CBC's at Erin. They started training in December 1916.

CBC commanded two battalions (a 'brigade') for the battle of Arras (Map 1) but the 8 tanks became stuck before reaching the front line. Yet they were 'helpful' in the event, and also did well at Messines (Map 4) in June 1917 (Mark IV tanks were then in use). But they were still generally regarded as a 'stunt'.

At the Third Battle of Ypres in the initial assaults they were more successful than expected despite the appalling ground conditions. They did very well at St. Julien (north-east of Ypres) on August 19 showing they could adapt to the mud. There was further success in September and October. Then followed the triumph at Cambrai (Map 1) in November.

BEHREND, ARTHUR (1895–1974)
As From Kemmel Hill
An Adjutant in France and Flanders, 1917 & 1918
Eyre & Spottiswoode, 1963

Arthur ('Charles') Behrend served as an infantry subaltern in Egypt and Gallipoli but was sent home on sick leave in 1916. The BEF was short of artillery officers and so he was re-trained, and joined 279 Siege Battery, Royal Garrison Artillery, on Kemmel Hill, (Map 4) south of Ypres.

There is no evidence that he kept a diary (either on the Western Front or in Egypt or Gallipoli). The account of the period of the German offensive and after is based on a file of messages and signals which he kept and a unit log book. He wrote up the account of the German attack in March, 1918 and had it printed ('Nine Days', 1921). He possibly wrote the rest of 'As From Kemmel Hill' from memory around 40 years after the war.

His first taste of battle was at Messines in June, 1917 after 19 huge mines were exploded under the German front line. After this they moved to Ypres and Behrend became Adjutant under a new Colonel, Thorp. Thorp was wizened and bandy-legged but a remarkably fine leader and artillery expert. He was fearless and totally dedicated to his work.

On the down side he never praised anybody and was short-tempered. He hated being criticised because he thought he was always right (he usually was). But if his gunners needed support and sympathy he was always there to offer it. He also had a sense of humour, making up code words from old-fashioned girls' names. His only hobby was a fanatical interest in Salvage. He had no friends and received two letters a year from home.

As the Third Battle of Ypres developed the Battery (firing heavy howitzers) fought an intense artillery duel with big enemy guns, a crucial part of the battle. Firing these big guns day after day was an exhausting task and in the autumn they moved to Bapaume (Map 2) for rest.

They were called into the action at Bullecourt (south-west of Arras – Map 1) in October and then the tank battle at Cambrai (Map 1) in November and December. The artillery played a big part in halting the German counter-offensives. Heavy artillery was then re-organised into larger units – Brigades co-ordinating the work of 5 Batteries. Colonel Thorp was chosen to command a Brigade with Arthur Behrend as his Adjutant.

A large enemy offensive was expected in the spring of 1918 and the brigade rested at Gezaincourt (next to Doullens – Map 2) after Cambrai. A notable event occurred here when a drunk gunner assaulted a priest late at night thinking he was a girl.

For the expected assault Behrend had to set up reserve positions for the 5 batteries (or 'Tocs'). The big enemy bombardment came on March 21, and its infantry massed ready for advance around Queant (near Arras – Map 1). Following the barrage the German artillery was able to follow its rapidly advancing infantry as Allied defensive plans fell apart. On the 22nd the whole artillery brigade was retreating as fast as it could go, and Behrend had to field panic-stricken messages and requests for help and guidance. Brigade HQ moved back west of Bapaume (Map 2).

It was a hectic job getting petrol up to the Batteries, replacing broken lorries and trying to move along congested roads. The Expeditionary Force Canteen was quickly emptied before the Germans arrived and officers drank a lot of gin, whisky and champagne. Because he kept the file of messages Behrend was able to recall the dialogue between artillery officers – 'a confused medley of hilarious, hostile and welcoming shouts'.

But from their new positions the howitzers of the 5 Batteries blazed away throughout March 23, trying to damage the enemy big guns and stem the forward flow of German infantry. Enemy planes swarmed overhead and the din was horrific. It did not bode well for March 24: another huge German attack was expected.

But, in the event, the enemy paused – 'overreached itself'. But the artillery used the break as an opportunity to get rid of a lot of superfluous materiel and then retreat further and seek out better positions (a slow business along packed roads). Information pouring in was confused and soon out of date: how far away was the enemy infantry?

They reached Achiet-le-Grand (Somme) and carried on. Colonel Thorp informed the brigade Major that he needed 500 gallons of petrol and food for 700 men – quickly. 'The utter absurdity of the situation seemed to dawn on them, and both grinned'. Not only did such supplies have to be located (when everybody was in desperate need of them) but they had also to be transported to where needed…

March 24 brought fresh German advances – Combles, Morval and Lesboefs (Map 2) fell and the brigade were ordered back a further 10 miles, via Acheux (where the Y.M.C.A. Canteen was quickly emptied) to Forceville (north-west of Albert – Map 2). But now Albert had fallen, only 6 miles away, and the howitzers moved further back to Orville (next to Doullens – Map 2) on March 26.

Yet the impetus of the German onslaught was fading: although March 27 brought more withdrawal – to Merzeville – that was as far as it went. 'The great March offensive burnt itself out like a forest fire'. The howitzers moved back east in April and the front line hardly changed after that until August. Perhaps, then, the most notable event for the Adjutant was a row with Colonel Thorp in June. "I think you're an unreasonable and obstinate man," Behrend angrily shouted. Following this, the Colonel told him to pack his bag. But early the next morning Thorp told him "I am not changing my Adjutant".

'It was the nearest approach to an apology of which he was capable'.

On this Ancre front the final Allied offensive was launched in August, on a front from Bucqury to Beaumont Hamel. (north of Albert – Map 2). Bapaume was re-captured on August 29. During September and October the brigade advanced nearly 40 miles.

BLACKBURNE, HARRY W. (1878–1963)
This Also Happened on the Western Front
The Padre's Story
Hodder & Stoughton, 1932

This book is made up of extracts from the hundreds of letters sent by Harry Blackburne to his wife. Later notes were added, along with the names of units, people and places (originally censored in the letters). Because of these almost daily missives the text has the appearance of a diary, but there are no dates, except that each year is given a separate chapter.

Harry went to France in 1914 as a Chaplain to an Infantry Brigade, and was later Senior Chaplain of a Division and then Assistant Chaplain of a Division. He served for the whole of the war, arriving in France on August 22, 1914.

In the headlong retreat from Mons and Le Cateau he dug graves in cemeteries at night when the shelling had ceased, and held 'wonderful' and 'ripping' services, sometimes four in a row to different Battalions. A shell landed between his feet but failed to explode (97 Chaplains were killed during the war and 69 died later as a result of their wounds).

As he left the River Aisne battle scene to move to Ypres he sent to HQ a full list of the funerals he had conducted with map references marking the graves. In Ypres he also served as an anaesthetist. He remembered the introduction of motor ambulances to take the wounded to hospital, replacing horse-driven ones, saving many lives. In Ypres he made his own cemetery outside the town – the shelling made it impossible to erect anything within it.

At rest in Locre (Map 4) he was instrumental in organising concerts and paper chases. At Christmas he gave out the King's Christmas cards and Princess Mary's chocolate boxes to wounded soldiers. Back in the front line near Béthune (Maps 1 & 4) he helped out with the numerous cases of frost-bite. In a cemetery he made here he spent hours painting names on crosses (on the ones at Ypres he had had to use pencil but he had all the map references of the graves).

It was a devastating and depressing task to pray alongside dying boys, such as the one from the Sussex Regiment who said the Lord's Prayer simply as he died. Another painful duty was to be with men condemned to death. Early in 1915 Chaplain Blackburne was awarded the Military Cross for bravery.

Out of the front line again at Béthune (Maps 1 & 4) he worked from 7 a.m. to the evening seeing as much as possible of all the battalions in the brigade, taking services and confirmations etc. One diversion was a 'slap-up tea' with the Bishop of London near the trenches, cakes provided from patisseries in the town. Harry also distributed Good Friday Cards in the trenches, where the troops were greatly amused by his 'barrel-organ' (harmonica)

The pervading spirit of Blackburne's account is that he thinks everyone is 'marvellous' or 'splendid' or 'wonderful'. The text is crammed with the names of numerous brigade officers (added on later). After the Battle of Neuve Chapelle (Maps 1 & 4) he wrote many letters to the mothers of the lost men.

Blackburne became Senior Chaplain of the 1ˢᵗ Division. The battalions of the division always expected the chaplain to produce what they needed in terms of refreshment and entertainment out of a hat. His best effort was probably the Cellar Club providing tea, buns and cigarettes for passing troops. Although this fare was sold at just above cost price there was still enough profit to buy a cinema and all its equipment.

Early in 1916 he became Senior Chaplain of the First Army. He worried about living in comfort whilst the troops suffered in the trenches. But he was told to 'Go and sleep in a trench if you want to, but you won't be able to supervise the work of the chaplains from there'. So he began to see a greater number of generals and chaplains than ever. He was a prime mover in getting more Church Army and Y.M.C.A refreshment huts.

Just about the first complaint he made about anybody appeared on page 93 about a lazy chaplain, or 'Pink Eye'. One chaplain complained to him that he didn't think the troops wanted religion; Harry's answer was 'go and make them want it!'

He delivered many lectures, especially on the need for religion in the front line. He had the idea of a Chaplain's School where they could go for courses. He completed a 'Mission' in 1917 – dozens of officers' meetings with him.

He also held many chaplain's meetings: topics included how to keep men away from brothels and to stop excessive drinking. But he was still available to serve tea at a horse show. 'I feel rather like a commercial traveller, always going round and pushing some particular thing'.

BLACKER, CARLOS, PATON (1895–1975)
Have you Forgotten Yet?
The First World War Memoirs of C. P. Blacker
Edited by John Blacker
Lee Cooper, 2000

C.P.B. wrote diaries and letters during the war but wrote this memoir in the 1960s. His son, John, reduced it by a half. C.P.B. enlisted in the Coldstream Guards in July 1915 (despite poor sight in both eyes). He crossed to France on October 5 to be posted to the 4th (Pioneer) Battalion, in which he stayed till 1918.

This very full, detailed account is presented in the fluid style and competence one would expect from such a well-educated, sophisticated and urbane man. It is clearly based, at least, for most periods, on daily entries, and the large number of letters he wrote (he wrote to his mother every day). It is a long and reflective book (agonising in places); some of the material is about the general progress of the war and there are many pages about fellow officers and their relationships.

In October 1915 the battalion was at Vermelles behind the Loos battlefield (near Lens – Map 1) where his brother had just been killed. This affected him very deeply. The 4th Battalion spent the whole winter in the Pas de Calais and spent much time helping in the mining operations between Loos and Lens (November). This was dangerous work because the shaft openings were vulnerable to shellfire: direct hits could result in men being suffocated or drowned down below.

C.P.B. was worried about doing nothing whilst his men worked pumps and filled sandbags all night but no one wanted officers to join in, especially those doing the work. Later the repair and re-construction of trenches around Loos took up most of their days. The main problem was the bad weather.

1916 began with clearing three redoubts near Laventie (Map 4). In March he was in charge of a detachment from several battalions wood-cutting in Clairmarais Forest near St Omer, guided by French foresters.

He was back with the main battalion near Poperinghe (Maps 1 & 4) in July, moving to the Somme at the end of the month, building light railways and roads. They were right up in the front line in September near Montauban (Map 3). The other battalions were to attack from Guinchy (Maps 3 & 4) and the Pioneers were needed to construct an earth road behind them for supply vehicles.

C.P.B. searched the area for a suitable route and was nearly shot by a sniper. When work started German guns spotted them and fired and a fellow officer was killed (September 15). For this action C.P.B. was awarded the Military Cross. He was promoted from Ensign (one star) to Subaltern (two stars). They returned to Montauban on October 5 to build a 'corduroy road' under fire from a long-range, high velocity gun of substantial calibre ('Quincy Dick'). One shell just missed the tent in which C.P.B. was sleeping but apart from being blown out of his bed he was unhurt.

November brought rest at St. Maulvis and very cold weather in December along with Colin Bain Marais, a South African who only wore underclothes once (probably to avoid lice – he was obviously well-off). There at Waterlot Farm near Guillemont (Map 3) their job was to mark out a new trench with tapes on a freezing night and under enemy shelling.

In December the battalion was in Combles (south of Bapaume – Map 2) and C.P.B. was ordered by some 'remote planner' to construct a very long communication trench vulnerable to enemy guns and to bad weather. The work stopped after several days and was replaced by a duckboard road. Their trench at Waterlot Farm was never used as the Germans retreated to the Hindenburg Line in 1917. At Corbie (April–May – Map 2) there was a month's training, sport (C.P.B. liked boxing), swimming in the Somme canal and concerts.

They moved north to Locre (Map 4) in May repairing communications just behind the support line. Old Etonians, including C.P.B., held a riotous dinner at St Omer (June 4), wrecking the dining hall. His morale declined markedly in the second half of 1917 (and he thought this was general amongst the troops) as they sensed that another huge battle awaited them. Indeed, the failure in July to break through in the Salient depressed everybody even more, along with the incessant bad weather.

A Canadian 'Scottie' helps a motor machine gun man out of difficulty.

C.P.B. felt that the work he was doing was too easy and safe, despite the fact that he suffered two near misses at Elverdinghe (Map 4) in August. He felt no more involved at Cambrai (Map 1) in December, erecting barbed wire defences in the face of the German counter attacks in December. He regretted that Pioneers were not used as infantry in emergencies like this (they were in 1918). Casualties at Cambrai were 3 killed and 34 wounded. The losses in the three infantry battalions were obviously much higher and he began to contemplate applying for a transfer to one of them so that he could do his bit.

At Christmas he was promoted to Captain: they were near Arras (Map 1) until March, for once not threatened by shelling. There followed the six German onslaughts (March–July). He gives a general account of these admitting that his personal records were sketchy and his memory of the period 'hazy'. He did remember helping to construct the 'Purple Line' of defences behind Arras in case the Germans broke through.

In June 1918 he transferred to the 2nd Battalion after a lot of agonising (he was worried about how his parents would feel having already lost one son). So he was with the infantry in the trenches in July (Bailleulmont) next to American troops. When the 2nd Battalion attacked on August 22 (Battle of Bapaume – Map 2) he was on a Lewis gun course and he was mortified to hear of the death of the officer who had taken his place, amongst others. There was a further assault on August 27 (at St. Leger) but he played no part in this.

Flanders, 1917, men of the East Yorkshire Regiment on their way to the line

They moved to near Lagnicourt in the Cambrai battleground (Map 1) and C.P.B. went over the top leading his Company in the Battle of the Canal du Nord on September 27 (from Amiens to St. Quentin – Map 2). Men were killed around him and he was hit in the head but able to continue and even fired a Lewis gun. Finally, he was ordered back for treatment as he was losing a lot of blood from an artery. He went to hospital and did not return to the 2nd Battalion until October 22.

BLUNDEN EDMUND (1896–1974)
Undertones of War
Penguin, 2010

Edmund Blunden was trying to remember his war experiences six years after the Armistice. An earlier attempt to do this (whilst the war had not ended) had petered out for some reason. He professed that he would think about this war for the rest of his life.

He went to France in 1916 as a 2nd Lieutenant in the 2nd Battalion of the Royal Sussex Regiment. There was a bad start when the Sergeant Major demonstrating how to detonate a grenade blew himself up on the training ground at Étaples. Near Béthune (Maps 1 & 4) he learnt the trench routines of a subaltern. None of the junior officers seemed to believe that the war would ever end (except to guess that it would be when the Germans sent up four black lights at night) and were more concerned about 'Blighty Albert' and 'Quinque Jimmy', two highly dangerous enemy machine guns opposite them.

Blunden was then at Festubert (Map 4) behind the line for a 'rest' when he and his platoon slaved away digging communication trenches. There followed a course in how to deal with poison gas which was more of a rest than the 'rest'. At Cuinchy (Map 4) in the trenches under hellish shellfire he was sent requests such as' What is the number of Loan Boots in your Company?' He did admit, however, that these trenches had very clear signs.

There were a further round of 'rest' with harassing training programmes but still preferable to the front line. Here, at Neuve Chapelle (Maps 1 & 4) he had a nagging fear that he would be shot or shelled by a British gun. During one night he had to crawl out along a disused sap trench and then into no man's land for a fearfully long time. When he returned the sentry fired off a few rounds at him. An attack took place in June 30, 1916 (one of very few dates supplied in this narrative) along the La Bassée road, when 'mad ideas of British supremacy flared in his breast'. Three Germans were captured. Apparently, the plan was to draw the enemy away from the Somme.

He then experienced trenches with a roof near Loos (Lens – Map 1) to keep out mortar 'pineapples' whilst Cambrin (south-west of Cuinchy – Map 4) was terrifying all day and night except for a brief respite in the afternoons. During the following rest he had to account for every screw picket large, every screw picket small, every pick, every mallet etc. with which he had been entrusted.

No man's land was always a jumble of holes, stumps and myriad other objects, and being out on patrol at night was a hazardous and bewildering undertaking. They were continually lit up by flares which invited volleys of shots from in front and from behind.

It was safer to be in your own trench where there was also always the chance of recovering a watch or some other valuable from a corpse. Blunden's C.O. became ecstatic when he spotted poems by Blunden in the 'Times Literary Supplement'. The Somme Blunden found to be completely devoid of civilian life and completely in the hands of the military. The ruins of villages stood starkly against the skyline.

Blunden thought Beaumont Hamel (Somme – Map 3) more terrifying than anywhere else so it was unwise to don pyjamas. It was a wonder to be alive at the start of every day. As autumn was reached a relative tranquility transpired. There followed the struggle to hold on to Thiepval against fierce and persistent attempts by the Germans to re-take it. The sergeant major did for himself by drinking pints of rum.

Thence to the Ypres Salient, where Poperinghe (Maps 1 & 4) was 'one of the seven wonders of the world'. Blunden was now a Lieutenant in charge of a company but was turned down for further promotion on account of his 'offences against propriety and demeanour'.

For a long spell in 1917 he was a Tunnel Major in charge of conditions for miners. Real rest only arrived in the form of courses. His work underground saved him from the worst of the Third Battle of Ypres, but still 'instant destruction threatened' from all around. He and his fellow officers agreed on December 31 that 1917 had been bad and that 1918 did not look any more promising in the 'sepuchral citadel' that was Ypres.

Chronology, for Blunden, was difficult but topographical and personal impressions remained clear. He remembered keeping up his spirits by reading 'Night Thoughts on Life, Death and Immortality' by an 18th century philosopher.

Blunden was sent home for 6 months real rest in February 1918.

BROUGH, JOHN (born 1894)
A Marine in the Great War
John Brough
Book Guild Publishing, 2012

Private John Brough of the 2nd Battalion of the Royal Marine Light
Infantry wrote a diary during the war but this was lent to a friend and never
returned. However, his son, who edited this book, discovered the diary
of his time as a prisoner of war from October 1917 in the Royal Marine
Museum at Southsea. John Brough was captured on Passchendaele Ridge
(Map 4). He was taken to near Roulers and put in a small room with 60
other prisoners.

There was little food and they had to cook this themselves (luckily
some cooks had been captured) but kind Belgian citizens brought them
more. They were moved to Kortrijk where at least they could have a
bath (but there was no soap or towels), fresh clothes and they were given
blankets.

They were in danger from British artillery and aeroplane raids. They
could send home cards and letters and managed to get hold of a packet of
cards. Sadly, no letters or parcels arrived from home.

He sold his jerkin on November 11 for 10 marks with which he
bought food and drink for their move into Westpahlia. During this long
journey they were only given a bowl of thin soup and a quarter of a loaf of
bread each per day.

The diary is obviously full of detail about food and drink, or what
there was of it, because it was the main concern of these prisoners. The
writing style is basically in note form. Someone stole his money – he
found out later that the culprit was one of his fellow marines but he was
not able to discover which one. However, on November 14 they got
Red Cross parcels. The German soup was terrible but any slops they left

were quickly devoured by the Italian prisoners. Even the electric light was unreliable so on many nights they had to go to bed when it got dark. However, there was some good news – Passchendaele Ridge had at last been captured.

They were often inoculated – they got more needles in them than food. There were fleas in the small, thin blankets. John managed to buy some soap (this was a normal German barracks with a canteen). He was able to play draughts with a soldier from Brindisi – they were eventually quartered with the Italians. Sometimes they got coal for a fire and sometimes not.

He received portions from two food parcels and also attended church. There was a great deal of theft but the food was improving. They had to work – down the local coal mine. It was a hard grind – filling up trucks with stone for long hours with still very poor food. At last John got hold of a book.

He found the going in the mine very hard – it gave him backache and headaches. On December 14 his close friend collapsed under the strain. Some of the Germans were nice fellows, others not so nice. The prisoners were paid a few marks a day. At Christmas the Russian prisoners had a concert and all the prisoners got some biscuits, an apple and 10 cigarettes. There was also a Christmas tree with lights but on Christmas day they were utterly miserable. They all wondered whether the next one would be at home with their families. A comrade who suffered from Quinces died in hospital. The prisoners often fainted underground.

One day the Russians refused to work and were left outside in the snow without greatcoats all day (January 2, 1918). The beetroots in the soup on January 3 were rotten. Someone stole the bread ration (January 6). A German guard hit a prisoner with his rifle for not moving quickly enough. John's boots were stolen and he had to wear clogs which crippled him. He had to go into hospital with swollen legs on January 14. He had to share a bed with an Italian but at least there was butter on the bread – in fact, the food and drink was marvellous compared to the barracks. Most of his diary were about food and drink (and the bad weather) but this is not surprising when you consider his situation – where was the next grub coming from and what would it be like?

A lot of food packets (from BEF units) arrived for 'John Brough' but, amazingly, there was another John Brough in the prison and they were for him.

John still had received no communication from home. He was in hospital again on February 17 with a poisoned hand. He had to have two operations on it but at least he got some new boots. The sister said that the Germans had captured Paris but this was on April Fools' Day!

Back in the barracks the main enemy was bed bugs. The last daily entry in the diary was on April 16, 1918. 'I did not keep the diary being too idle'. He was sent to a rest camp but this consisted of working all day at market gardening (near Dusseldorf).

He left there on November 19 bound for England via Holland.

BRUCKSHAW, HORACE (1891–1917)
The Diaries of Private Horace Bruckshaw
Royal Marine Light Infantry 1915–1916
Edited by Martin Middlebrook
Scholar Press, 1979

There were two diaries – the first was in a stiffly-bound notebook 159 mm long and 97 mm wide, made up of 250 feint-ruled pages written in pencil in a clear, flowing hand. Horace had received a good elementary education (which usually included calligraphy) and worked as a draughtsman (the diaries have competent sketches and diagrams).

The second diary was a slightly smaller but equally well-bound notebook with 224 pages (see illustration). The wording was often in note form; e.g. 'Morning broke fine but stiff breeze' – a simple commentary of an ordinary man caught up in the most extraordinary circumstances. Yet he could break out into more detailed descriptions with ease. He wrote the account to provide a record of what he had experienced for his family to read, never dreaming it would finish up as a book.

The last entry is for Sunday November 12, 1916. He brought the diaries home on leave and left them with his new wife. He may have carried on writing until his death in 1917 but if he did it was all lost along with his remains. His wife kept the diaries for over 50 years. They were then auctioned and sold, and later published. Martin Middlebrook edited the work.

He decided to leave the text as it was with minor corrections. He also divided it into dated sections (Horace had provided all the dates). The editor also added a preface, introduction and a historical commentary and a postscript.

Private Horace Bruckshaw volunteered for the Royal Marine Light Infantry (Plymouth Battalion) and travelled to Gallipoli early in 1915. He served there for over a year, coming to the Western Front in May 1916. He then wrote a diary entry for every single day till October 1 when he was sent to a casualty clearing station and later to hospital suffering from very nasty boils. He returned to his unit on November 9.

Horace had a good sense of humour, as befitting a marine. When an elderly French lady lifted up her skirts to show where she had been shot by a German soldier to him it was 'enough to make a pig laugh'. He was ready to joke about his dreadful boils – 'The Doc carving up my mush again this morning. I shall be glad when the blessed boils have disappeared'.

When you consider the death date of most of these diarists it is truly sad that this one (like Bernard Adams) did not see the end of the war in which he valiantly fought in Gallipoli and the Western Front. He lies somewhere in France, possibly with a diary only he knew about.

Bully beef and dog biscuits. Drawing by Horace Bruckshaw.

BUCKLE, HENRY (1882–1954)
A Tommy's Sketchbook
Writings and Drawings from the trenches
Lance Corporal Henry Buckle
Edited by David Read
The History Press, 2012

Henry had been a part-time volunteer soldier since 1900. He joined the 5th (Territorial) Battalion, The Gloucestershire Regiment on September 2, 1914. The battalion travelled to France in March 1915.

The remarkable feature of Henry's record of his service for a few months in 1915 was the numerous watercolour paintings (he was also a keen photographer) which he produced of the front lines and back areas where he served. He took part in no major battle but nonetheless the 'quiet fronts' on which he fought were extremely dangerous places and in the end he succumbed to serious injury.

This occurred in October 1915 and Henry wrote his diary on many days between March and October. For some reason, probably because diaries on the Western Front were not officially allowed in case the enemy obtained vital information from them, when Henry typed up his diary following his medical discharge from the Army he left out all the dates and place names. David Read restored these from Battalion records (plus information provided by Henry on the paintings).

Despite the fact that Henry was a well-read man David Read had to do considerable work on spelling, grammar and, particularly, punctuation. Also, Henry made mistakes about events and places and the editor again corrected these using official records.

Henry was promoted to Lance Corporal soon after his arrival in France (April). The battalion went to Ploegsteert Wood (Map 4). Here, he was in charge of No. 15 Section in 34 Trench (April 15). If he heard any strange noises from no man's land Henry had to fire a rocket from a pistol, giving off a bright light. The men quite liked this diversion because the pitch blackness and silence were unnerving.

The section proved an inventive group, for instance making a 'decent fireplace' in the side of the trench on which to cook bacon and make some dumplings, all done without producing smoke, which would have provoked rifle fire from the Germans.

Henry described a quiet front as a 'huge game of chess... we are the pawns, but no idea whose move it is now...' On April 20 one of his Section was shot in the head. Senior NCOs had no hesitation in giving Henry responsible jobs, such as 'orderly Corporal', which entailed a five-mile walk taking around orders to all platoons of a Company.

Some of the trenches the Gloucesters were put in were shallow and in a poor state of repair, in sharp contrast to deep and well-maintained German defences. This was the case when they moved to near Messines (Map 4) and had to do constant repairs and improvements. It was this lack of proper protection that caused the loss of so many of Henry's comrades on these 'quiet' fronts.

In July there came a very long march south where the battalion was to take over part of the French front line near Hébuterne and Gommecourt Wood (north-east of Bapaume – Map 2). These trenches were even worse than the ones they had left in Messines (Map 4) and 'the spade became mightier than the rifle'. There were even no dug-outs to provide special shelter from the hails of grenades the Germans hurled over, so this proved a mammoth task of ceaseless labour at night.

Henry became quite lame and was unable to walk back to his billet and had to get on a horse, something he had not done for a long time and so he became sore elsewhere, too. It was in these areas – Hébuterne, Gommecourt Wood, Sailly-au-Bois and Bus – that Henry produced a whole series of pictures, an amazing visual record of this environment.

Late September became a hectic time as the Battle of Loos (Lens area – Map 1) raged nearby. During one period of 6 days Henry was under constant shelling – 'a nearly continuous scream of shells over our heads,dense masses of yellow smoke... clouds of earth... heaps of timber and earth going skywards... bursts of machine gun fire...'

Henry was finally wounded in October. He was 'buried in the trench and twisted up...' He eventually reached hospital. At first, he seemed to be classed as a 'walking wounded' case but he was largely bedridden. In hospital in Rouen there were 'ACTUAL BEDS' (previous 'beds' had just been straw mattresses on the floor). He also got some pyjamas.

'… am now in a sort of straight jacket one side…' But then he was on crutches doing jobs in the ward. He didn't seem to have a clue what was wrong with him. Anyhow, the doctors put him on a boat for Blighty. He went to hospital in Cheltenham: he was there for Christmas. It is obvious that he was in some sort of serious condition.

BURRAGE, ALFRED McLELLAND (1889–1956)
War is War. Ex-Private X
Pen and Sword, 2010

Alfred McLelland Burrage was a well-known short story writer for magazines and periodicals. He volunteered for armed service with the Artists Rifles (1/28 Battalion, London Regiment) in 1917. He wrote 'War is War' anonymously in the late 1920s and it was published by Gollancz in 1930. He concealed his identity and used fictitious names in the text in order not to upset anybody.

Burrage hoped to get a commission but he remained a Private throughout his 1917–1918 service. He could have avoided conscription because of his age and the fact that he had dependent relatives but '… hated being thought a funk… I was willing to die for my country'. Most professional writers who served in the BEF became officers.

Burrage was trying to remember events which happened ten years before. 'I ventured to set down what I remember'. It was thus a chronological narrative in which most place names were recalled but very few precise dates although the reader will have a rough idea of when he was writing about.

Incredibly, he continued to write short stories for magazines even when in the front line near Arras and in the Ypres Salient and Cambrai in 1917 and the Somme in 1918 when the Germans were on the rampage. 'In trenches when my fingers were too numb to hold a pencil, when I was worn out with work and sleepless nights… I was the only front-line man in the battalion who had been in every stunt with it. This was rather wonderful luck.'

He went to the front line at Gavrelle near Arras (Map 1) in the Summer of 1917 but contracted trench fever without ever being in a trench. Before he was really recovered he was sent back to Gavrelle, supposedly by this time 'a quiet front' but Burrage and his comrades suffered very dangerous and uncomfortable conditions. They were liable to be shot or shelled at any moment. Many diarists were of the view that junior officers endured the same terror but Burrage wrote that they were 'not of them and could not fully appreciate their sufferings and hardships'. Higher Command he regarded as 'fools in red tabs'. French peasants were genial, dirty and obscene and about two hundred years behind English peasantry.

At Passchendaele (Map 4) late in 1917 Burrage was part of the British force who went over the top in support of Canadian troops trying to capture Passchendaele Ridge. The first 'ripple' of British infantry was 'blotted out'. Burrage finished up in an ex-enemy stronghold with a few other survivors after hell-raising escapes from near death. At one point the heavy and continuous German shelling made him cry out, "Oh, Christ, make it stop! Oh, Jesus make it stop! It must stop because I can't bear it." When he had shouted thus everything suddenly became quiet and it seemed that God would indeed save him.

His experience during the great German offensive in the Spring of 1918 was similarly frightening. He was a stretcher-bearer at this time rescuing wounded men whilst under fire. Eventually he was hit in the back and sent back to England. Burrage's accent and willingness to say what he thought in an articulate manner meant that he fell out with some of his comrades although he was very fond of some of them, especially 'Dave', a rough-and-ready Cockney with an eye for the girls. He was 'the only man I ever cried over' wrote Burrage (at a time when Dave was blown up and missing). Burrage recounted being on leave in London and staying at his Club. Members either thought he was 'a splendid fellow' or someone who was a lucky lad to be on such a picnic or wondered where he had got to. Dressed in his tattered uniform he played cards with some friendly officers.

BYRNE, CHARLIE ('GINGER') (born 1896)
I Survived. Didn't I?
The Great War Reminiscences of Private 'Ginger' Byrne
Edited by Joy B. Cave
Lee Cooper, 1993

Joy Cave tape-recorded Ginger's war story in 1977. He read and amended the original typescripts but died before the book was published. Ginger's son, Young Charlie, put in some amendments that he thought his Dad would have liked.

Ginger joined the 2ⁿᵈ Battalion of the Hampshire Regiment after volunteering for service in 1914. He went to Egypt in 1915 and France and Belgium from 1916 to 1918. His most critical moment was going over the top with the Newfoundlandlers on the fateful day, July 1, 1916 on the Somme at Beaumont Hamel (Map 3). Despite the terrible losses suffered by the Canadians Ginger miraculously survived (didn't he?).

He was in the Somme area in May 1916, then a 'quiet' sector. But the extent of activity behind the lines made Ginger think that a big battle was in the offing. The Hampshires worked closely with the Newfoundlanders in training and just before the big day he was sent across to the Canadians to join one of their machine gun teams as 'Number Three' – which meant he had to carry about the ammunition and get it ready to arm the gun.

Ginger's account of the first day of the Battle of the Somme is totally gripping. One thing that it demonstrated clearly was how little the ordinary infantryman knew what was happening except what they could see and hear. From the start it was terrifying as Ginger scrambled over the top lugging along two heavy boxes of ammunition and his rifle. His officer was shot dead in front of him immediately and 'there were blokes laying everywhere'. He run on into a hailstorm of bullets; to survive in these circumstances was a miracle but those who did kept running forward.

His fellow machine gunners were both hit and killed instantly. Ginger reached the German wire as a persistent Jerry machine gunner tried to gun him down. But Ginger managed to fall down a shallow shell hole, its front parapet inches above his head. Looking back he could see where he had come from but running across was inviting a speedy death from a German bullet. Wounded men out there who did try to move were soon mown down.

Thus, he lay there all day, the training exercises they had been following for the past few weeks of no use at all as the enemy machine gunner tried to get one bullet into the shell hole. The Jerry certainly was not going to come out any closer.

Night arrived and the Germans fired up their usual Very lights to illuminate no man's land so Ginger's chances of escape remained slim. But between each flare he crawled along on toes and elbows in order to keep himself as low as possible and got to a larger shell hole. He crawled on and reached a trench but still insisted on going back with a stretcher-bearer to rescue a soldier laying out there. So Ginger survived the worst day suffered by the BEF and one in which the Newfoundland Regiment was decimated.

The 2/ Hampshires moved up to Ypres later in July. Here, Ginger was saved again after scrounging a gas mask from an officer which was superior to those carried by the other ranks. The result was that comrades around him were badly gassed whilst he escaped.

He was then transferred to the Machine Gun Corps (88 Brigade) and back on the Somme in September and fought in the action at Gueudecourt (near Flers – Map 2) on October 12. In 1917 his Division was involved in the Arras (Map 1) campaign. He was 'as happy as a sandboy' in the Machine Gun Corps, which was made up by a 'cosmopolitan crowd' rather than the inward-looking men of the Hampshires who had mostly served in India before the war and tended to be hostile to newcomers.

Ginger had a great affection for mules and rode south to Arras on one. Later he adopted a mule he rescued, and named her 'Monchy' (after Monchy-le-Preux, where he had pulled her from a wrecked wagon).

Ginger was at the Battle of Cambrai (Map 1) late in 1917. He admitted that it was difficult for him to remember place names to tell Joy Cave where he was at particular times. They had not given him a map and there were no signs up, he pointed out. A lot of the villages were just piles of rubble, anyway. But one very welcome skill he learnt was that he could usually find his way around complex battlefields. "Ginger knows the way," his mates said.

After leave he was back in the 'muck heap' that was the Ypres Salient. His 'queer luck' stayed with him as a German plane machine gunned dozens of men around him when they were marching. Ginger did not say much about 1918 to Joy. But he did refer to Sir Douglas Haig's famous 'backs to the wall' order on April 9, rather politely pointing out there was no 'wall'. Other soldiers were rather more forthright. Wall or no wall Ginger and his mates kept on fighting. He finished up in the Army of Occupation in Germany, which he enjoyed because the grub and the fags were much better.

CAMPBELL P. J. (born 1898)
In the Cannon's Mouth
Hamish Hamilton, 1979
and
The Ebb and Flow of Battle
Hamish Hamilton, 1977

Although 'The Ebb and Flow of Battle' was published first it was about 1918, whereas 'In the Cannon's Mouth' was about 1917.

P. J. Campbell wrote these highly detailed and descriptive narratives 60 years after the events they covered. The story is delivered in a series of episodes, including highly specific dialogue, almost in novel form. It is as though Mr. Campbell is referring to a diary he wrote at the time. There is abundant material on the personalities and actions of fellow officers.

He arrived in France in May 1917 on the Somme battlefield at Miraumont (north-east of Albert – Map 2). What immediately struck this 19-year-old 2nd Lieutenant was the rumble of far-off artillery, still firing in this region. He was listening out for the guns because he had joined an artillery column delivering ammunition and supplies to the guns.

He depicted the utter desolation here – mile after mile of a crater-filled landscape. The only sign of vegetation was a few patches of coarse grass. It was crammed full of rubbish – cartridge cases, unexploded shells, empty tins, vests and shirts and scraps of uniform, picks and shovels, rusty rifles and broken and abandoned wagons. Amongst this mass of debris were hundreds and hundreds of wooden crosses.

When the column moved up to Flanders about the time of the Battle of Messines (Map 4) in June Campbell was transferred to a Royal Artillery Field Battery to run a Section of two guns, about fifty gunners and drivers and horses. He was much happier here with friendlier officers and highly skilled gunners. It was a new experience for him – a boy educated at Public School working alongside older working-class men. Although he now came near enemy artillery fire he had not yet seen the other side of this dreadful war – corpses, the cries of the dying, fear and demoralisation.

C Battery became part of the bombardment opening up the Third Battle of Ypres. But trying to move forward to new positions was soon abandoned because the artillery had themselves torn up the sodden terrain into a mass of holes. Someone suggested they could try going up in boats. It was a relief to get into dry clothes and to an evening in Poperinghe (Maps 1 & 4). The guns continued to pour shells into the shell holes and the ammunition had to be hauled up by the poor struggling horses day and night over the mud.

2nd Lieutenant Campbell tried to show he was brave by turning out during the unloading but the Sergeant said " Don't be so daft. How do you think it's going to help us or anyone if you go asking to be hit?"

He took his turn as Forward Observatio Officer (F.O.O) sending back information to the guns about the progress or otherwise of the infantry. This was near the Steenbeeke stream. In fact, this attack was a terrible failure but the artillery was obliged to keep up their onslaught. There were no intact signalling wires to send back up-to-date information.

At this point Campbell and his fellow observer were in severe danger from enemy shelling. Now he heard the cries of the dying as the missiles fell all around him, and he was paralysed with fear as he stared at Zonnebeke church.

The young man later reflected on the deep fear he had felt but came to the conclusion that to be afraid was a waste of useful energy. But he 'never conquered it'.

Back in the comparative safety of his wagon lines his Major announced that the war had lasted too long and that he was going to make a separate peace with the Germans. At rest, they enjoyed football, sports days and riding races. He met a pretty girl called Suzanne (he remembered he was a virgin at the time) but she rejected his advances. Then he was intoxicated with Paris but resisted the temptation to pay two hundred francs for a prostitute.

He returned again to the Passchendaele battle field for a 24–hour stint as a liaison officer with the infantry. On his way up he was machine-gunned by a Jerry plane and in the front line a shell landed between his feet and he was only saved by a deluge of swamp which covered him from head to foot.

The precise dialogue between himself and fellow officers might suggest he did keep a diary in some form to note how often he was at the guns or at the safer wagon lines. Otherwise the authors of these memoirs written so long after the war must have incredible recall.

As an artillery liaison officer he met different sorts of responses from infantry officers. For instance, the Grenadier Guards would ask him if he was a Regular soldier and if he went to Eton, and then proceeded to ignore him. A county Regiment, on the other hand, 'exhibited warm-hearted bustling, lovable inefficiency'.

We find that the text is in November and that the Canadians capture Passchendaele Ridge. C Battery was then off to Cambrai (Map 1). From the early hours of their New Year 1918 looked 'a hopeless dawn'.

'The Ebb and Flow of Battle' is also a narrative (memoir) with no specific dates. Early in 1918 he had tonsolitis and was not back on duty till March – at Nurlu (south-west of Cambrai – Map 1). Detailed dialogue with fellow officers carries the story forward.

"Jerry's through," shouted a fleeing infantryman. "He's in Epehy, we've got no officers left." This must have been on March 21. Firing the big guns was deemed useless because of the confused situation and the foggy conditions. But Lieutenant Campbell did order "Fire!" and he was awarded the Military Cross. The citation read that he had 'inflicted heavy casualties on the advancing enemy' but he pointed out in his book that this was simply not true, yet he grew to be proud of his medal.

Then followed a frantic retreat, mingling with fleeing refugees: perhaps the only relief was picking up food and drink etc. from abandoned canteens. They finished up in Lavieville but further German offensives did not move them back any more following the heroic re-capture of Villers Brettonneux (south-east of Corbie – Map 2) by the Australians.

'August. We were about to attack. It was our turn now'. But poison gas practically blinded Lieutenant Campbell in September: he refused the opportunity to take a Blighty One. By the time he got back to his Battery it was the middle of October. He was promoted to the rank of Captain but he had become so attached to his Battery that he was very reluctant to go. Yet he soon acquired a similar affection for the new Battery (it was in the same brigade). Chapter 15 does have a date – November 10–11, 1918.

CARR, WILLIAM (1884–1985)
A Time to Leave the Ploughshares
A Gunner Remembers
Robert Hale, 1985

Elizabeth Marshall, William Carr's daughter, persuaded him to recount his experiences as a gunner and taped his responses and edited this book. She checked his account against official records and got the material into chronological order.

William clearly remembered many dates and all the places where he fought, and, amazingly, some of the dialogue of the gunners. He was a farmer in Scotland when at the age of 32 he decided that he wanted to fight for his country. He arrived in France with the 169 Infantry Brigade, Royal Field Artillery, as a 2nd Lieutenant in June 1917 as the BEF was attempting to storm Messines Ridge (Map 4).

He became part of 377 Battery further south in a quieter front near Armentières (Map 1 – Rue Flourie) and was very quickly in action, trying to hit a registered target and learning about SOS rockets – sent up by infantry in difficulties and requiring artillery support. He found that gunners were a jolly crowd, with relations between officers and men very relaxed. They enjoyed capers like raids on honey farms (written up by Carr as a precision military report). Lieutenant Carr became known to his fellow officers as 'Carlos'.

The relative peace of Armentières (Maps 1 & 4) was shattered in September when German artillery almost flattened the town. They were then called south to Cambrai (Map 1) later in the year to support the big tank offensive. They moved south with a 'special' caravan – a rickety old gypsy affair needing daily maintenance, but filled up with crates of whisky in order to entertain visiting senior officers. The big daily question was –'Is the caravan all correct?'

46

It was just as well they had their lighter moments: this was going to be a huge offensive and the gunners were filled with feelings of anxiety and foreboding – although there also was excitement and expectancy. A gun battery moved at about two a half miles an hour (and only at night): all transport was provided by horses, which had to pull huge gun limbers. Looking after the horses was a vital part of battery life, and the gunners were very fond of them – they were prepared to go hungry themselves as long as they could feed the horses.

They reached Metz en Couture on the Cambrai front on November 16, 1917. The Battery was given its target late on the 19th and at first light they caught their first sight of the tanks – 'how impressive these caterpillar-tracked monsters appeared to us'.

At 6.20 a.m. on November 20 377 Battery was part of a vast line of artillery firing thousands of shells against the Hindenburg Line. A gap was smashed in this fortress and Carr went forward to reconnoitre a new gun position beyond it. His first sight of corpses (mainly German ones) was a shocking experience for him. At least he found some decent wine in the German dug-outs.

377 started firing again on November 21 but the new position was spotted by a German plane and the Battery was targeted. One gun was immediately blown sky high with its crew. A large shell landed between Carr and his Major but it was a dud. Eventually, he went for a bite to eat and during his absence his own gun was struck and members of his crew killed. To make matters even worse, the Battery accidentally killed a fellow gunner at the Battery in front of them and the brigade C.O. (CRA) came over to raise hell over it. The dead gunners were buried where they fell.

The Cambrai batttle ground then fell quiet for several days; the initial gains of the tanks were not substantiated. Also, at the end of the month the Germans launched their own furious bombardment and wide counter attacks. The British artillery stood its ground until it was in danger of being engulfed. Eventually, the gunners had to abandon their guns and run for safety. Many officers were killed or wounded.

Without their guns the remnants of the Battery moved out to near Amiens (Map 2), where Carr was shown a report about his possible death and a Brass Hat turned up and tried to get Carr to sign a document putting some blame on him for the loss of the guns. Well, he refused to sign and heard nothing more about the affair. They were looking for scapegoats. Actually, he was eventually awarded the Military Cross for bravery at the action.

The battery got some new guns and moved to the St. Quentin sector previously held by the French in their Somme zone. The fresh German onslaught was expected on March 21 and the Battery officers decided to get into pyjamas on March 20 because it might have been the last occasion they could do so for some time.

But on March 21 they were part of a chaotic retreat before the German hordes. They kept going back for three days with just a few hours' sleep on the muddy ground and very little to eat – in fact, they almost starved and when another unit refused to hand over a tin of Maconochie Carr had to threaten them with a revolver to make them realise the gunners were more than hungry. In the village of Criosilles (south-east of Arras – Map 1) the battery was at one end of the village and the 'Jerries' were at the other end: they escaped but the 'Great Retreat' continued until finally 377 had gone back nearly 25 miles and everyone was exhausted and completely without food. The horses were in an even worse condition.

Yet a reinforced battery was back in action on April 11 to the north, near Arras. On the 12th the order was 'SOS three thousand yards, three rounds a minute', which was the highest rate of firing. But a Fritz balloon detected them and 377 was decimated; William Carr miraculously survived but he had lost most of his fellow officers.

Eventually a restored 377 was engaged in the Summer battles around Albert (Map 2). On one occasion Carr left his bivouac for a few minutes and while he was away a shell landed on it.

But Lieutenant Carr and the Allies began to move forward on the old Somme battlefield in front of Morlancourt (south of Albert) and Americans arrived. At 10 p.m. on the night of November 10, 1918 a single shot hit the Battery and killed one of the gunners.

CLAPHAM, HENRY SHEFFIELD (born 1875)
Mud and Khaki
The Memories of an Incomplete Soldier
Naval and Military Press, 2009

It was a bad start for a draft of the Honourable Artillery Company – marching over Kemmel Hill in full view of the enemy, a strictly prohibited route (January 13, 1915). This was a real diary of 1915 based around precise dates and written very soon after the events it described, and spanning from the date above to October 23, 1915.

It has a highly literate style; Henry Clapham was forty years old in 1915 and had been a partner in a firm of lawyers. So he could write 'our amateur cooks, who understand more of carburetters and centargos than New Zealand lamb'. There is an entry every few days with Clapham referring to the events of the intervening days.

The draft had marched out of Bailleul (Maps 1 & 4) and reached Kemmel village (Map 4). No one seemed to expect them to arrive, an abiding fate for drafts. In the ruins of the village Clapham and four comrades found wood for a fire and further up the road 'ancient smoke-dried crones' who supplied hot black coffee and Flemish bread'.

Henry was obviously just a Private despite his age and qualifications. A spent bullet hit the road by him and his war had started. Corpses still lay in the fields around them. They were just a few hundred yards from the front line and star shells exploded and bullets whistled above their heads.

By January 19 Clapham was in the trenches learning the business of where incoming shells were likely to fall – interesting for a while then frightening. Back in reserve at Locre (Map 4) there was Flemish beer and an estaminet run by Emma and Albertine. There were also lice-ridden children. Going back to the front put him as usual in 'a muck sweat'. He witnessed for the first time the death of a pal.

Diarrhoea broke out and it was battle between his gut and the ubiquitous Number 9 pill, designed to cure anything. The only really useful drink was rum. Private Clapham carried around his section's ration of it. This leaked, although no one believed it. At least, some relief followed – a concert in a local school and some curried Maconochie. But the beer remained inadequate compared to any English brew. He was discovered by the lice.

Back in the front line he spent days along with comrades soaked to the skin. His hands were very sore and if he wore gloves the wool stuck to the sore bits. 'Harrison's Pomade' arrived for the lice: it was effective but uncomfortable (February 22).

Sniping was a constant threat. But if anyone felt sorry for themselves they soon went downhill. A soldier in a Cossack hat always cheered them up with his jolly singing (until he got a Blighty one). Clapham provided no names for anyone.

Many Flemish people were still living in the area. Clapham did not like them (he and his mates called them 'Gonzoubu', the origin of which was lost). At their best they were surly, at worst, possibly spying for the Germans. But many of them had plenty of food and drink for sale.

When they got to Westoutre (Map 4) to rest 30 bags of parcels awaited them (March 16). His description of the undamaged countryside (that would soon change) ranks poetically with Graves or Sassoon: it is an extremely well-written account. Early in April, in the St. Eloi and Dickebusch area (Map 4), his feet also became very painful. A man not wounded badly enough to to be sent back to base yet still sick and expected to fight had a nasty time of it. The only thing to remind them of civilization was a letter from home.

Because the action was so fresh in his mind Clapham was able to repeat authentic dialogue (see especially page 106). It became cold in April and May. In June the battalion was in the ramparts inside Ypres: he described the town as 'a pink heap of brick and plaster'.

Their attack on June 16 captured enemy trenches but someone stole Clapham's helmet. Something moved under his feet and it was a a huge interred German still breathing. They got him out. Then they endured hours and hours of shelling as the enemy fought tenaciously to get back their trenches. A gas shell landed by Clapham's feet but he was unscathed as he was wearing his respirator. The bombardment went on and on and could drive men crazy. How they maintained their composure in such conditions is one of the miracles of the Western Front.

The 'Leaning Virgin' in Albert. The legend was that when the Madonna and Child fell, the war would end

They eventually withdrew back into Ypres but the shelling went on. Yet the cover was better and it was mainly the surviving trees that suffered. Their uniforms hang around their bodies in filthy rags. In July they were sent to the rear for rest and some clothes. Clapham was now a Lance-Corporal (meriting two stripes in the Honourable Artillery Company). He complained bitterly about staged newspaper pictures and articles which were 'pure nonsense' – almost as bad as 'latrine rumours'.

In August they were back in the line. At this time the recruits of Lord Kitchener's New Army were beginning to arrive. It was not all fighting: he received a parcel from a girls' school as part of the scheme in England to identify heroes and send them food, drink and clothing. He also did some boating in the Yser Canal until a shell plopped into it. His idea of recreation was to play cards. By this time the only alarms were the occasional shell, which still gave them the 'wind-up'. In some ways it would be worse to be hit by one of these than one part of a hurricane of shells. The natives remained 'sullen and Hun-like' (September).

In October Henry Sheffield Clapham became a Lance-Sergeant and on the 23rd he was granted home leave and that was when the diary ended.

CLOUTING, BENJAMIN (1897–1990)
Teenage Tommy
Memoirs of a Cavalryman in the First World War
Edited by Richard van Emdem
Pen & Sword, 2013

Richard Van Emden recorded Ben Clouting's memoirs in 1989 and 1990. He served on the Western Front from the very start of the war to its very end. The editor added historical notes. Ben signed up for the 4th Royal Irish Dragoon Guards in July 1913 when he was 15 years old. The Regiment left for France on August 14, 1914 and arrived in Belgium a week later. Cavalry patrols went out towards Mons and located German infantry and cavalry to the north.

There followed a small-scale clash at Casteau during which a few Germans were put to the sword or captured. A brief rifle battle ensued but both sides quickly withdrew. An infantry battle followed on August 23. The presence of overwhelming German forces was ascertained and immediate British retreat was ordered. On the 24th the British cavalry charged (at Audregnies) in order to allow the infantry to get away.

Ben remembered the charge as 'a melee, with shell, machine gun and rifle fire forming a terrific barrage of noise'. The cavalrymen later christened the event as 'Shrapnel Monday' or 'Joy Ride'. Ben was knocked off his horse and then he tried to help a wounded comrade but had to leave him to be captured by the enemy. Forced back the Dragoons tried to shelter in a sugar factory and behind a slag heap but the German artillery soon registered their position and they had to carry on retreating very rapidly. But they had allowed the infantry to get away.

Ben remembered the complete chaos of the this retreat from Mons, with the roads clogged up with troops and their transport and also swarms of refugees. The BEF went through Le Cateau to St. Quentin, to Noyon (near Amiens – Map 2) and beyond – around 30 miles. Scattered units tried to reform as they suffered severely from hunger and thirst. Farm animals were butchered, orchards plundered. The danger of being overrun by the Germans was ever-present. Ben spotted a signpost indicating that Paris was only 9 kilometres away.

But the Germans were unable to continue their advance to the capital and the situation stagnated as the French Army and the BEF re-grouped and prepared to fight back in the Battle of the Marne in September. Ben accompanied an intelligence officer operating behind the enemy front line on the Marne (and later the River Aisne) in order to ascertain their positions and strengths. The enemy was driven back towards Belgium.

Ben returned to normal duties caring for officers' horses at Longueval (Map 2). Eventually he became horse orderly for the new C.O. of the 4th Hussars later in September. They left for Ypres early in October as the weather grew colder and wetter. Ben trained with the cavalry to adapt to operate in trenches to the east if Ypres and eventually took up a position near Zillebeke (south-east of Ypres – Maps 1 & 4).

But it was the French more to the north of Ypres who bore the brunt of the Second Battle of Ypres in April 1915. Yet cavalry units had to fight near Potijze (Map 4) in May and suffered from heavy enemy shelling. Ben elected to become a stretcher-bearer. A fellow stretcher-bearer was shot dead beside him as they struggled to get a badly wounded man out of no man's land.

But Ben said, "I was lucky. For most of the war I was an orderly and had breaks from the trench."

Yet in a desperate German last-ditch attempt to break through on May 24, following a long bombardment, Ben was hit in the ankle by shrapnel as he tried to cross the Menin Road. He had been carrying an ammunition box and this had saved his life: many pieces of shrapnel were embedded in it. He was also suffering from gas poisoning.

He was lucky enough to find a farmyard broom to use as a crutch and managed to reach an ambulance in Ypres (as this pulled away a crumbling wall just missed it). By May 26 he was in hospital in England.

He returned to France in October but caught impetigo and was in hospital again till the last day of 1915. For a long time he was horse orderly for Lieutenant Colonel de Wiart, a heroic leader (he was wounded 11 times and won a VC on the Somme), at various Battalions.

Ben was near Arras (Map 1) in the Spring of 1917 when he was hit again by shrapnel. But his helmet and a thick skull prevented serious injury. In the Third Battle of Ypres he took rations up to the front line, a nerve-wracking job as the German artillery could usually spot them moving up the communication trenches (and sometimes the ration parties had to go up on top when the trench was damaged).

Later in 1917 he was at the cavalry training school at Cayeux-sue-Mer at the mouth of the Somme as horse orderly for one of the instructors. But he wanted to get back to the front line with the Dragoons. He actually applied for a Commission but apparently lack of an 'old school tie' failed him: he was given the compensation of one stripe. In the last weeks of the war Ben mounted his horse and cleared barbed wire using a lance adapted with cutters. He went to Cologne as a member of the Army of Occupation.

COLLINS, NORMAN (1897–1998)
Last Man Standing
The Memoirs, Letters & Photographs
of a Teenage Officer-Cadet
Edited by Richard Van Emden
Pen & Sword, 2012

Richard Van Emden constructed this volume from taped interviews with Norman, Norman's own taped memoirs, plus his letters (he wrote home to his parents and brother every few days) and postcards.

Norman Collins was commissioned into the Seaforth Highlanders in August 1916 and reached Forceville in the Somme region (north-west of Albert – Map 2) in late October to join the 6th Battalion to fight in the Beaumont Hamel area (Map 3).

The battalion was poised to engage in the Battle of the Ancre on November 13. He went into battle with them armed with a walking stick and a .45 revolver which he didn't know how to use, and some Mills bombs. Officers in battle were identified only by triangles in indelible pencil on their shoulder straps – although the stick must have been a giveaway. His duty was to shepherd his men out of the trench and into no man's land. "Knowing one's duty took one's mind off the horrible things," he said.

He was in a rear wave of infantry aiming at the second and third German defensive lines. But here the enemy had a formidable line of machine guns firing 'in a solid wall of lead'. But he leapt down into a German trench and tossed around his Mills bombs. They reached Beaumont Hamel, although nothing of it was left except piles of bricks.

He and his platoon found masses of German ammunition, supplies and food (which he lists in detail in the book). His gruesome task when the fighting died down was to bury numerous dead comrades, plus some

Newfoundlanders who had lain out there since the fateful day of July 1. He remembered that he carried out this dreadful task without any emotion, long since 'deadened' to such chores. Norman filled up dozens of sandbags with the pay books he collected.

Norman felt 'an intense bond' with the men under his command because they went through such terrifying experiences together: the soldiers relied on his unwavering leadership and bravery to sustain them. He had to write countless letters home to the parents of the dead men, sometimes as many as 60 at a time. Most of them he knew nothing about and he had to use, in his words, a 'kindly hypocrisy'. The parents often wrote back to thank him.

The 6th Battalion went to 'rest' at Auchonvilliers (near Albert – Map 2) but Norman had to return with a working party to their trenches almost immediately (December 8) to perform hard manual work . As they marched up the road to the communication trench a shell exploded amongst them, killing many and driving splinters of metal into Norman's back and thigh. At first they tried to dig these out with a hooked lancet. He finished up in hospital near Doullens (Map 2) and then in Brighton, England, where he spent his Christmas, 1916.

He was classed as 'walking wounded', but despite his cheerful letters to his family he spent most of his time bedridden in pain. He improved enough to take a trip up to London. He was pronounced fit for general duty in February 1917.

However, there were still bits of shrapnel in his body which had nearly severed an artery and he became very ill again and needed another operation. He was in Ripon in hospital and resting for two months.

He was back with the 4th Battalion on April 29; it had just suffered severe losses in the Battle of Arras (Map 1). This struggle had stagnated but still in May it remained a very violent affair of raids and shelling with little in the way of organised shelter apart from battered trenches and shell holes. They were in the vicinity of Roeux until the fighting finally ceased on May 17.

Norman remembered vividly the cries of dying men in no man's land. He had received instruction in how to go out and shoot these poor creatures but he was never able to raise the courage to do this. The strain he was enduring surfaced in his letters, which became less cheerful and much shorter.

The battalion moved to Fricourt (Map 3) in June and trained in pleasant weather for yet another battle. But they did enjoy a lot of sport at this time. Hope grew that this battle from the Ypres Salient would bring a quick end to the war.

They were moving up to the line at Pilckem (north of Ypres – Maps 1 & 4) but Norman was struck in various parts of his body by more shrapnel. He was sent to hospital in Paris Plage. He recalled how marvellous the Voluntary Aid Detachment (VAD) nurses were in the care of the wounded and in acts of kindness to them, and in providing entertainment. In August he was in hospital in London. He was never able to return to the Western Front.

CONGREVE, BILLY (1891–1916)
Armageddon Road
A VC's Diary 1914–6
Edited by Terry Norman
William Kimber & Co. Limited, 1982

William La Touche Congreve ('Billy'), a major by the end of 1915, won the Military Cross at Hooge in 1915, the DSO at St. Eloi (south of Ypres – Maps 1 & 4) in 1916, the French Legion of Honour and the VC after his death on July 1, 1916 at the Battle of the Somme.

Major Congeve came from a very military family and was educated at Eton and Sandhurst. He joined the 3rd Battalion of the Rifle Brigade in 1911. He kept a daily diary from July 28, 1914 to January 17, 1916, but two months of it late in 1915 was burnt in a fire. The account is clear and very much about the military action. It contains considerable criticism of the higher echelons of the British Expeditionary Force.

Billy Congreve reached France on September 13, 1914 and he went up with his battalion to fight in the Battle of the Aisne – which drove the German Army even further away from Paris. He was near his father – Major General Walter Congreve, VC, KCB, MVO (or 'Dads') and was often in the company of one General or another and given important tasks, such as showing Winston Churchill and the Norwegian Minister of Paris around the battlefield (the latter was nearly hit by a shell and covered in mud but was more concerned about publicity compromising Norwegian neutrality).

During the 'Race to the Sea' in October, Lieutenant Congreve described the burial of 'a very good friend', 'Hammy', who was Major General Hamilton, struck by shrapnel.

Primitive trenches were appearing late in October at the struggle around Armentières, La Bassée and Neuve Chapelle (Maps 1 & 4). Here, a sniper's bullet just missed Congreve whilst the enemy shrapnel was 'beastly unhealthy', especially for officers reconnoitring in the rear. It provided a good view of British infantry crawling across no man's land a yard a minute. Billy's attention was particularly caught by 'a great bearded turbaned fellow'. Sadly, after a while, he crawled no more (October 29). Lieutenant Congreve continued to lead a charmed life as a shell landed at his feet and failed to explode. There were terrible casualty figures but no ground was gained and Congreve was already wondering whether the fruitless loss of life was due to poor leadership.

He was in Ypres on November 9 and still the shells followed him around as the Germans prepared to storm the town and eradicate the British Salient. But the myriad woods to the east hampered their progress, along with the fierce resistance of the BEF

Captain Congreve described 'the hateful brew' of 'Black Marias' and 'Weary Willies' (German shells) on Ypres. The men were 'splendid' but 'weary and broken'. He did not know how they managed to stand up to it. But by November 20 the German offensive came to a halt in failure.

The Ypres Salient now settled into trench fortifications on both sides. Yet occasional attacks were still ordained by Sir John French, for instance, the one at Wytschaete (Map 4) on December 15, which resulted in the loss of great numbers of infantry. The British newspaper headlines the following day announced 'British troops hurl back Germans at Wytschaete'. On Christmas Day some Germans attempted to move out of their trenches for a truce but the Rifle Brigade start firing at them.

By the time of better weather in 1915 further attacks out of the Salient at Neuve Chapelle (Maps 1 & 4) and St. Eloi were attempted These were disastrous failures and there were furious rows in Higher Command as to whom was to blame: Brigadier General Ballard became the scapegoat.

The start of Congreve's entry for March 23 was, 'We are to take over the 27th Division line which embraces St. Eloi. What joy!' On April 12 he climbed down a rope ladder to visit some ex-Durham coal miners digging under the German lines. They were 'a jolly lot'. They blew up Hill 60 on April 18. But then came the second German attempt to destroy the Ypres Salient, now including the widespread use of poison gas shells. Captain Congreve was critical of the efforts of the French Army in this Second Battle of Ypres.

'It is not pleasant to sit so close to everything, he wrote on May 9.

'One longs to be up doing something'. But he lost many much-loved fellow officers. There was talk of a shortage of ammunition yet the Prime Minister (Asquith) denied this in Parliament. –'a lie', according to Congreve.

The Second Battle of Ypres petered out on May 25 but Higher Command still insisted on aggressive activity in the Salient, once more with little success and heavy casualties, particularly from lethal German shelling. Congreve moved into the General Staff (always likely). The numerous sketch maps in the book smack of close familiarity with the details of the battlegrounds.

There was a fire at HQ on November 27, 1915 which destroyed Billy's diary entry from September 11. The last entry was for January 17, 1916. He had became a Brigade Major and possibly his enlarged work load prevented him from keeping up his daily diary. He was shot by a sniper whilst in the front line.

COOPER, MATTHEW
We Who Knew
The Journal of an Infantry Subaltern during the Great War
Edited by A. M. Cooper
The Book Guild, 1994

Matthew Cooper kept a diary for 1918 and with the assistance of military documents for 1916 and 1917 wrote this memoir soon after the war ended. He wrote it for his 'own satisfaction' – to have a record of what had happened to him on the Western Front. His son, Anthony, discovered this 70 years after it was written: it had been kept a secret by Matthew.

It is a clearly written account (he was educated at a good school in Dublin) if plain and generally factual. There are only a few precise dates but the reader gets a rough idea of the chronology.

Matthew arrived in France as a 2nd Lieutenant in the Cameron Highlander Regiment on February 23, 1916 after volunteering for service in September 1914. He went to the front line in the Loos sector (near Lens – Map 1). It was a quiet front by this time but he still had to lead risky raids up to the enemy wire. By now the Loos salient consisted of a vast network of trenches and fortifications which stretched to within the ruins of the town. It was still a dangerous existence in the British trenches, where the troops were vulnerable to rifle grenades thrown by German raiders, mortar shells (which fell in a deep curve) and snipers.

The 8th Battalion moved around this sector, often near Mazingarbe (south-east of Béthune – Map 1). Much of the time 2nd Lieutenant Cooper was supervising working parties repairing and constructing trenches, and also helping the miners in their tunnels. The odd stray shell was a lurking menace and Matthew was nearly hit twice.

He developed a problem with boils on his head so missed a big gas attack in which the 8th Battalion took part. He was in hospital in

Rouen for six weeks. He was then away on a company commander's course when his unit joined the Battle of the Somme in August 1916 and fought hard at Guillemont and Ginchy (Map 3), suffering terrible losses, especially of officers.

He was back with them when they moved to Flanders, now a quiet front, and they enjoyed a very pleasant billet in an old hospice at Locre (Map 4) and trips into Bailleul (Maps 1 & 4), where there was an officers' club and a large canteen. Home leave beckoned but it was preceded by a British attack designed to keep the enemy on their toes, always nerve-wracking when home leave was imminent. On Boxing Day a football match was interrupted by shelling and one soldier was killed.

The battalion officers managed to get hold of a gramophone and the music was a popular relaxation (and officers from other units paid visits), especially in the freezing weather. Sniping was now becoming a serious danger in the trenches. A newcomer was alarmed: "Dem fellers would shoot yer," he announced accurately. Matthew was now 'totally fatalistic' about the prospect of sudden death, hoping that it would be instantaneous.

The 8th Battalion took part in raids preceding the offensive aimed at Messines Ridge (Map 4) on June 5, 1917. Matthew witnessed the detonation of 1,000 tons of TNT which blew the ridge apart on June 6, followed by a huge artillery bombardment. He was in the second wave of infantry charging into no man's land at the devastated enemy front line.

When on leave in Dublin in July he was detained in a military hospital because of more boils and general illness, and deemed unfit to return to France. He was not back there until April 1918 during the great German offensive. He had transferred to the 1st Inniskilling Fusiliers and was on the canal bank next to Ypres on April 29. There was a serious possibility that Ypres would be abandoned but the BEF managed to hold on to it as the German pressure lessened.

One of the men in Lieutenant Cooper's platoon (he did stand in as a company commander at times) refused to leave a pill box and the officer had to threaten to shoot him. Later, he placed the same man under arrest after he knocked down the Sergeant Major at a pay parade.

Matthew provided a detailed account of what he did on May 28, 1918 (obviously from his diary). The sector had gone quiet by June and war seemed to be replaced by morning parades, training, games in the afternoon and recreation in the evening. But then they had to move to opposite Messines Ridge (now in enemy hands along with the town of Bailleul – Maps 1 & 4) as it seemed that there would be a fresh enemy assault.

But this did not happen and the Allied fight back gathered momentum and the battleground of the Ypres Salient fell silent. Lieutenant Cooper went past Passchendaele in a train. He was in Dublin with his wife and new baby on Armistice Day.

COPPARD, GEORGE (1898–1984)
With a Machine Gun to Cambrai
A Story of the First World War
Cassell Military Paperback, 1999

George Coppard wrote this memoir from the diaries he kept during the war and sent it to the Imperial War Museum in 1968 – and it was published as 'With a Machine Gun to Cambrai' in 1969.

Noble Frankland (Secretary of the Museum in 1980) was impressed by the 'power of spontaneity' of Coppard's text. Also, Christopher Dowling, the Keeper of Education and Publications, referred to the book's 'emotional intensity', and its demonstration of a private soldier's 'helplessness' in the grip of a military system which demanded unquestioning obedience.

Although George did not get a secondary education he was a highly literate writer by the time he was in his 60s. It is a clear and straightforward text. Dates are precise.

He volunteered in 1914 when he was 16 years old, pretending he was 19 (August 27) and joined the Royal West Surrey Regiment, or Queen's 2nd of Foot. He went to France in June 1915 as a member of Lord Kitchener's New Army.

They were soon in trenches near Armentières (Maps 1 & 4). His early experiences were like any other Tommy – he was scared stiff but fell into the routines of the trench and the learning curve of survival in this terrifying environment. And here was yet another soldier who found himself in 'Plugstreet' (Ploegsteerte) Wood (Map 4), where he had his first taste of the enemy artillery – a new shock to the nervous system. But this was a 'quiet zone' where the enemy would not fire at you if you didn't fire at them.

'Rest' consisted of lots of work but at least there was nightly sleep in a bed and the possibility of a bit of spare time in an estaminet. Real war followed and he lost his first pal – a shattering shock. At the Battle of Loos in September 1915 (near Lens – Map 1) he was put into a machine gun section as a Number 3, which meant lugging about heavy boxes of ammunition, plus rifle and equipment in the vicinity of the Hohenzollern Redoubt.

Here, there was a further introduction – to the terrifying 'Minnenwerfer', an enemy shell which caused a major assault on nerves and morale. There were also snipers and lots of rats.

The Queen's were out of the front line for a spell late in November but before the end of the year they were opposite hostile Prussians but at least rum was making an appearance. George's uncle back home appealed to the War Office to have his nephew released on account of his age (George didn't find out about this until after the war – his book has a copy of the official letter turning down this application in February 1916).

In the same month George became part of the new specialist Machine Gun Company and back to the Hohenzollern Redoubt he went. But there were nice breaks in Béthune (Maps 1 & 4), a bustling town he loved. But on the Somme he saw the dreadful results of the carnage of July 1. He went into action himself on July 3 north of Contalmaison (Maps 2 & 3) where he realised how strong and intricate German trenches were in comparison to the British ones.

In the assault on Thiepval in August the main torment was the 'whizz-bang' German shell which travelled faster than sound. He was in the devastated Trones Wood (west of Guillemont – Map 3) in September with 'hellish' German shrapnel and lethal bombing from enemy aircraft. George's great mate 'Snowy' accidentally shot him in the foot (October 17, 1916) and he was sent to a hospital where they investigated whether the wound was self-inflicted (or the result of an arrangement with a pal). That was an awkward few days but they exonerated him eventually. He was out of the war for six months.

He arrived back with the 37th Machine Gun Company on May 8, 1917, now a Number One in a gun crew still in action in the Arras sector (Map 1) enduring heavy and sustained enemy artillery fire and bombing from the air.

He was promoted to Corporal and became part of the great tank offensive at Cambrai (Map 1). But on November 22 a bullet went clean through his thigh from an enemy machine gunner who continued to fire at him but he escaped further damage.

He was in a field hospital within an hour, and in Birkenhead in a week. He was awarded the Military Medal in 1918. An appendix to the book shows letters written to George by ex-soldiers who had enjoyed the story and recounted their own experiences.

CULL, WILLIAM
Both Sides of the Wire
The Memoir of an Australian Officer
captured during the War
Edited by Aaron Pegram
Allen & Unwin, 2011

This book is based on the memoir 'At All Costs' which Cull wrote shortly after the war. Cull was badly wounded and captured on February 26, 1917 on the Somme battlefield in the attack on Malt Trench near La Barque (Map 3). Only 4 Australian POWs (out of 3,867) wrote an account of their captivity.

'At All Costs' was published in 1919 at a time when the British Committee on the treatment of Allied prisoners was making its early enquiries. Aaron Pegram kept Cull's story largely intact, but added an introduction, endnote and epilogue.

In his book Cull admitted to 'no pretence of chronological order, just an impression of observation and incident written as they as they are recalled'. His memory was 'blurred because of his injuries and maltreatment' in German hospitals and camps.

Cull was in the 23rd Battalion of the Australian Imperial Force in Egypt and later Gallipoli (where he was also wounded). He arrived in Marseilles in March 1916 (he gives the occasional precise date). The battalion went to trenches near Armentières at Fleurbaix (Map 4) struggling with the enemy for control of no man's land.

They moved to the Somme and Cull was promoted to Captain in the 22nd Battalion. He was in the assault on Pozières Ridge (Map 3) on July 30.

Later in the year the 22nd was in Sanctuary Wood near Ypres and early in 1917 at the action at the Butte de Warlencourt (Map 3). By this time the Germans was ceding land in the Somme battlefront in order to take up positions in the new Hindenburg Line of fortifications. Cull's was one of many Australian Companies detailed to find out where the Germans were with the possibility of taking over their trenches.

'At All Costs' then has chapters on 'Psychology of Battle' and 'Men and Episodes', where praise is heaped on his senior officers.

As part of their retreat strategy the Germans were maintaining some formidable strongpoints to impede the Allied advance, along with numerous and ingenious booby traps all over the terrain. Malt Trench near La Barque (Map 3) was one of these German defences. But Australian commanders appeared to be unaware of the strength of the Malt Trench defences and planned to send in companies like Cull's without the usual artillery support. Cull made preliminary probes to find out exactly how strong the German defences were in this area and became certain that they were in for a nasty surprise.

But his seniors insisted that he went ahead and the result was that Cull and his men were met by a hail of rifle and machine gun fire. But the survivors ploughed on, hacking their way through the first line of wire and making for the next. Cull was leading his men when a shell blew away one of his hips.

German surgeons operated on him and were obviously surprised when he survived. He was sent to hospital in Cambrai (Map 1) and later Bochum, He lay for days on his own in great pain, with little sleep and in a filthy bed, and with bed sores, his wound still a gaping hole.

Life improved a little when they moved him around and exercised him. But generally his captors were not pleasant to him. It was many weeks before he was shown any kindness at all by medical staff. He was transferred to Karlsruhe into a tiny, rat-ridden cell but then he went to hospital and met other Australians. The food was poor and tasteless – enough for a slow starvation had it not been for Red Cross parcels and some expensive but weak wine and beer.

He was moved south to prison camp at Freiburg (October 1917), then Heidelburg and then to internment in Switzerland (Montreux) after Christmas. The Swiss made a great fuss of them as they now opposed the Germans. In January Cull's nervous system broke down and he was very ill again for a month. There was no chance of restoring his hip, which was completely shattered. He was repatriated to England just as the German Spring offensive was launched in 1918.

DOLDEN, STUART (born 1893)
Cannon Fodder
An Infantryman's Life on the Western Front 1914–18
A. Stuart Dolden
Blandford Press, 1980

Although Stuart had graduated in Law he was a private in the London Scottish Regiment when it reached France in July 1915. He kept a day-to-day diary throughout the war. Men from various regiments in Rouen found themselves temporarily in the Number Four Entrenching Battalion, which was despatched to Doullens (August 6 – Map 2).

Stuart got back to the London Scottish at Vermelles (south-east of Béthune – Maps 1 & 4) after a couple of weeks constructing trenches but he was not pleased at having to do even more digging – this time in no man's land within sight of snipers. He also had to contend with lice and noisy, spitting French soldiers.

There followed a month's training near Lillers (August 31–September 21 – west of Béthune – Maps 1 & 4) for the Battle of Loos – marching, practice assaults and 'belly-flopping' (getting down on the ground quickly). But there was some rugby and swarms of wasps.

Trenches at Loos (Lens sector – Map 1) were not good, with no room to even sit down let alone lie down. It was wet and cold and to try and sleep behind the trench on sodden ground with a groundsheet over them (they had no greatcoats) was distressingly uncomfortable. Stuart was a bomber but the primitive detonators on the grenades were rendered useless by the rain. Also, lying on the useless bombs was not comfortable.

They went over the top in front of Loos with enemy fire coming from sides (some of it 'friendly') as well as from the front. All seemed lost as large numbers of the attackers fell dead or wounded. But a large force of Germans in front of them – many hundreds – suddenly surrendered, apparently unnerved by the kilts. Success seemed to arise out of confusion rather than tactics. Thus the German front and second lines were captured. Yet the London Scottish had 300 casualties out of 540.

The survivors was forced to dig shallow ditches during a bitterly cold night. Enemy retaliatory fire became lethal in these inadequate defences. They could not retire because they were called across to help block a German counter-attack to the left at Hulluch. This involved more digging in and yet another night in the front. They finally came out on September 29.

They were back in the Vermelles (south-east of Béthune Maps 1 & 4) sector early in October. Stuart had two very close escapes from shells and on a bombing raid a bullet went through his water bottle and kilt (October 13). Since September 25 the brigade had lost 4,400 men out of 5,000!

They then rested near Lillers, west of Béthune (Maps 1 & 4), where he was called upon to defend a man at a court martial. He contracted impetigo in November and was sent to hospital (where there was an epidemic of diarrhoea). He avoided that but not laryngitis, which kept him out of action into 1916.

He eventually rejoined his battalion at Forceville (February – north-west of Albert – Map 2) and then they were in Doullens (Map 2) from March to May – 'a pleasant stay'.

In June the London Scottish were in the defences around Hébuterne (between the Somme and Arras – Map 1), repairing and developing trenches under enemy shelling. They were in the assault at Gommecourt (north-east of Bapaume – Map 2) on the infamous first day of the Battle of the Somme but Stuart was not directly involved because he had become a cook. His battalion lost three quarters of its strength at Gommecourt and Stuart had to go back in the line as a bomber in this emergency (July 16).

But by the end of July he was back with the cookers (his quartermaster boasted that his cooks were nearer the front than the cooks of any other battalion in the whole brigade). So Stuart was still in danger, even cooking in the transport lines, and definitely when he was dishing out food and tea in the trenches.

In October he was offered a commission in the Paris HQ Staff but decided to remain as a cook on the Somme because 'a post in Paris would require great strength of character if one was not to be undermined morally'.

Stuart provided an immense mass of narrative detail in his memoir because it was based on a daily diary. Date and place are always there. Perhaps comment on the general battle situation is lacking but this is probably the best account of how cooks worked on the Western Front.

They appeared to spend a lot of time finding their own accommodation since it was not organised for them. Stuart actually got into a bed on October 20 (he tossed for it with the other cooks). Sometimes they lay in open ground soaked to the skin! They did a crucial job – endeavouring to keep the infantry fed and watered in difficult and dangerous circumstances. But I still can't believe that Stuart turned down that job in Paris!

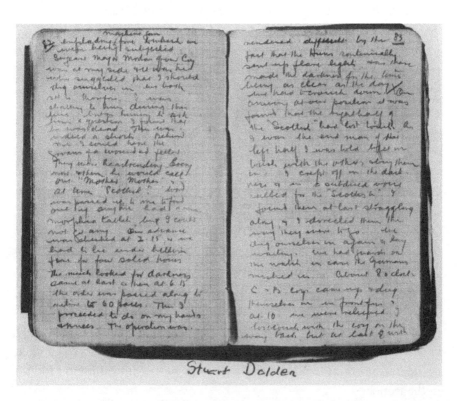

Pages of the author's diary with notes of the attack on the Hollenollern Redoubt at Hulloch during the Battle of Loos, 13th October, 1915

DOUIE, CHARLES (born 1896)
The Weary Road
Recollections of a Subaltern of Infantry
John Murray, 1929

This volume was first published in 1929. Charles had written a series of memoirs for the journal 'The Nineteenth Century and After'. After some editing by Charles the book was published by John Murray.

Charles's memoir appears to be entirely based on memory: there are very few specific dates and only in a very general sense does the reader know what month (sometimes months) to which he is referring. Also, beyond 1916 it becomes rather like an essay rather a memoir.

However, there is quality in this account by a young and enthusiastic subaltern, a sketch of what he endured and detail about fellow officers and NCOs. Charles reached the camp at Étaples with the 1st Battalion of the Dorset Regiment late in 1915 just after he had become 19. He was frustrated at first, like other young 2nd Lieutenants at this period, by being put in charge of men digging trenches (Entrenching Battalion). He wanted action in the front line not 'strolling up and down a hundred yards of sodden grass for 8 hours a day'.

Finally, he was returned to his battalion but it was difficult to find them (another common and frustrating experience of the Western Front) and had not yet 'learnt the art of making himself comfortable in unpromising surroundings'. He was rescued by the quartermaster, an NCO of the very best quality. For 4 years this soldier led the battalion's supply wagons wherever they went and he was with every ration party that took supplies to trenches. He deserved his Military Cross.

Charles was very happy to be with a regiment (his uncle had served in it, too) which valued the traditions and strong discipline of the pre-war Army. The battalion had an unusual profile of action between 1915 and

1917: it was on the Somme at Hénencourt (west of Albert – Map 2) before the end of 1915, fought at the Somme in 1916 (with heavy casualties), but not at Arras, Ypres and Cambrai (Map 1) in 1917. In 1918 it went to Italy.

The memoir is unusual in having quite some detail about the Somme from before June 1916. The battalion served in the trenches beginning as support at the Usna Reboubt and in Dunfermiline Avenue (where Charles's Sergeant was not happy unless he was in the most dangerous trench).

Under the first barrage he endured Charles was 'almost wild with fear'. Men were hit around him and he vividly remembered the 'cry in the night', the blinding flashes and the nauseating smell of blood. It was bliss to go back to the sanctity of Albert (Map 2).

Back in the trench there was the 'grim humour' of receiving a letter from a very young cousin to ask Charles how he was. Shortly after, Charles optimistically joined a raid, waiting in a shell crater for the order to advance behind the first wave of raiders. The British artillery opened fire behind him and the enemy artillery replied immediately. His enthusiasm began to fade, even more so when German machine guns opened up on both sides. The Germans knew all the details about the attack. By the dawn light Charles saw the corpses of a fellow subaltern and his own servant hanging on the enemy wire.

The battalion took over the trenches in front of Thiepval in the Spring of 1916. One of Charles's first tasks here was to go over and rebuke British gunners for dropping shells on his troops. He was received with 'good-natured sarcasm' but he had the last word when he took charge of a dud shell that they just slung in a trench. On his way back he was knocked flying by an explosion: you could die at any second on the Western Front.

The battalion suffered casualties on July 1, 1916 but that 'was only one day in three months'. He observed that a daily record of these three months would be intolerable because it would have 'constant reiteration of attack and counter-attack'. He could remember 'no order of time or place'.

He can remember that he was at Serre Ridge (near Beaumont Hamel – Map 3) in November 1916 and Nieuport (Map 1) in October 1917 (after July 10, he reported, this was a quiet front).

DOWNING, W.H. (1893–1965)
To The Last Ridge
The World War One Experience of W. H. Downing
Grub Street, 2002

W. H. Downing published this book in 1920 but the publisher went bust and he received lots of copies of it in lieu of royalties. All but one copy was destroyed in a fire.

He was involved in all the sixteen battles fought by the Australian Imperial Force on the Western Front. He had tried to enlist at the start of the war but was rejected 8 times because he was too short. Then his mates stretched him with weights on his feet and he managed to get accepted in September 1915. He was placed in the 7th Battalion, AIF.

In Egypt for final training he was offered a discharge on the grounds of a dislocated and cracked bone in his right arm. He turned this down and was then transferred to the 57th Battalion. By the time he arrived in France in 1916 he had been promoted to the rank of Sergeant. He was offered the chance of a commission but did not want to leave his pals. He was awarded the Military Medal for bravery during the Battle of Polygon Wood in the Ypres Salient in 1917. He remained a front line soldier for the remainder of the war on the Western Front. Brigadier – General Elliot, Downing's Divisional Commander (and later his partner in a law firm) described 'The Last Ridge' as 'the true picture – the monument we still want for our rich dead'.

This current edition of the book was edited by Downing's grandson with only minor changes from the 1920 original. Explanatory notes are kept to a minimum. The text is in the form of a narrative with only a few dates although place names are usually provided. Soldiers' names are fictitious for some reason.

The 57th Battalion suffered along with the rest of the AIF in the

Battle of the Somme. Downing wrote that, 'One accepts the immediate present… the deeper one dug the more bodies one exhumed. Hands and feet protruded from the slimy, toppling walls of trenches…'

The savage weather of January and February 1917 also took its toll on morale. 'Australia has forgotten us', he wrote for January 27 when the temperature was 25 degrees of frost and there were no blankets. He was in and out of the front line at Ginchy (Maps 1 & 4). 'It's a hopeless business – weeks in and weeks out of the trenches…'

The structure of 'To the Last Ridge' is unusual for having interludes or essay chapters. For instance, Chapter VI is entitled 'Trench Mythology.' Bullecourt (south-west of Arras – Map 1) in April and May 1917 raged hideously for five weeks. In September and October it was the turn of the Ypres Salient. Downing was a Sergeant as they battled for ridge after ridge towards Passchendaele, including the frantic struggle around Polygon Wood. He did not mention the fact that he won the Military Medal here.

The next diversionary chapter (X) is a comic interlude about Downing and his funny mate 'Bluey ('a person of parts'). The 57th saw out the rest of the winter in front of the Messines Ridge (Map 4) and was in place to meet the German onslaught in the Spring of 1918.

As a result of the ensuing battles Villers-Brettonmeux (south-east of Corbie – Map 2) became a shrine to Australian military history. Here, hordes of marauding Germans were slaughtered during a heroic defence on April 25 (the village still has its famous sign – 'N'oublier jamais l'Australie' – 'never forget Australia'). Downing recorded that the 'rare thanks' of Field Marshal Haig was the order of the day.

Chapter XIV is another comic break – 'A Shot on the Wrong Target' in which Downing and his mate Bluey drove off in the Brigadier's Mercedes from outside Brigade HQ. In yet another break from the main story one of Downing's officers, nicknamed 'Puss in Boots', is involved in an embarrassing scene in an estaminet bedroom.

The German push was eventually defeated. Chapter XVIII – 'Some Characteristics' – is about the nature of the Australian infantryman.

DRINKWATER HARRY (1889–1978)
Harry's War. The Great War Diary of Harry Drinkwater
Ebury Press, 2014

Harry, from Stratford-on-Avon, volunteered to join the 2nd Birmingham City Battalion ('Birmingham Pals' – later the 15/ Royal Warwickshire Regiment) at the outset of the war. Along with many thousands of others of Lord Kitchener's New Army, he arrived in France in late 1915. However, unlike the vast majority of them, he tried to keep a daily diary of what he was experiencing at home and abroad (later in the war he served in Italy). Some days were missed for one reason or another.

The final form of his diary was a foolscap-sized leather-bound diary, which was eventually bought at auction by David Griffith. Then Jon Cooksey edited the book.

Harry survived some of the worse battles of the war and his account is a most vivid description of what he and his pals suffered. He could write well, having been educated at King Edward VI Grammar School in Stratford. He came from a family of Methodists with strong moral values (quite a number of the diarists had a similar upbringing). Such 'muscular Christianity' helped Harry through the terrible ravages of trench warfare.

The various stages of the diary went from a few scratched notes in pencil carried around in his tunic pocket, written up when away from the front line. This went into small notebooks, and there were six of these by the time he was finished.

Later, in the 1920s, he reviewed what he had written and entered the final form into the big book, embossed with the title 'War Diary'. The review had additional observations – often his retrospective feelings about what he was describing.

The 15/ Royal Warwickshire Regiment arrived in France in time to endure the horrible conditions of the 1915–1916 winter in flooded, freezing, rat-infested trenches. Respite from this took place in very uncomfortable billets. Harry depicted the ruined countryside and its bedraggled citizens.

To sit in these water-filled holes in the ground and scribble notes for posterity under the flickering light of a single candle (if he was lucky to have one) became a type of duty for him, one encouraged by his Christian and disciplined upbringing.

One day in December 1915 his attempt to write was defeated because his hands were stiff with frozen mud and there was no nowhere to sit. 'We lived every minute in a state of fever and, in an isolated case or two, delirium'. On January 29, 1916 he was in a billet near Arras (Map 1), sharing a candle with a whole platoon of men, many of them trying to write letters home. Harry had a few spells helping with mining operations near Arras, and found this convenient for writing notes as he waited to fill the next bag with spoil.

There was good news in April 16 when a divisional canteen opened up and Harry could get stacks of candles. 'Here I am', he wrote on May 24, 1916, 'back to my billet, writing like the dickens – 2 a.m'.

'No amateur pen can faithfully portray the conditions we were in when we got back into the trench' (June 14, 1916). The Birmingham Pals were back on the Somme in the autumn, when there were desperate struggles to move forward and then hold back the enemy. By this time Harry was in a machine gun team. He reached the rank of Sergeant in 1917. In 14 months he had not missed a day's duty.

He returned to England to train as an officer, coming back as a 2nd Lieutenant in the 16th Battalion of the Royal Warwickshires, in August 1917. This Battalion was then moved to the Italian front but back on the Western Front to meet the German onslaught in the Spring of 1918. In June he was shot in the knee and brought back to England.

DUNHAM, FRANK (born 1897)
The Long Carry
The Journal of Stretcher-bearer Frank Dunham
Edited by R. H. Haigh & P. W. Turner
Pergamon Press, 1970

Frank Dunham wrote an immediate account of most days during his war service, and expanded this in 1922 with more detail. The editors left out some entries to 'avoid the very sameness and monotony of trench warfare'. They also added some footnotes.

Frank came from a middle-class family in Norwich and received a good secondary education and wrote well. The detail in his diary is intense, a sort of blow-by-account of each day – an early 20ᵗʰ century Facebook, you could say, except that this was not a bit of fun but a very dangerous and frightening experience. Indeed, his style is understated, plain, not really conveying the horror of it all; but we know it was there. The fact that he became a chain-smoker, like so many other infantrymen, indicated the constant tension he was under.

One wonders how Frank managed to find the time to produce all this material but stretcher-bearers tended to get separate shelter and billeting and had more time for their own pursuits, exempt from parades and drilling.

The information provided a clear indication of time and place – every village and camp. He arrived at Havre on October 25, 1916 as a volunteer in the 25ᵗʰ Battalion of the London Regiment (a Cyclists' unit). In November in Ypres he was transferred to the 7ᵗʰ Battalion (the 'Shiny Seventh' because they liked to shine up their buttons brightly). In 1917 he moved to the 6ᵗʰ Battalion. There was a great deal of swapping around battalions because of the heavy loss of life and limb: these particular Tommies were generally happy about it as long as they were in a London regiment.

His first task in the front line south-east of Ypres was to help to carry a wounded man 600 yards through thick mud.

They moved in December to take part in work (they were not excused from fatigues!) in the system of tunnels being constructed south of Ypres for mining operations under enemy lines. It was quite a dangerous place to be because there was constant artillery fire aimed at the vicinity of the tunnel entrances. Relief came with trips to Poperinghe (Maps 1 & 4) and football games.

Frank was part of a highly successful raid on enemy trenches near Hill 60 in February 1917. According to him it was 'the most successful raid by any British forces during the whole war'. 118 prisoners were taken (important for garnering information about enemy plans and formations and whereabouts) although there were 70 British casualties and Frank and his fellow stretcher-bearers were very busy and constantly in the thick of the action. Of the 31 stretcher-bearers Frank served with only 6 survived the war.

The fronts in the Ypres Salient remained relatively 'quiet' during most of the early months of 1917. But action intensified in May as the assault on Messines Ridge (Map 4) neared. This began on June 7 with the detonation of the mines under the Ridge. As the infantry moved forward the stretcher-bearers followed close behind, their first incursion into no man's land and then enemy territory. Frank's entry for this day is ten pages long.

There was much cricket in July and the stretcher-bearers won all their games partly because they had more time for practice. They had to do their bit on working parties – digging trenches, repairing roads etc. But there was time off in St Omer and some decent meals and concerts.

They were then involved in the offensive near Hooge (south-east of Ypres – Maps 1 & 4) on September 7. There were a lot of wounded men to pick up. The stretcher-bearers constantly looked death and mutilation in the face: could they save this man? Was it best to treat this man? Could this man get back on his own? There was no distinction between friend and foe – they did the same for wounded Germans. Through this day, too, Frank was suffering from the flu. When they struggled back at the end of the day it was still dangerous because the back areas were constantly shelled.

Later in September the battalion moved south to the Arras front (Map

1) – now 'quiet' with occasional shelling. Frank wrote that the stretcher-bearers thus had 'an easy time' with plenty of sport, baths and time in the estaminets. It was 'posh' and 'cushy'.

A 12-inch howitzer is prepared for action

But then they went on to Cambrai (Map 1) late in November as part of the big tank offensive. There followed the shock of the German counter-offensive, Frank's first experience of facing a general enemy assault. In the headlong retreat the loss of stretcher-bearers was high because it was a far more dangerous job on the retreat for they were constantly under heavy shelling, bombing and machine gun and rifle fire.

Stretcher-bearers were obviously under the direction of the Medical Officer and part of their job was to help with first aid at the Aid Post. Out of action they would help there with general tasks, such as inoculations.

In January 1918 Frank was transferred to the 1/19 Battalion where he found there were less privileges for stretcher- bearers, such as separate dug-outs, and he had to take part in more work, such as bringing up rations from the back areas, an arduous and dangerous task. Even though Frank was the senior stretcher-bearer he still had to do it. Eventually, however, his experience in first aid became so invaluable that the medical officer moved him permanently into the aid post.

Frank was in the big retreat of March and April 1918 (he was near Ytres) and eventually got to Albert (Map 2). Late in April the battalion went even further west. Frank was given a stripe – but no extra pay with it! But when he moved across to the sanitation section (dealing with latrines etc. and also under the direction of the medical officer) he accepted a second stripe but only after being paid for it. They began to move east again.

DUNN, JAMES, CHURCHILL (1871–1955)
The War the Infantry Knew
A Chronicle of Service in France and Belgium
Edited by Keith Simpson
Abacus, 1994

Dr. Dunn kept a coded diary of his service and also wrote hundreds of letters during this time. However, these were not available to Keith Simpson, the editor of this volume, probably because Dr. Dunn had destroyed them. He also used contributions from men who served with him: these are listed at the beginning of each chapter. Dr. Dunn compiled the narrative but remained anonymous in the 1938 book 'The War the Infantry Knew' despite writing much of it in the first person singular. His actual name appears only thee times in this book over 588 pages. One of these is a reference written by Siegfried Sassoon –' The MO. was strolling along the trench with the detachment of an amateur botanist'.

Robert Graves wrote of Dr. Dunn 'as the bravest and coolest man under fire that I ever saw in France'. He had served as a trooper in the Boer War (before qualifying as a doctor) and was posted to the 19th Field Ambulance on July 23, 1915 and as Regimental Medical Officer to the 2nd Battalion of the Royal Welch Regiment (RWF) on November 7, 1915. 'The War the Infantry Knew' is divided into chapters with headings indicating the period covered. Many specific dates are included and the book has the appearance of a diary. It is also possibly unique in being a Battalion memoir rather than one about a particular soldier – but not to be confused with official Battalion histories.

The period before Captain J. C. Dunn joined the battalion is thus covered by contributions from men who had served it at this time, although Dr. Dunn would have had other sources. Unlike the 1st Battalion the 2nd had not suffered badly in 1914 or 1915. It thus had many pre-war regular soldiers still in its ranks and thus preserved much of the traditional discipline of a pre-war unit. It was obvious that this type of regime suited Dr. Dunn.

The book is a marvellous testimony to the life of a battalion on the Western Front, its characters (such as 'Fizzer') and the daily trials and tribulations. Dr. Dunn writes in an amusing (because these soldiers were funny) and whimsical manner. It understates the horrors witnessed by a busy doctor often in the thick off the action. The detail is incredible: you can find out about the rising price of sandbags, for instance.

When he joined the battalion it was in Béthune (Map 2), which remained 'a cheerful town' with popular canteens, recreation rooms and a good theatre. But 1916 looked likely to become much grimmer: the battalion losses started to accumulate in the Cuinchy and Cambrin sector (Maps 1 & 4) as commanders stepped up the action with raids on enemy trenches. Arthur Conan Doyle visited to get 'local colour for his new pot-boiler' (June). At Givenchy (Map 4) the Germans detonated their biggest mine of the Western Front and one company lost two thirds of its strength.

German prisoners were able to tell the battalion where and when it was going to attack on the Somme. It was engaged between High Wood and Martinpuich (Maps 2 & 3) on July 15, and the casualties piled up with 'ear-splitting' enemy artillery fire aimed at virtually unprotected troops who could smell the reek of the dead in Mametz Wood. The High Wood (Maps 2 & 3) action was so intense and hectic that individual accounts of it are difficult to connect. Shells could also arrive from behind as the ranks of experienced gunners were depleted.

It was back to working parties in August (still very dangerous and exhausting) and Bienvillers (September) – 'the inhabitants have gone, the louse and the rat swarm in it'. However, later in October Lecheux (south-east of Doullens – Map 2) was a 'delight' (apart from the dysentery and the French habit of chaining up their farm dogs).

When they got back into the front line in the assaults on Le Transloy (north-east of Albert – Map 2) in October results continued to be frustrating and the losses just as bad. But Dr. Dunn noted that many of the replacement troops were of good quality, especially from the Yeomanry. There was haggis on January 1, 1917 (popular with Southerners) but prices in Vauchelles (near Amiens – Map 2) were high because the Australians had just left.

Siegfried Sassoon was in the battalion for a month and contributed a chapter on the Spring of 1917 when the battalion joined the Battle of Arras – 'a blurred personal experience'. He was courageous during a trench raid but was wounded and sent to Scotland.

At Arras (Map 1) another third of the battalion was killed or wounded. 'April 27 – What a treat to have a mattress' (we presume this was about the medical officer!). The official report on the late April campaign at Arras made 'very entertaining reading. What artistry!'

In May there was horse racing and a shooting competition. The creeping barrage rate was altered to 1 mile an hour in poor conditions (about half the previous rate) and 2 miles an hour in good conditions. 'No one was excited' by this news.

The summer was generally quiet – more sport, entertainment etc. Arraines (on the Somme) was nice and so was the French coast (diarists tended on the whole to remember the good things about the Western Front). In late summer the plans for a new front in Flanders developed and the RWF went to Nieuport (August – Map 1) but this front did not materialise and the battalion was back near St Omer in September. Dr Dunn has a couple of highly entertaining pages on estaminet names.

They joined the Third Battle of Ypres. They were in the Glencourse Wood action on September 25. Dr. Dunn went 56 hours without food and 73 without sleep. Out in Messines (Map 4) an enemy shell hit HQ but the Germans had built it and it was hardly cracked. According to Dr. Dunn the battalion was changing – 'November 5 – All around here there is slackness and want of efficient supervision from above'. But he was still impressed by some of the replacements coming in from the Yeomanry, standing for hours before Passchendaele Ridge in appalling weather and under dreadful artillery bombardment.

The battalion was down in Estaires (Map 4) following the bitter winter – digging. Higher Command was obsessed with the need for new defence lines as the anticipated German onslaught took shape. The 2nd RWF was not involved in the fighting in March and early April but faced the enemy across the River Ancre late in April. The earlier impetus of the German attack had now faded and they were unable to get across the Ancre (April 22 – 24). 'April 30 – The Ambulance is resting'. This message came in response to Dr. Dunn's request for more dressings. 'Poor devils!' he wrote.

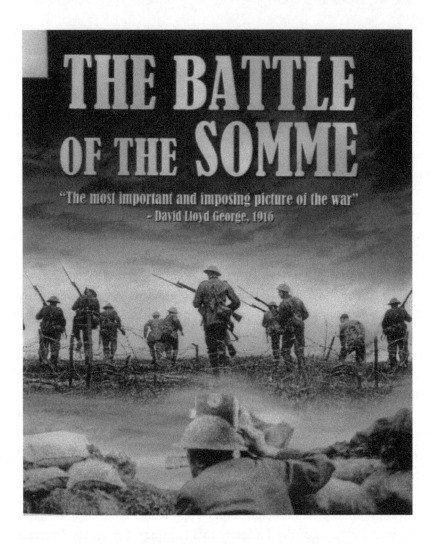

It became very hot in Bouzaincourt (Map 3) and the village was raided for white shirts. The MO acquired a black-flowered sunshade. On the whole 1918 was not a good year for Dr. Dunn. He became increasingly annoyed with falling standards in what was regarded as one of the best battalions. He was put out of action by gas on May 22 and when he recovered in June he went to another battalion. He did not mention this in the book but continued with the history of the 2 /RWF until 1919.

EWART, WIFRID (1892–1923)
Scots Guard on the Western Front 1915–1918
Wilfrid Ewart
Strong Oak Press, 2001

Wilfrid enlisted as a subaltern in the Scots Guards at the beginning of the war but delays meant that he did not go to France until February 1915. He kept a diary intermittently, sometimes leaving gaps of several weeks. He obviously consulted the diary (when he did so he tended to write in the present tense) but added a lot more for this memoir (in the past tense), written before 1923 (he was killed in Mexico in January of that year). The memoir was first published in 1934.

What distinguishes this rather erratic or even eccentric account are the vivid descriptions of environments, particularly of the battlefield. Every so often he breaks out into these somewhat poetic passages. His memoir is one marked out by individual images.

He was in trenches first at Saulty (north-east of Doullens – Map 2) and then Estaires (Map 4) in March. He watched men shuffling out to fight –'March 11 – a bright beam of light shooting out from the doorway discloses… men heavily burdened with great-coats, packs, haversacks, water bottles, entrenching tools… Strange figures they look in the dim light'. This was at the battle of Neuve Chapelle (Maps 1 & 4). They climbed over the breastworks out into open country against a hail of bullets. Men fell like stones around him. He was shot in the leg. Shrapnel burst around from German batteries. 'And the groans, the moans, the crying of those who lay around!'

He crawled back through the continuing hellfire. He got into a crater and a head appeared offering to carry his pack. But he had a marked map in it and did want this to fall into the wrong hands. He dragged himself along a trench and past a field of corpses laid out in lines for burial. Finally he came across two stretcher-bearers 'apparently none too keen to enter the fray'.

Even in the ambulance clattering along Wilfrid described the scenes he passed. In the casualty clearing station in Estaires his label for England was attached. But in hospital in Rouen another doctor decreed that he must stay in France. The bullet had made a neat hole in his leg but missed the bone .However, in the event, they did send him to England.

He was there for six months before returning to the same section of front line he had left (Aubers Ridge, November 1915 – Map 4). As soon he arrived he was ill for a week. He got a parcel for Christmas – tobacco, pies, chocolate, a pound cake, bedroom slippers and a knitted scarf. There was a Christmas truce – 'grey and khaki figures surge towards each other as one man… They mingle, shake hands, pat each other'. Gifts were exchanged but two Bavarian officers came out and gave the Tommies five minutes to get back. A few of them did not make it and were wounded by shrapnel.

In February 1916 Wilfrid was with the 7th (Guards) Entrenching Battalion in the Somme area. He was then ill again and not back with his battalion in the Ypres Salient till May. He gave a detailed description of supervising a working party digging a new trench in no man's land at night. They dug frenziedly to get themselves under ground level, not easy in the waterlogged ground. Around them was the 'sickly stench of bodies… Strange and fearsome things are dug up'. This included a British machine gun converted by the Germans.

An enemy machine gun traversed the area every few minutes, immediately firing across in the opposite direction, so it was wise to keep prone. Occasionally there was a loud explosion. A bird cried and they could hear the rattle and grating of enemy transport, trolleys along the light railways and the Germans' pet dogs barking.

There were other shadowy figures shifting about – were they friend or foe? A shot rang out and someone screamed. A cuckoo called. A digger was hit in the ankle. "Is it a Blighty one, d'ye think? Tea. Breakfast. Sleep.'

In June and July it was lively along the banks of the Yser Canal by night – it could have been a 'backwater in Venice'. But when ordered to leave the brown ditches they were glad to go to the rolling hills, woodlands and hedges of the Somme. Exhausting months in these trenches were followed by marches of up to 30 miles in a day and a barn running alive with big black beetles.

There was a 'kit-strafe' and Wilfrid's hair oil and deck chair were confiscated along with his collapsible bed and bath. At Bus-lez-Artois (near Amiens – Map 2) they trained (August). He was in hospital with enteritis in September and by the time he returned 11 months later his battalion was engaged in the Third Battle of Ypres.

He fought in the trenches and in no man's land during the German attack of August 4, leading a company when its commander was killed. Paris was better in September (some nice descriptions) and also company commander training in October plus trips to Amiens. Wilfrid was getting 'a new zest for life, the holiday spirit'.

'December 8th 1917 and six weeks and three days since I made an entry.'

He was at Bourlon Wood near Cambrai (Map 1) on November 23 going forward in open territory but halted by the machine guns of the Third Prussian Guards Division. They were sent back to try again. Wilfrid and the only other three survivors were saved by a convenient oak tree. The Prussians threw phosphorous bombs at the wounded on the ground. Wilfrid managed to squirm back on his stomach with bullets miraculously missing him. The British advance was ended.

In January 1918 he was near Arras (Map 1). In February he had violent neuralgia and flu. In May he was appointed as a liaison officer with the French and he was back in Paris with more extended descriptions of life in the capital. In June he had trench fever but was back for the Battle of St. Leger (south-east of Arras) on August 4, then had a riding accident and was back in hospital.

EYRE, GILES
Somme Harvest
Memories of a P.B.I. in the Summer of 1916
The Naval & Military Press, 1991

This narrative first appeared in 1938 and is a memoir of 2 months during the battle of the Somme. Giles was in the 7th Battalion of the King's Royal Rifle Corps (KRRC) and reached the Western Front in May 1915. He was invalided home in December 1915 and when this account opens for May 1916 he had transferred to the 2nd Battalion resting at Mazingarbe-les-Brebis (Lens sector – Map 1).

The narrative has page after page of precise dialogue. Giles was writing 21 years after the events described and he can probably recall the gist of these conversations but elaborating it in this way gives the book the feel of a novel.

Up in the old Loos trenches Giles remembered the creaking of the German supply limbers. There is detail on the French people with whom they billeted (Giles could speak French – and he had studied Latin at Public School). He described the rum ration as 'one of the few inspired measures higher command hit upon'.

Out on patrol in no man's land they were moving round a building ('Red House') when they came face to face with a German patrol. They stared at one another wondering what to do; then, as if by combined instinct they fled towards their respective trenches. Giles also told another tale in which a German with a pronounced American accent offered to barter cigars and schnapps for bully beef, jam and biscuits. The sap trenches were just a few yards apart so sandbags full of the goodies were flung across. A further treat from across the way was a concert given by a classical violinist, but this attracted some Stokes mortars and that was the end of fraternisation. Snipers also opened up and a British sniper was shot in the eye through his loophole.

Soup and Poulet de Perigard back in billets was a welcome relief. Here, the riflemen were impressed with valiant and interesting French soldiers they met for a drink. Henri Picard was a true patriot and also a good pianist. They returned to the front met by the cheery news that a big raid was going to take place. They were to attack 'The Triangle' (a railway intersection).

Mines were detonated just in front of the German line and they had to scramble over the resulting mass of debris. They bombed, stabbed and destroyed. Often when a section of enemy trench was captured the defenders ran to right and left to other parts of the trench. Thus the Rifles needed to build trench blocks to shield them from the enemy, who were trying to bomb them from these flanks.

Giles's pal, Marriner, was blown to bits beside him, and Giles was smothered in his flesh and blood. Enemy shelling of his position became ferocious. They had to get out of it fast but orders were conflicting. They had to make their own decision: run for it!

They were at rest but then came the expected call from the south and they marched to near Albert (Map 2), arriving in time to hear the pre-Somme bombardment (which began on June 24). They moved into captured trenches between La Boiselle and Fricourt (Map 3). 'Rod' Rodwell of Giles's platoon was scathing and resentful about their predicament. "… if we ever live to see the end of this," he said, "we'll soon find out if we've been tricked."

The whole platoon was selected as a bombing group to join the Leicester Battalions for the forthcoming attack on Bazentin Wood (Somme – July 14 – Map 3). The Wood was 'stiff' with German machine guns and dug-out emplacements. At least there was some Chablis left and Giles quoted Dante. But there was also tear gas and the area was full of gasping men. Giles refused a stripe as he wanted to stay with his erudite platoon, who could sing 'Vesti la guibbe' and read 'Three Men in a Boat'.

The attack was preceded by an enormous barrage. Giles's mind could not grasp the magnitude of it – '… countless tons of lethal steel… flying, like a monster hosepipe vomiting a stream of water…' Then they got over easily to the German first trench ducking under raking machine gun fire. They were called forward again taking prisoners but they never bayoneted captured or wounded men. They were running out of bombs. The enemy shelling intensified and the lieutenant was wounded. Giles dragged him into some shelter because he would not have survived if left where he lay. 'Men fall, rise, come at me, melt away.' 'Rod' Rodwell, philosopher and D.C.M. was fatally wounded and died in Giles's arms.

Back again with the KRRC for the attack on Pozières Ridge (from July 22 – Map 3) there was a preliminary task of trying to reduce the heaps of corpses, dangerous because the Hun was half round their position. But a party of Germans was also out performing this grisly job. They waved to each other.

They were joined by bronzed Australians. Giles was appointed a runner, a role with a very low life expectancy. The colonel would be in the thick of it, too. "That was the place for a Colonel of the Rifles," he said. Times were desperate because they had no Lewis guns and bombers. They went over. 'Tac-tac-tac' fired the enemy machine guns. Two more pals died – '… useful, good, dependable lads…' but Giles had to '… plunge back into the activities of the moment'. Giles also could not stop for a wailing corporal hit in the groin. They entered the first trench and the Germans scattered left and right. Giles went back to the colonel but the C.O. was shot in the chest. Should they go on?

Giles ran with the Adjutant. But it was a perilous situation because they heard that the battalions of either side of them had failed and they were in danger from the flanks. There was a rush to get back and Giles and a few others were left stranded in the German trench. These were nearly all newcomers and voted hastily to run for it. Giles would have preferred to stand his ground but had to run with them.

There was activity in the shell holes ahead of them and once again these inexperienced troops called out frantically who they were. The men in the holes were German! Giles was still prepared to fight but was quickly surrounded by 'threatening faces'.

FEILDING, ROWLAND (1871–1945)
War Letters to a Wife
France and Flanders, 1915–1919
Edited by Jonathan Walker
Spellmount, 2001

Rowland Feilding did keep diaries but these were not available. Instead, we rely on the enormous number of letters which he wrote to his wife and daughter. Because of censorship he had to leave place names out of letters but these were added later from his diaries. This collection was first published in 1929.

The editor has had to leave out some letters for this edition because of limits on space but otherwise he lets the letters speak for themselves but adds a little information to maintain a narrative.

In August 1914 Captain Feilding was in the 2nd Battalion, City of London Yeomanry ('Rough Riders') – a territorial unit. But he joined the Coldstream Guards and left for France on April 29, 1915 after some additional training.

He was in the 3rd Battalion at this time and went to near Béthune into the Givenchy trenches (Map 4), then the Cuinchy brickstacks. In this vicinity big German mines were wrecking hundreds of yards of the front line and replacing them with huge craters which the armies scrapped over. In May he became a company commander in the 1st Battalion.

Captain Feilding's letters were often long accounts of the battered countryside and villages and of the spirit and resilience of his fellow officers and men. He loved their humour. "I wish my father had never met my mother," said one unhappy soldier. "Perhaps he didn't," came a call from behind.

Nearby at Cambrin in August enemy trenches were just a few yards away and Feilding helped to throw bombs at them after a British band had serenaded them with 'Die Wacht am Rhein'. The Germans were very unhappy because they had applauded the music.

A new Guards Division was created late in August in preparation for the Battle of Loos (Lens sector – Map 1). Because of his involvement here there were no letters for over a week. A bullet lodged in a wad of letters he had in his pocket. A very long letter of October 2 described the courageous advance of his company. He was caked with mud and his uniform was in tatters, his face black from the smoke and brown from the showers of earth which fell on him. An 'immense Major' lay on the battlefield for several days because they could not get a stretcher to him: he had no food and the rain soaked him continuously. 'He was quite cheerful'.

'… bring some of our professional hypochondriacs… they might witness the appalling wastage of the best manhood' (October 4, 1915). Trenches were littered with gas pipes and cylinders, discarded rifles and equipment, bombs, small-arms ammunition boxes and the dead. In them the confusion and congestion at night was a 'shambles'. Rowland Fielding made no attempt to hide the ghastliness of it all from his wife (unlike some letter-writers) because she the had expressively told him not to.

He found the diary of a dead Bavarian – Otto Arnermaaier, who had hated this hell on earth. Trenches at La Gorgue (north-west of Neuve Chapelle – Maps 1 & 4), which the Guards took over, needed digging deeper because the previous occupants had been Ghurkhas (November 11).

In December Captain Feilding was invalided home with a poisoned knee and did not return until April 1916. Soon after his arrival he ate whitebait with a General, fish caught by the latter's batman with a gauze net on the end of a pole in the Somme.

A promoted Major Feilding watched the Battle of Montauban (Map 3) on the famous July 1 and noted how pleased British troops were to give German prisoners bully beef and cigarettes. Until August 24 Feilding was left in an Entrenching Battalion but then came the call to command the 6th Battalion of the Connaught Rangers (September 6). This Battalion had fought bravely to capture Guillemont (Map 3) on the 2nd and was decimated in the process.

His first order was to attack Ginchy (Maps 3 & 4) with many soldiers just drafted in and without battle experience and under severe bombardment. His Adjutant was only 18 years old, but good. They went over the top against ferocious enemy fire (September 10). Casualties amongst the officers were devastating. After the successful attack they were shelled for three more days but these staunch Irish stood up to the onslaught. Major Feilding became Lieutenant Colonel Feilding.

They then moved to the Ypres Salient. He was shadowed by his batman, who had been in the Irish constabulary, where he had been taught to keep his eyes and ears open and his mouth shut. At Locre (Map 4) in January 1917 the defences were battered walls of shredded sandbags withstanding numerous German assaults. Lieutenant Colonel Feilding was ordered to attack on February 19 when he was missing vital officers. The result was a prolonged attritional struggle. At its conclusion the Germans called out "Send out your stretcher men" and there was an impromptu truce.

A bright idea from above re-classified the infantry as Lewis gunners, bombers, rifle grenadiers, riflemen etc. A visiting general at Rossignol asked one man if he was a Catholic. He followed instructions. "I'm a rifleman, sir," he replied dutifully. But Colonel Feilding had nothing but praise for his officers and men apart from a few who misbehaved hoping to be sent to the safety of prison.

The Connaught Rangers provided 'mopping up' and carrying parties for the highly successful attack on Messines (Map 4) in June but the Corps General still looked miserable. Rowland Feilding had a riding accident and he was in hospital and convalescing in England – July–September 1917.

The Rangers were in the Arras sector (Map 1) for many months engaging in spasmodic warfare. February 17, 1918 brought 27 letters from his wife due to postal difficulties and 15 of them were censored by the French. They were back on the Somme to meet the German offensive but Feilding slipped and dislocated his elbow (March 27) and finished in Dorchester House Hospital in Park Lane.

While he was absent the 6/ Connaught were 'destroyed' in the German onslaught and Lieutenant Colonel Feilding went on to lead the 1/15 London Regiment (August 16). By then more Germans than Allied troops were being killed in the Somme region. Late in October he was in Lille (Map 1) listening to descriptions of German brutality during its long occupation.

FLOYD, THOMAS HOPE
At Ypres with Best-Dunkley
BiblioLife, 2008

This is a narrative run along with extracts from his letters and his diary of 1917. For some days he uses both sources. Thus the account is one of great detail, almost like an early 20th century Facebook.

Thomas had been a private soldier in the Royal Fusiliers in 1916 at the Somme but was brought back home to train for a commission. He became a 2nd Lieutenant in the 5th Battalion on March 1, 1917. He arrived in the Ypres Salient near Brandhoek (Map 4) on June 4 when the guns were having a day off. So when they resumed their onslaught later in the day it came as something of a shock because this was far heavier than on the Somme. It went on for 17 days – the Allies were building up to a big attack and the German artillery always responded enthusiastically.

The officers of the 5th Battalion were accommodated in the Ypres Prison, a cell for each of them. But the town was never a healthy place to be – around 1,000 casualties every week. It was essential to avoid the gates, registered to an inch by the enemy guns. The unpopular C.O., Colonel Best-Dunkley, returned from leave. He called the officers together and proposed to buy a new band, with subscriptions from officers and men. But not a soul supported the idea.

Thomas wrote much detail about fellow officers, especially the Colonel, and NCOs. He also supplied information about his meals, his bedtimes and getting up times. At rest at Westbecourt he particularly remembered the champagne. Very few days are missed in his account.

Back in Ypres (July 1) four Lieutenants went up to survey the portion of line they were to take over and did not return. All of them were badly wounded and one died soon after. There was a dangerous task for Thomas as he supervised the construction of forward trenches at night under perpetual threat from snipers and machine guns. If anyone made a noise they had to fling themselves down as machine gun fire swept across no man's land.

July 5 was very lively as the Cheshire Regiment next door began a large-scale raid and the Germans threw everything at them. But the nightly patrols and work had to go on in this war of tense attrition as the Germans knew that a full-blown assault was imminent. Enemy planes also stepped up their bombing raids. Thomas was up to knees in water but he hardly noticed it as he concentrated on his work with an eye open for the next shell or bomb.

However, he did like to discuss the wider war situation when the opportunity arose, managing to get hold of out-of-date newspapers and trying to keep up with what was happening in other theatres of war. He was often asked when the war would end because of his knowledge. The answer was 'not yet – Germany still pursued hopes of annexation, or at least indemnities'.

The more immediate concern was that the Germans were now employing mustard oil gas, starting on July 12. A gas bomb hit the soap factory accommodating the Fusilier other ranks and over 100 of them had to go to hospital. The officers discovered an old mine shaft, which, although damp and dirty, provided succour from the gas. Thomas was still out in no man's land on many nights, fearing that the latest trip would be his last –a nightmare without end and with gas. At least the rain on July 15 got rid of the stink of gas.

A good sing-song down the mine helped morale. A further boost to Thomas's mood was that Colonel Best-Dunkley liked him, called him 'General' (the adjutant called him 'Field Marshall – all on account of his knowledge of the war). There was argument over the appointment of Winston Churchill to the cabinet post of Minister of Munitions: Thomas thought he was very able, others disagreed (July 19). Thomas was less enthusiastic about the royal family changing its name to 'Windsor'.

The battalion moved to Watou (July 21 – Map 4). Reports of the condition of officers and men affected by gas continued to come in. There was also news of a son for the colonel. "Poor little sod," commented someone. "To think there's another Best-Dunkley in the world to look forward to." Not a soul worried about Best-Dunkley being hurt or even killed in the coming battle. He certainly worked very hard on the preparations for it. The impression Thomas got was that he was getting ready for glory and even death.

From July 25 Thomas used his diary to convey the narrative. They were endlessly instructed on the battle plans. They went into the concentration trenches on the 29th – the day when his diary 'abruptly closed' and he turned to the letter he wrote later when in England in hospital.

Thomas commented in this letter that he thought that the fighting between July 1 and 20 rendered the battalion incapable of sustaining a major offensive, at least, for very long. There were reinforcements to replace the large number of casualties but these were not battle-hardened troops.

Zero hour for July 31 was 3.50 a.m., when a huge bombardment crashed out. German prisoners began to pour past them. One asked for the nearest train station for England. Thomas went over with his platoon near St. Julien in column. Amidst shot and shell they advanced over fields, trenches, wire, fortifications, roads, ditches and streams, all strewn with wreckage and corpses. 'It was hell and slaughter'. The colonel strode on armed with a walking stick.

Finally, it was hardly possible to stand up without being shot. Thomas's platoon just vanished from around him and he was shot in the leg at 10.20 a.m. He huddled in a crater expecting second by second to be blown up but miraculously survived. Colonel Best-Dunkley was posthumously awarded the VC.

FRASER-TYTLER, NEIL
Field Guns in France
Lieutenant-Colonel Neil Fraser-Tytler
Edited by Major F. N. Baker
The Naval & Military Press 2009

Captain Fraser-Tytler was given command of a Royal Field Artillery howitzer battery which arrived on the Somme on December 4, 1915. This edited collection of letters to his father first appeared in 1922.

Down by the river (Ancre) in the Vaux Valley it was relatively quiet at this time so the shrapnel shell bursts on December 12 came as a nasty surprise – 'a curiosity', according to The captain. His first trial shots were 'very interesting'. More so was a 'weekly big joint strafe' in unison with other batteries on December 14, aimed at Sand Redoubt in front of Serre (near Beaumont Hamel – Map 3).

Their zone in January 1916 stretched from Mericourt to Herbécourt (Map 2): the French front was across the river and artillery action had to be co-ordinated with them. The captain's French began to improve. The work of an artillery chief entailed keeping observation open – selecting and maintaining Observation Posts (OPs), shifting them when necessary and ensuring that telephone wires to them were kept working.

The front began to get less quiet in January as the Germans prepared an attack on Frise (west of Peronne – Map 2) and eventually captured it (January 29). There ensued a big artillery battle as the French prepared to win back their lost territory. In February they packed their trenches with 'dirty, tough' Colonial troops (in front they had no protective wire). The British gunners were called upon to co-ordinate closely with their French neighbours.

The captain was a hunter; these enormous howitzers actually 'sniped'.

There was a bird's eye view of the whole German front facing them. Their big telescopes (eventually including a 7 foot monster from the Lady Roberts' Telescope Fund – through which they could see the badges on the uniforms of the German soldiers) could pick out targets like enemy machine guns and swiftly obliterate them. The attritional struggle astride the river continued in February and March.

But The captain, as befitted an Old Etonian, had time for nice lunches and dinners in Amiens (Map 2) and picked the early primroses. Despite Allied willingness to co-operate the river was proving a severe hindrance to plans to advance. The decision was taken for French infantry and artillery to move across the river, which meant a shift of position of the British artillery to the east in order to accommodate them.

The captain provided an almost minute-by-minute account of a typical day –the slogging match with the German guns blazed on. There was no let-up because the frenzied preparations for 'The Big Push' proceeded in May and June. This entailed new roads, mazes of new trenches etc., 'without the Hun noticing'.

The great bombardment commenced on June 24 ('U Day'). Thirty tall poplar trees in front of the battery, which had been a good shield, were now in the way, and they were the first to go. For The captain it was a 'cheery and useful' afternoon: the stupendous noise was 'wonderful'. This was the view from the gunners; the tens of thousands suffering below had a different opinion of the artillery (of both sides).

June 25 to June 29 was planned as 'V Day' to 'Y Day' but the heavy rain caused a postponement and so the 29th became 'Y2 Day'. The gunners could watch the Allied infantry crawling over the ground, an advance of 700 yards by 9 a.m. (this was the most successful of the July 1 fronts because the Germans were not expecting it to stretch so far south). The gunners could see the flags of the successful infantry in the German trenches. There was a lull for two hours then more progress in the afternoon. Subsequently, the German artillery fired all night so the British guns were obliged to reply.

Within the next few days The captain was able to move his gun forward 1,500 yards. There was little rest because there was also 'night work' to be done – 'tickling up' roads, railways, dumps and villages and ration parties. The battle for Trones Wood (west of Guillemont – Map 3) ensued from July 8. Observation for the gunners was more difficult because the skyline had been captured and German use of gas also obliterated views. But the big guns kept going forward.

But by July 22 Delville Wood (Map 3) had been lost to an enemy resisting fiercely. The action of enemy artillery also created continual difficulties in keeping the telephone wires to Trones Wood intact. The battery had been shooting for a month and so they were taken out to recuperate at Béthune (Maps 1 & 4), playing football, fishing and holding splendid horse shows.

Their next Somme zone was near Flers (Maps 2 & 3) with a full view of 'Hunland' on the ridge around Bapaume (Map 2). The captain reckoned that the British taxpayer got more for his money than the German, and that this better use of resources came from the time in 1915 when the Royal Artillery was severely short of shells and had to ensure the best use was made of the ones they had.

On October 12 there was 'a shoot of a lifetime' and 'good killing'. But the extent of the enemy shelling meant a constant vigilance over telephone wires. The captain had to keep taking out large parties of signallers and frequently leaving them in pairs in shell holes to check on sections of wire. It was all 'fine sport', also the task of hiding gun positions and OPs from German eyes.

Montauban (Map 3) in November was 'rain and mud, mud and rain' (batteries needed a lot of water to keep going but not this much). Eventually they 'shut up shop' on the Somme and retired to Doullens (November 16 – Map 2)). But The captain was a 'bitter' man in December because there was a big re-organisation of the Royal Artillery and his battery was split up.

This may have been the main reason why he wrote no more letters till March 1917. By this time they were following the Germans back to their Hindenburg Line. There followed the Battle of Arras (Map 1) and with his new battery The captain was engaged for several weeks at Henin Hill. Finally, a 600–yard section of the Hindenburg Line was captured.

The war now shifted to Flanders and so the battery began to operate from Dickebusch Lake (Map 4) in June. They got a fearful reception, with lots of gas shells. A 'fiendish ten days' ensued at Vlamertinghe. Attack from the air was also intensifying. From Potijz Chateau (Map 4) there were many artillery battles. August and September The captain described as 'hopeless and endless' and 'much ado about nothing'. The joy of fighting on the Somme seemed to have disappeared. He said that killing Germans was much more difficult here.

In October there came the assault on Houthulst Forest (Map 1 – north-east of Ypres) but the battery was decimated by poison gas. The captain was badly affected (eventually in 1918 he finished up in hospital). In December 1917 he accepted a post as instructor at the Fifth Army School and spent most of 1918 there.

FRENCH, ANTHONY
Gone for a Soldier
The Roundwood Press, 1972

Anthony joined a London Regiment of Territorials after the recruiting office failed to check his birth certificate. His C.O. was known as 'The Bollocker' and the 'Canaries' (NCOs) at the base camp in Étaples were 'contemptible'.

This is a memoir with hardly a place name and no dates apart from September 29, 1916: the date when Anthony came round after his leg wound. But these are the recollections of a very good writer almost in the form of a series of essays on life on the Western Front from the view of the infantryman. Some of it is almost poetic, moving and very funny. The only other memoir which is like it was by the writer Alfred McLelland Burrage in his book 'War is War'.

There is an extremely sad scenario of how Bert Bradley became Anthony's pal, how Bert died on the Somme beside him at High Wood (Map 3) in September 1916, and the receipt of a harrowing letter from Bert's father.

They were urged on by 'The Bollocker' and an ironic comment came from behind Anthony: "O, what a world of ill-favour'd faults!" Then they marched and marched but sang in harmony and bantered cheerfully amongst themselves and with passing units. "Well, strike me pink if it ain't the boys what eats off plates."

"Sweep on, you fat and greasy citizens!" added The Voice. They arrived at a farmyard and called for 'the dancing girls' and Madame responded by bringing out a bull and a cow to fornicate. Even the bouncy Londoners were silenced by that one.

When the going was harder and the weather worse the songs became more critical. "No more soldiering for me..." The weariness and resignation of the infantryman after a long footslog is graphically depicted in Anthony's account of arrival at billets.

Amiens (Map 2) had too many flies but nice French people and estaminets where the object was to spend every centime before the Germans got hold of it. Anthony's skill on the piano was well-rewarded with many a sing-song, and even classical recitals. At a lecture the Major fell off a damaged stool. "And when he falls, he falls like Lucifer. A wretched soul, bruised with adversity," intoned The Voice, who was, in fact, Nobby Clarke of Hammersmith.

News from those back from leave was eagerly awaited. They discussed what they were fighting for. "It goes a long way back. I think we can't help ourselves," said Bert. The next day he might be scavenging for matchsticks under the duckboards. There was a big debate on how to dodge Minnewerfers. This gave rise to deep mathematical calculations: the solution was 'it's round and it bounces'. Similar work had to be done on when to go to the latrine and how to spend the least possible time there since they were located in the most exposed spots.

Dusk and dawn were 'treacherous hours' and sentry duty was nerve-wracking – Anthony's account is the best I have read. Anyway, the following night was at rest and they were able to start the formation of 'An Ancient Order of Trench Rats', discuss the motion 'Money is the root of all evil' with the Padre and listen to Nobby Clarke reciting Shakespeare.

Anthony was at a lecture given by a staff Captain who said he had been in Berlin the previous week.

He also demonstrated an armour-piercing bullet and a tank. Shortly afterwards the battalion went to Mametz Wood (Maps 2 & 3) following its capture. They plodded on to High Wood, passing the men whom they were relieving. "Cheerio, see you in Berlin."

The 'trenches' were just shell holes strung together. Officers encouraged them by saying that the Germans had even less protection. They prepared to go over the top. Anthony remembered the young Lieutenant's instructions word for word. Who would forget such words?

The creeping barrage opened up and over they went. He has a vivid and most moving picture of the death of Bert by his side. You feel Anthony's utter sense of loss. He cradled Bert's head in his arms but was ordered on as mortar bombs, shells and bullets came for them. They reached the enemy trenches (which were, in fact, even worse than the British) and

Anthony was 'floundering, turning, firing, scrambling, cursing, firing, running, falling, turning, re-loading, firing, scrambling, cursing, joking, panting…' He was shot just above a knee.

Corporal Bachell carefully gave him first aid. Anthony crawled along inch by inch from dusk till dawn. In all, he did this for two days, making sure he was pointing north and dragging himself to his left. Finally, he was spotted by a machine gun crew, themselves isolated in no man's land.

It was a further day before the stretcher-bearers arrived. He remembered a tent and then some nice Australian doctors and nurses. They said he had been asleep for twelve days. He was back in Étaples. But The Voice was silenced for ever. At the end of the war Anthony was preparing to take a commission in the Tank Corps. He arrived on the parade ground at Chelsea Barracks in a taxi just in time for the Colonel to announce that the war was over.

GARVIN, ROLAND, GERARD (1895–1916)
We hope to get word tomorrow
The Garvin Family Letters 1914–1916
Edited by Mark Pottle & John G.G. Ledingham
Frontline Books, 2009

Roland Gerard ('Ged') Garvin was commissioned into the 7th (Service) Battalion, South Lancashire Regiment in September 1914. Between then and July 23, 1916, when he lost his life, he wrote many hundreds of letters to his parents and they both responded with equal enthusiasm and endearment. His father was editor of the 'Observer' newspaper.

Later generations of the Garvin family looked after the letters until they were placed in the British Library in 2003. The editors of this book have written a prologue and added explanatory historical notes to help the reader understand the context of the letters.

Ged went to France on July 17, 1915 and on to the Lys front. He soon heard that he was promoted to Lieutenant and learnt how to handle a machine gun (Marville – south-west of Bailleul – Maps 1 & 4)

'These trenches expose one to hardly any vestige of risk' (Festubert–Givenchy front, August 16 – Map 4). In billets at Vieille Chapelle (August 18 – near Neuve Chapelle – Maps 1 & 4) he recorded his recipe of crushed sardines and Quaker oats. 'I am somewhere in France about 2 miles south of somewhere else in France' (August 23) – an indication of the continual battle against censorship.

His three main worries at this time in the trenches north of Festubert (September 17 – Map 4) were that he could not wash his feet, look round at the countryside, and vermin. Shelling was spasmodic and snipers were more of a nuisance (one shot his servant).

He was not directly involved in the fighting at Loos (Lens sector – Map 1). 'I'm perfectly safe', he wrote on October 2 and asked for some nice long, thick socks (his mother sent him piles of food and clothing). He supposed that he might have to start smoking in order to give his jaw some exercise. He went out on a night patrol and lost his revolver (a Smith & Wesson .45) and asked his mother to order him another one and send his British Warm, soup tablets and iodine tubes.

In November Ged's trenches were knee-deep in water and he was continually helping to rescue men stuck fast in the mud. He made a handy hot water bottle out of an empty rum jar. His father, in touch with leading politicians, wanted to hear news 'of the action' but Ged pointed out that there was not much to tell (November 28). He spent some time training his men in sniping and observing.

Billets were in the Marville – Lestrum area. 'The rain it raineth every day' (December 3). He was not taking off his pyjamas during the day. Relief came with a 'trench training' course at Linghem in the Pas-de-Calais. He complained about his 'witless' major. He admitted to a shell striking a wall a few feet from him. During January 1916 he became commander of a company. He requested some more Tiptree jam on February 9.

Enemy rifle-grenades were becoming a problem: it was all right if you heard the 'phlop' of them being fired. This 'quiet' (Festubert – Givenchy – Map 4) front still required a great deal of hard work and little sleep, perhaps worse for officers than men. Ged complained of being perpetually weary. It was amazing how much he was able to read (listed at the end of this book of letters).

Preparations for the Somme began in April with intense training in the Pas-de-Calais. The battalion eventually moved south in May 6 towards Amiens (Map 2). They were near Albert later in the month. Ged gained some work experience at Divisional HQ in June.

In his absence the battalion helped to capture La Boisselle (July 3–4 – Map 3). Ged returned to the fray on July 13 (having been promoted to Captain). He was at Hênencourt Wood (west of Albert – Map 2) and in command of his company as it went up to Mametz Wood (Maps 2 & 3) on July 19. An attack out of Bazentin-le-Petit (Map 3) was planned in the early hours of the 23rd.

As they went over the top Ged was killed by machine gun fire as he led his men towards heavily fortified German positions north of Bazentin-le-Petit.

He was 20 years of age. I am writing this on the centenary of his death.

GIBBS, CHARLES COBDEN STORMONT (1898–1969)
From the Somme to the Armistice
The Memoir of Captain Stormont Gibbs, MC
Edited by Richard Devonald-Lewis
William Kimber, 1986

Richard Devonald-Lewis assembled this book from the memoirs of Captain Stormont Gibbs, which he believed were written about 1930. He substantiated these from 'Battalion War Diaries' and other sources.

2nd Lieutenant Gibbs (educated at Radley College) arrived in France to join the 4th Battalion of the Sussex Regiment as part of a large replacement draft during the Battle of the Somme following the loss of about half of its strength at High Wood (Map 3).

Stormont Gibbs had detail about how he (a very young subaltern) was initiated into a battle-hardened unit. Near Fricourt (Map 3) he took out a working party to dig a new trench in no man's land and his fellow subaltern lost his nerve. Gibbs had suddenly to decide whether to march the men back through shelling or wait till it had eased off. 'How should I know?' he wrote. Working parties out in no man's land were in great danger (Siegfried Sassoon had a poem about it – 'The Working Party').

On August 16, one of the few dates provided by Gibbs, the battalion went into the front line between Bazentin–le–Petit and Longueval (Maps 2 & 3). He experienced unexpected shocks – a dark night and contorted corpses in a trench, being fired on in no man's land by his own artillery, officers inviting 'Blighty' flesh wounds etc.

During the attack of August 18 he also discovered that seeing dreadful wounds was far worse than seeing dead men. 'War was filthy and horrible beyond words. It is torture'. Some of the survivors on August 18 after disastrous losses were 'mad with fear' and would keep running till they dropped. The next dreadful event for Gibbs was the death of friends – only two officers apart from himself were left. 'There was much mismanagement,' he claimed.

He still had to go out into no man's land to supervise the construction of new trenches. Gibbs admitted to great difficulty in 1930 remembering chronology but he recalled in vivid detail a personal gun battle with a lone German in a trench the Suffolks had captured. They expected to be overrun by a counter attack at any moment and Gibbs threw a rocket roughly in the direction of the enemy but whether this stopped them in their tracks he would never know. As to the question of whether he was frightened – 'I was too much a public school boy still to dare to be frightened'.

His memory then goes blank for the next two weeks. In September they went to a quiet line near Hébuterne (south of Arras – Map 1) where despite his youth he was promoted to Adjutant of the battalion. He was initiated into the mysteries of 'office work'. His recall then 'deserts' him and the story is basically picked up at the Battle of Arras (Map 1) in the Spring of 1917 (the editor, however, sustains a narrative from other sources).

There is insight into the interaction between a C.O. and his adjutant, in this case between a Boer War veteran and a young and relatively inexperienced officer, though an obviously smart and enterprising one. Gibbs appeared to have more up-to-date technical know-how than the 'Old Man' and possibly more common sense. But at least the C.O. realised he had a good assistant and let him make decisions for the battalion.

At one point the 4/ Suffolks were cut off after an attack at Arras (no date) and awaited imminent death or capture. 'As I write of these far-away events I wonder if they all happened in another existence. I can't really believe they happened to me'.

The Adjutant's work was never done: after escaping from this predicament he had to arrange for new drafts to replace the killed and wounded Suffolks. 'After April 17... as the war proceeded I am able to be far less chronological and all sorts of memories are mixed up'. It is apparent that he kept no sort of diary. Memories of Passchendaele and March 1918 are 'hazy'. There is the occasional recall of a vivid event but it is the editor who sustains the narrative from other records.

GIFFARD, EDDIE (1887–1918)
Guns, Kites & Horses
Three Diaries from the Western Front
Edited by Sydney Giffard
The Radcliffe Press, 2003

Eddie Giffard was the 7th born in a family of 11 children (6 boys – 3 killed in the war). In 1914 Eddie returned from a sheep station in Australia to volunteer for military service.

His diary was kept in the attic of his sister's (Maude) house for over 50 years. It was written in 5 pocket-sized notebooks. There is some uncertainty about some words and phrases because the pencilled writing has faded.

Like Jack Giffard, Eddie's account was tersely composed in note form; e.g. 'Thursday, 4 November 1915. 3 p.m. Left Waterloo for Southampton. D, P, M, J and M to see me off. Stayed night at Railway Hotel'. Eddie was a 2nd Lieutenant in the Royal Field Artillery.

He arrived on November 13 in La Gorgue, near Laventie (Map 4) at the Artillery Guards Division HQ. His daily entries consist of very brief military style notes (1 to 6 lines) as he joined the bombardment of the enemy. But he did have plum pudding for dinner on November 25 and 'buzzard cake' for tea on the 25th. The snow which fell on November 26 was the first he had seen for 5 years. On most days he reported on the weather. On December 9 it was 'Wet as usual'.

2nd Lieutenant Giffard did a lot of work in the OP under German howitzer fire. There was some fraternisation on Christmas Day but enemy shells soon put a stop to that. A German request for a truce to allow them to bring in the wounded was turned down. Eddie had a haircut on January 8, 1916. Some shrapnel grazed his arm on the 13th but a spot of oidine solved this problem.

Eddie's is a 'local' diary in the sense that he does not describe the condition and strategy of the front line. He did not write when on leave – February 1 to the 9th.

'February 11 – OP all knocked out'. They moved to rest at Eringhem and played football in the snow and held a horse show. They moved to Ypres on March 14 – 'first taste of the salient'. Here, the artillery on both sides was much more active as they battled for the mine craters at St. Eloi. 'OP was pipsqueak (ed) during day' (April 15).

He slept in Talbot House, Poperinghe (May 1 – Maps 1 & 4) before more home leave (May 2 to 13). In the summer Eddie started missing out some days because 'nothing much happened'; e.g July 1–7. He was promoted to Lieutenant.

His battery was at Colincamps in August (near Amiens – Map 2), and Trones Wood (Somme near Guillemont – Map 3) in September. The intense fighting around Ginchy and Guillemont resulted in an entry of 11 lines on September 9. There must have been casualties but he does not often mention them.

Eddie was in a Royal Artillery rest billet for a week in November followed by more leave. A letter stuffed into the diary was from the C.O. of the 7/ Lincolns praised Eddie (FOO Lieut. Giffard) for his observation work and constant and concise reports. Conciseness was a virtue in this field. The diary became a daily one again.

'6 February 1917 America breaks off Dip relations with Germany; very cold wind'. He received a gramophone on February 8 and he was promoted to Captain with a position at staff HQ. The Germans began retreating to their Hindenburg Line. They were burning villages and destroying the countryside, which made it extremely difficult for British artillery to move up into new areas.

The battery returned north in May and were in reserve for the attack on Messines (Map 4) in June. They were directly involved in the bombardment preceding the Third Battle of Ypres and thereafter fully engaged in the violent artillery duel which was a background to months of infantry battle.

'Got a cut & bruises behind right ear myself and bled a bit' (September 21). It didn't sound much but in fact it was a Blighty One. There was a letter in the diary from Colonel Bethel – 'You have had a very hard time and got hit twice'.

Eddie did not return until November 30 and then joined another battery south in the Arras sector (Map 1) but then he attended a long course at Shoebury and Salisbury till February 1918. His military entries became longer at the time of the German onslaughts in March and April but he was still able to say where and with whom he had dinner on many days. He also played a lot of cricket. The final Allied advances progressed and Eddie was at Lagnicourt (south of Arras – Map 1) in September and Cambrai (Map 1) in October. He was hit on the left arm on October 13.

'8 Nov 1918. All sorts of rumours of Armistice: Bosch deputation reported to have entered the French line'.

But Major Edmund Giffard was killed by a shell just before the Armistice.

GIFFARD, JACK (1884–1956)
Guns, Kites & Horses
Three Diaries from the Western Front-line
Edited by Sydney Giffard
The Radcliffe Press, 2003

Lieutenant Jack Giffard was a Regular Army gunner in the Royal Horse Artillery, which sailed for Boulogne on August 16, 1914. He was badly wounded at Nery (near Rouen) and returned home a month later. He kept a daily diary of this time.

In this book Sydney Giffard edited not only Jack's diary but also those of his two brothers, Eddie and Walter (Sir Sydney Giffard is Walter's son). There are two separate entries for them.

Jack's diary has its own story. He hid it in the rafters above his head when the Germans occupied his dressing station. He brought it home and his sister made a copy. She kept this in the attic of her house for 50 years (along with Eddie's diary). It is not known what happened to Jack's original.

Jack had an entry for every day from August 16 to September 17. It is composed in note form; e.g. 'Sunday 16 August 1914. Arrived in S'hampton 10.a.m. with left half battery, Sclater- Booth & John Campbell – remainder 1 hr later. Fine. All aboard by 5.0. a.m.'

In Boulogne (August 17) he went around in a fiacre and a tram. On August 18 he reported the death of General Greison (this happened on a train – a critical loss because he was regarded as the leading expert on German military theory and practice).

Jack, in common with other gunner subalterns, had much to do with horses. On the train to Maubeuge he had 'awful trouble' with them in 'barborous trucks' (August 19).

He got near the German cavalry on August 21 after being' showered with flowers, cigars, eggs and all sorts of food' by the generous French people. He saw his first German shell burst at 2 p.m. on Saturday, August 22, near Mons.

Late on the 23rd they were moving south quickly but on the 24th at least they were firing their guns and stopping the enemy and enabling the remnants of the British cavalry to disengage. Jack was very relieved that only 30 of his battery were lost. They went a further 15 miles back to Villers Pol.

There was another close escape on the 25th as the battery was blocked in a sunken road by fleeing transport with the Germans closing in. On the 26th there was an artillery duel – the Germans using high explosive shell whilst the British relied on shrapnel still. Jack retreated another 10 miles and had only 50 minutes of sleep. 'We were all sleeping on our horses, the men absolutely done up'.

On August 27 they approached St. Quentin: everywhere was littered with ammunition, stores, harness etc. French citizens did all they could to help and the gunners slept briefly in a big farmhouse at Seraucourt (near St Omer). Apparently, their baggage wagon was 30 miles in front of them. The Germans caught up on August 29 and the gunners were under threat from artillery, cavalry and infantry (Berlancourt). Jack sat in an apple tree, eating apples and directing raking fire. But the vastly superior number of Germans continued to press forward and the battery retreated another 10 miles to Baillie.

They billeted by the River Aisne on the 30th in a nice house (Madame had fled to Paris with her three cars). Nery was reached on August 31. Here, quite unexpectedly, as Jack was tending a lame horse, the battery came under a surprise storm of shells and bullets.

Desperately, they managed to get two guns firing, but all Jack's crew were put out of action and he was hit by many pieces of shrapnel and gun fragments in his head, body and limbs. British cavalry and infantry rushed up and after heroic fighting (three VCs were won here) they drove off the Germans.

But the battery was 'knocked out' – men and horses. Jack was taken off in a Field Ambulance to a temporary dressing station at Baronne, just 30 miles from Paris. His numerous wounds were dressed and he was given morphia to ease the pain, which must have terrible (although he never mentioned it). But despite this he was left behind when the bulk of the patients and staff were moved to the capital (September 1).

The next day the Germans arrived in Baronne and ransacked all the possessions of the wounded soldiers but Jack managed to hide his in the rafters (plus his diary). There was 1 doctor and 13 orderlies to take care of 140 wounded. The Germans otherwise treated them well, giving them good food and drink and care.

Dr. Warrington took a large number of pieces of metal out of Jack. The fighting could still be heard going on all around them. 'Is Joffre at last beginning to cork up the neck of his much talked of bottle?' (September 5). Jack shaved off his beard with a 'heavy mowing machine' (September 6) and got hold of a toothbrush.

On the same day the French re-took Baronne and in the subsequent confusion groups of German, French and British troops filtered in and out of the area. Two French soldiers were shot in cold blood by Germans with revolvers – 'dirty dogs'.

On September 8 there came the prospect of transport to Paris but in the event they were diverted to Rouen (September 9). Here, he was well cared for by elderly ladies of the Croix-Rouge. He reached Havre by the 10th and had English visitors and newspapers.

Doctors worked hard on removing more metal and keeping his many wounds clean. He was moved to a house owned by a rich Englishman. A 'villainous old man' tried to shave him with a blunt razor. 'Never again!' (September 15). Jack's father arrived with a nurse to take Jack home and he arrived in Southampton on September 17.

Jack's twin brother, Bob, was killed on the Western Front in October 1914. Brother Sydney lost his life in Gallipoli in May, 1915.

GIFFARD, WALTER (1896–1971)
Guns, Kites & Horses
Three Diaries from the Western Front
Edited by Sydney Giffard
The Radcliffe Press, 2003

Walter lost a leg in an accident before the war but he had an artificial leg fitted at Roehampton and he remained very agile. Eventually, the RFC accepted him as an observer in a balloon in April 1917. He was posted to the Second Wing behind Ypres late in 1917, when the Third Battle of Ypres was still very much alive.

His diary, consisting of two notebooks, was found in his desk after his death. He noted in the second book that the war was 'the most colossal battle, both in magnitude and importance, that the world has ever known'.

Walter sometimes wrote in note form, like his brothers, but for many of his entries he wrote with more expression e.g. 'December 6, 1917. We tried to sleep six in a carriage. But, as Bairnsfather put it, we had to get up and rest every now and again'.

He travelled to the 2nd Wing HQ at Bailleul (Maps 1 & 4) and went up in the air straight away. There were frequent threats from enemy planes but big enemy guns firing from many miles away were even more lethal. Also, the weather had to be clear and calm for the sausages (long balloons had replaced round ones) On December 15 a British plane thought it was 'awfully funny' to dive at his balloon for a joke. Walter was also sometimes in danger from his own artillery trying to hit marauding planes and nearly hitting him.

The wind on December 28, at 56 m.p.h., was lifting the winch off the road (if it was strong enough it could lift everything, winch crew and all, and fly away with the lot). Also the strain on the winch engine was too much and Walter had to get them to engage to low gear for it to work. It took 25 minutes to get him down.

'29 December 1917. Thick fog: went for a walk' – another 'dud' day. 1918 brought a fresh menace – an accurate big enemy gun firing from 9 miles away. The called it 'Clockwork Charlie'. On January 3 it shot down 4 of 7 balloons in the area.

The kite company and the local artillery were supposed to liaise but it was obvious that the gunners did not think balloon observation and information was accurate enough to take out enemy positions. One consequence of this was that they sent over useless gunners to work with the balloonists.

The winch was prone to all sorts of accidents. On January 13 it skidded into a ditch. Walter wrote in his diary every day (with a few gaps) except when he was on leave, like his brother Eddie. 'Clockwork Charlie' downed two kites on January 19 and shot them down again after they were patched up and sent aloft once more. The cable on a third balloon was cut and the crew had to bale out. British planes shot this down as it was heading to German lines in the wind.

On January 23 a mouse fell out of Walter's rigging but he failed to catch it and put a parachute on it. He noted that enemy balloons came down straight away when shelled.

A long entry in February was about the batman who wanted to polish Walter's leg and the gunner who went up with him and brought up his breakfast, lunch and probably dinner, as well. But the quality of the liaison gunners was improving and Walter's hopes of a fruitful partnership blossomed.

March 4 Walter spent trying to convince the artillery that his observation of 'OK' hits was reliable. On March 7 he had to come down and patch up after 'Clockwork Charlie' hit his basket and balloon. On the next evening he was stuck out on the Menin Road after his transport failed to arrive. This was not a healthy place to be on foot and also his leg became too painful to walk on and he had to crawl a few hundred yards at a time. Luckily, he got a lift on a truck.

Even on misty days HQ ordered Walter up to test visibility – most 'aggrannoying' was his comical opinion of that. Unlike Eddie, Walter made many comments about the men with whom he worked – good and bad. Lardiner, for instance, was a good fellow but he talked shop all the time.

Walter had a very long description of a dramatic day on April 5 when

'Clockwork Charlie' forced him down twice but then he managed to locate where it was. He contacted the artillery and they hit this position. But then another big gun located him as he had drifted eastwards and hit the balloon But he decided to let it drift down. Then it began to go down too fast for comfort. So he climbed up in the rigging as the basket landed with a big thump.

The German gunners had saved 'Clockwork Charlie' and it proceeded to strike Walter's kite 5 times in 3 days.

The German offensive opened up in the north and the kite balloon companies had to collect all their stuff together and retreat rapidly west and south to St Omer, and beyond – to Desvres (near Boulogne). Balloons were out of action for the time being. But a Canadian Colonel persuaded Walter to take hum up, and whilst aloft he lit up a cigarette!

Walter was transferred to another unit for a while to work as a Recording Officer. He quite liked the job – much safer and more comfortable. But he refused to apply for a similar position permanently because it was not 'playing the game'. A fellow balloonist was killed (between May 24 and June 1 – he used just one entry for this period). On one day he saw 11 crew baling out at the same time. This may have convinced him to take the reporting job. He was under great pressure to do this. It was obvious that the strain on him was immense. The last diary entry was for June 4, when he came home on leave. Perhaps, as the editor observed, Walter thought that as a reporting officer, he was no longer playing a proper part in the war.

GLADDEN, NORMAN
Ypres 1917: A Personal Account
E. Norman Gladden
William Kimber, 1977

Norman kept a diary but did not write it up on all days. Norman joined the battle of the Somme with the 7th Battalion of the Northumberland Fusiliers at a time of the wild disorder in the front line during the capture of Le Sars (north-east of Martinpuich – Maps 2 & 3). The later stages of this struggle was a highly depressing experience for Norman. He found organisation chaotic and thought that it grew worse during the assault on the Butte de Warlencourt (Map 3) in November. He spent 26 days in forward areas with a minimum of shelter and practically no cooked food. He complained of a serious lack of leadership from officers and NCOs.

He caught trench fever and went into hospital on Christmas Day in Rouen in time to enjoy the decorations and the festivities. 'No treasure cave of Arcady could have appeared so wondrous to my eyes as the gaily-bedecked ward'. After a month in England he left again for the Western Front on May 1, 1917.

He got a warm welcome from his new battalion – the 11th – at Zillebeke (south-east of Ypres – Map 1) – with a humane sergeant-major! There followed a 3-day 'intensive nocturnal apprenticeship' in the trench (May 23-25). It was all much better organised than the Somme front of 1916, also safer and more comfortable.

Norman volunteered for machine gun duties and in his account gives a detailed description of each team member. They left for Ypres in motor lorries on 28 May. They came under a heavy German bombardment – the ever-present threat of death was no different here. But the Bunde of Zillebeke (sandbagged banks around a small lake) had been skilfully constructed to make a dangerous area comparatively safe. From this vantage point Norman had a good view of the shattered city of Ypres: no sign of human movement as shells still pounded into it.

At the end of the month he moved nearby to Hill 60 and suddenly the sniper became the chief threat. The hill was honeycombed with tunnels and the throb of engines digging even more of them. Overhead the artillery of both sides pounded each other, particularly on June 3 – attrition to interrupt the tunnelling work. Norman's job was to pass along filled sandbags into one of the mine galleries but he was under serious threat of a direct shell hit.

The 19 great mines exploded on June 7. Norman's battalion followed in the first wave of infantry attacks. A shell landed next to him and rendered him witless. He dug in at Battle Wood still shaking from head to foot. On the 9th Messines Ridge (Map 4) was secured.

They were taken out to the Mont des Cats (Map 4) where 'the man called to read the meter' (it was an inspection by the Divisional Gas Officer with a dark green band around his hat).

Back at Hill 60 a few days later there were further nervy nights in highly vulnerable trenches – shells at night, sniping by day. Everyone was scared stiff at their position outside the tunnels. It was such a relief to get inside a tunnel in support.

Norman, back in reserve, 'discovered' Harrison's Pomade (for the lice). They retired to camp at Le Thieushouk for cleaning-up, inspections and bomb-throwing competitions. Norman had time for some rambling (late July 1917). They got even further away from the front at Quelmes (August – west of St Omer) but the incessant rain became depressing. It stopped when they got to a more comfortable farm at Serques (west of St Omer).

But a new campaign for the Ypres Salient was planned for September. At least the Poor Bloody Infantry had a good idea of what was planned as they were shown at Poperinghe a large model of the proposed battle area – Dumbarton Lakes and Tower Hamlets Ridge.

It all started on September 20 when the battalion raced forward with a formidable barrage behind them. But there was also a furious response from the enemy artillery. Norman was in the second wave of infantry, struggling along with Lewis-gun ammunition. Men fell in droves around him and in terror he lay in a shallow pit. But he forced himself up (he could not just lay there like a few others did, much to his disgust). He finally reached a trench and leapt down on a great heap of dead and dying men – British and German. He ran to the comparative safety of what was left of Dumbarton Wood.

The most advanced British troops were now over the Tower Hamlets Ridge but all Norman and a the miscellaneous collection of men sheltering in the wood could do was wait for orders. They had to wait a whole day with no food and little water before being called out (September 21). For a little while as Norman ran, still carrying the machine gun ammunition, he lost touch with everyone – and he was beside himself with fear, not knowing where he was (he could be running towards the enemy).

Somehow he found his way back; his mates thought he had 'snuffed it'. But he had lost close friends. Indeed, half his company was lost.

Replacements had to come in and because of shortages men from transport and service corps had to be drafted in. They were very unhappy at becoming infantry! A new threat in the back areas was air raids and especially the new incendiary bomb. They were glad to get back to Le Thieshouck at the beginning of October. But the shortage of troops in the Salient was becoming more and more desperate and so they were quickly recalled to the devastated area around the Menin Road. Their mission was to get wounded men back for first aid as the RAMC was overwhelmed by the number of casualties laying out in the battle areas.

They sat in makeshift trenches below Passchendaele Ridge for several days, highly vulnerable to enemy shelling. They were in perpetual fear and when at last they were called in they ran like 'rabbits' to get away from this frightful position. The ridge still loomed ahead – still not captured.

GLUBB, JOHN (1897–1986)
Into Battle: A Soldier's Diary of the Great War
Cassell, 1978

The famous 'Glubb Pasha', who commanded the Arab Legion in Transjordan from 1939 to 1956, found his 1915–1918 diary 60 years after the end of the First World War, written in exercise books. The pencilled writing was faint with age.

The majority of days have an entry apart from when he was wounded or ill. It was written in trench dug-outs, bivouacs or billets. Places where he was are clearly named and there are good maps and diagrams. To prepare for publication General Glubb copied out the original without alteration He did add an introduction and some extra notes – always denoted by italics.

General Glubb's writing is clear and concise with detailed descriptions of the devastated environment. His good sense of humour is evident and was much appreciated by the men he commanded, along with his willingness to ensure they enjoyed relaxations such as parties, concerts and sports days.

His diary provides a rare insight into the critical part played by the Royal Engineers in supporting the front line, especially during the Battle of the Somme. The engineers frequently had to endure the dangers of the front line, especially from enemy artillery fire whilst they helped to construct defensive works and communications.

His father was a general in the Royal Engineers and John (educated at Cheltenham College and the Royal Military Academy, Woolwich) became a 2nd Lieutenant in the 7th Field Company, Royal Engineers aged 18. The diary commenced on November 24, 1915, when he was on his way to France. By the end of the month he was working near the front line in the Ypres Salient.

On December 20 Glubb suffered his first wound – a smashed big toe. He spent three weeks in hospital at Hazebrouck (Map 1). Shortly afterwards he was struck by a shell splinter in the neck. On return, he became second in command of the company as an acting Captain under the command of Captain McQueen. But he went down with appendicitis and was on sick leave in England until August 1916.

He re-joined his company on the Somme. John Glubb had a deep sense of duty – to the point where he felt that it was his destiny to be involved in this conflict. For instance, on January 14, 1917, he wrote, 'Suddenly I had my whole self overwhelmed by waves of deep and intense joy, which it is impossible to describe' – an amazing revelation on a wet and miserable day when he was exhausted.

Captain Glubb was much admired by his sappers, such as Corporal Cheale, who was absolutely fearless and with a morbid interest in corpses, or 'property owners' as he called them. Cheale also managed to get married to a French girl who could not speak a word of English and he had no French.

Of the Somme Glubb wrote, 'No word of mine can describe the dreariness and hopeless desolation of the scene, wrapped in mist and rain' (January 1917). The 7th Field Company later moved up to the Arras sector and a new battle. Glubb agreed that he must have been irritating to Captain McQueen, being 'adolescent and arrogant'. McQueen was a devoted officer and leader – but he had no sense of humour and had no interest in parties, concerts and sports days. On August 21, 1917, a shell exploded next to Captain Glubb and smashed one side of his face. He was in England recovering for nearly a year and only returned to France in July 1918.

GRAVES, ROBERT (1895–1985)
Goodbye to All That
An Autobiography (1929)
Penguin, 2014

Robert Graves claimed that he wrote this book as a way of forgetting the war (an endeavour which failed). He enlisted in the Royal Welch Fusiliers at the beginning of the war and went to France in May 1915. He was wounded on the Somme in July 1916. Subsequently, recovering in England, he wrote of his experiences on the Western Front in the form of a novel. He reconstituted this as history in the late 1920s. He also made use of letters written in late May and June 1915.

Graves was gratified to be commissioned in a famous old regiment and thus rather disappointed to be bundled with other reservists into the Welsh Regiment and sent to the trenches at Cambrin (south-west of Cuinchy – Map 4). This was at a stage in the war when trenches were still regarded by the BEF as shelter rather than places to exist in: both the French and the German Armies were far more advanced in their use of trenches.

The first corpse Graves encountered was of a soldier who had committed suicide after becoming 'a bit queer'. Mostly Tommies waited for 'the cushy one' – the wound that would get them back home. Later in May Graves was in the dangerous salient sticking out around the Cuinchy brickstacks, shared with the Germans. The enemy line was so close that they lethally employed rifle grenades and trench mortars. A grenade landed right beside him but, improbably, had landed the wrong way down. He could soon work out all the different types of explosions and the ones to disregard.

In June they rested in Béthune (Maps 1 & 4), where troops were forbidden to bomb fish in the canal. Graves's men were mostly tough

Welsh miners able to joke about most calamities but not a comrade who took 3 hours to die after having the top of his head blown off. A later billet nearby was in completely wrecked Vermelles (south-east of Béthune), where the officers played the sergeants at cricket using a parrot cage as a wicket (the dead parrot was still in it).

British trench life was slowly becoming more organised and disciplined. Graves could work out when a whizz bang was going to arrive even though it did so before he could hear the bang of it being fired.

At the end of July Graves was finally called to the Royal Welch 2nd Battalion at Laventie (Map 4), but found these tough Regular Army officers extremely unfriendly (they called 2nd Lieutenants 'warts'). He gained some respect by going out on a night patrol and infiltrating an enemy trench. He had actually deduced that the best way to last out the war was to get wounded, and that night patrols in the open was a good way of getting wounded. In any case, to do an officer's job effectively meant taking severe risks all the time, and RWF officers took more risks than most because they considered themselves superior fighters to the Germans.

On leave in London in August Graves was surprised to find how indifferent people were to the war. He returned to France for the late September offensive at Loos (Lens sector – Map 1), a costly fiasco. They had gas cylinders with lids that failed to unscrew at the critical moment. Five months at the front knocked the stuffing out of Graves: no longer was he anxious to get hurt. Every additional month at the front made officers less and less efficient and more likely to become wounded or sick. Graves was at least transferred to the more amenable 1st Battalion – at Festubert (Map 4) – in November. Here, he also met Siegfried Sassoon.

In the early weeks of 1916 Graves was a training instructor at Havre. When he returned to his battalion in March it was on the Somme at Fricourt (Map 3). After a nose operation in England he was sent back to the 2nd Battalion at Martinpuich (July 9 – Maps 2 & 3), due to attack High Wood. Before they were able to do this they were assailed by a huge enemy bombardment. A piece of shrapnel passed straight through Graves's upper body and he was reported as dead. His C.O. wrote to his mother to tell her that her son had been killed.

In fact, he rather miraculously survived a bleeding lung in hospital in Rouen, then London. 'The Times', which had announced his demise, had to announce that the news of his death was premature. He also had to persuade his bank that he was still alive to get paid. The officers of his battalion had been decimated at High Wood (Map 3).

In December 1916 Graves turned down the offer of more sick leave in England and returned to the Somme in January 1917, and was put in charge of the HQ Company of the 2nd Battalion. But he developed bronchitis and was sent to hospital in Oxford. There, he became an instructor in the Officer-Cadet Battalion in Wadham College.

GREENWELL, GRAHAM (born 1896)
An Infant in Arms
War letters of a Company Officer
Allen Lane The Penguin Press, 1972

This collection was first published in 1935. Graham Greenwell made the selection from an enormous number of letters he sent to his mother. In this 1972 edition John Terraine has written an introduction.

He noted how happy and cheerful Graham was from the first letter in September 1914 to the last in December 1918. Apparently, in 1935 the book was much criticised for this, going against the then current tide of disillusionment with the Great War (Lloyd George's 'War Memoirs' had just been published in this vein). However, there are many, many letters which describe Graham's deep depression, anxiety and fear.

He travelled to Havre with the 4th Battalion of the Oxford and Bucks Light Infantry on May 11, 1915. He was only 18 years old and soon having a 'ripping day' in Ploegsteert Wood (Map 4), although there was the odd bullet flying about. All letters are headed with place names: he must have added these in the post-war editing.

British and German working parties were out in no man's land at night but it was 'not considered etiquette to fire'. Graham was devastated by the death of an officer friend, Hermon – shot through the head by a sniper (May 28). Trench mortars were another menace – 'a new devilry'. Life was 'depressing' and 'boring' but sometimes 'exhilarating'. On June 6 there was something resembling a battle following a colossal British bombardment – a mountain gun, howitzers, rifle grenades and trench mortars. The enemy was 'thoroughly cowed'.

Having moved around quite a lot in June and July (Allouagne, Noeux-les-Mines etc. – near Béthune – Maps 1 & 4) they settled for many months in the Hébuterne trenches. Graham reported that he was in a fancy little dug-out with lace curtains (August). When he became particularly depressed he kept repeating to himself, "Thank God I didn't go to the Dardenelles'" and this soon made him feel a bit better.

They searched for safe spots to put in loopholes to snipe the snipers. 'The further back you get from the trenches the more promotion and plums you get', he complained on September 22, a typical grouse which belies this idea that he was blissfully happy and content.

Still at Hébuterne (south of Arras – Map 1) October 28 was another disturbing day. He had to take up his platoon from the support to the front trenches when there was a fear the Germans would infiltrate. The way was across open ground which was registered by the enemy artillery. He was knocked off his feet twice but it could have been much worse. The enemy action turned into a furious and prolonged bombardment which left them all 'utterly demoralised – utterly cowed'.

But he was doing well in the eyes of senior officers and became Assistant Transport Officer (November 6). He was also Mess President so on the 7th the C.O. sent him off to the Expeditionary Force Canteen to order all the supplies for the regiment's canteens. He had to balance the accounts later, a massive job covering 'millions of different articles'.

He was sent to the Sailly-au-Bois Bomb School later in November. By the end of the year he was complaining about blasts from the British artillery, which caused massive retaliation from the German guns on his men who had little proper protection from the shelling.

February 1916 (still at Hébuterne – billets at Courcelette – Maps 2 & 3) was marked by a series of German trench raids, which made everyone jumpy. Graham complained about the shrapnel helmets which they had to wear except when sleeping – 'most unpleasant soup plates'.

On April 14 he was 'very much depressed'. On the 19th he was nearly caught in the open by machine gun fire. But a few days holiday at Bayencourt (between Amiens and Arras – Maps 1 & 2) cheered him up. There was a lot of training out of the front line. But on July 2 they were in 'a field behind Mailly Maillet' (Somme) being passed by lines of big guns and ammunition limbers. From the other direction came fleets of ambulances and crowds of German prisoners. The din of the Battle of the Somme was utterly deafening.

They were poised to join it on July 4 but they were pulled out when the German trenches they were about to attack were vacated by the enemy. By the 8th Graham was more depressed than ever because of the ceaseless rain. Worse to come: on the 19th they were in the storm of battle at Bouzincourt (Map 3), caught out by German artillery when in an exposed position – just a ditch really. Graham had been held back in reserve. By the 24th their losses were getting horrific: in Graham's company the commander was killed and two other officers wounded along with nearly all the NCOs. 63 men were left out of 150. Another company lost all its officers. The battalion was then taken out of the line. Graham had the job of training up almost a new company.

Rest at Agenvillers restored morale a little and rows with the 'vile Dubosc' (a drunk old French owner of their mess) livened things up. Graham threatened Dubosc with 'Monseiur le Baron' (Lieutenant Carew Hunt, seven feet tall and fluent in French). But by August 13th Graham was in the Ovillers trenches (north-east of Albert – Map 2) with many men who had been in the army just a few months. 'I have seldom felt such a miserable wreck' (August 14). The battalion's casualty list continued to be devastating and there were constant fears of being overrun by enemy infantry as the Germans fought desperately over every yard of ground and shelled heavily and persistently. Graham's letter of August 16 ended with 'now feel as cheerful as possible' – which was probably not all that cheerful. The ex-German trenches which they were occupying were an absolute hell of a mess and a stink.

Somewhere along the line it was obvious that Graham had a wound of some sort which he was trying (unsuccessfully) to hide from his mother. He was promoted to Captain. They rested in the Bus and Warlincourt area (Map 3) before going to the Le Sars trenches in November. The C.O. told him to 'cheer up' (nicely – he thought a lot of Captain Greenwell) on the 7th . But a few days later he was in hospital and there are no letters from November 15 to January 13, 1916 (or Graham chose not to include any from this period).

But he was in trenches at Hérbecourt (Map 2) in February as the Germans retreated to their Hindenburg Line. Graham reported 'open warfare is in full swing'. The battalion became part of a 'flying column'. His company was in the forefront of attempts to seize villages before the Germans could destroy them. But the enemy would not give up their campaign of devastation easily: Roissel (east of Peronne – Map 2) was captured from them but then lost again. Graham drew praise during this period from Higher Command for his daring exploits in pursuit of the enemy. The C.O. sent him some champagne.

'…the trenches are in an indescribable state…'
Col. Robertson returning from 'rounds', January 5th 1915.

Then came the move to the Ypres Salient in August. Again, the battalion was suffering badly and Graham was promoted to be Adjutant of the brigade Company. But Langemarck on August 18 brought more heavy losses. In his old company every officer was hit except for two subalterns.

They were in a 'chaotic state' and it was 'difficult to keep cheerful' (August 24): enthusiasm was replaced by 'dumb and disciplined resignation'. He reported from Vlamertinghe on the 29th that the previous day on the canal bank at Ypres was 'the worst expression of modern warfare I have ever struck'. He was awarded the Military Cross at some stage, whether on the Somme or at Ypres is not clear.

On November 24 he was on a train to the Italian Front.

GRIFFITH, WYN (1890–1977)
Up to Mametz Wood
Wyn Griffith
Gliddon Books

'Up to Mametz Wood' was first published by Faber & Faber in 1931. Wyn became a Lieutenant in the 15th (London Welch) Battalion and served for the whole war.

Before the war he was training to be a lawyer but answered the call straight away to join the New Army. His narrative begins in December 1915 when the battalion was near Aubers Ridge (Map 4). Wyn writes very well: the earlier part of his account tends to be factual, descriptive, but increasingly lively for 1916. He was able to repeat many a dialogue with fellow officers and the men, whom he much admired. The book thus becomes more and amusing and engaging. Twelve years after the war he was able to recall the places where he served but provided few dates. Yet the reader knows roughly when he is referring to.

Arriving in a support trench he wondered, 'Why I am not afraid?' He remembered that this was because of 'a sequence of minute experiences, each in its turn claiming concentration'. But it did unnerve him to have go up on top to supervise some work. He felt very vulnerable even though the enemy was several hundred yards away.

On Christmas Eve he awoke in his dug-out floating in water. A prevailing theme in this account was the terrible state of the British trenches. He believed that High Command was not really interested in comfort for the troops because their basic plan was that they were going to attack the enemy – sooner or later. The Germans, on the other hand, were going to make sure their troops were well-entrenched and comfortable because it was defence that was their pre-occupation.

So Wyn found himself behind low, evil-smelling walls of wet mud, standing on undrained sump pits and ramshackle dug-outs built on the lines of a child's one-room house – no foundations, unstructured with no framework.

There were German calls of "Merry Christmas, Tommy" and replies of "Merry Christmas, Fritz,' and men stumbled out with presents. But the British got as near as possible to the enemy defences in order that their own lack of protection was not revealed. The Brigadier had been round earlier making threats about any fraternisation and so the affair was short-lived. But these men did not not hate another; they did hate the artillery of both sides.

They moved to Richebourg St. Vaas (south-west of Neuve Chapelle – Maps 1 & 4) but the artillery must have spotted them because they were greeted with an hour of 5.9s raining down on the already wrecked village. Wyn was terrified but fought to 'maintain an appearance of unconcern'. After all, he was their Company second-in-command (and had been gazetted as a Captain – but he had to wait a long time for this to come through).

Trenches at Richebourg l'Avoue were only marginally better than the previous ones. Everywhere there was water to wade through. A mortar was fired at the Germans. "You bloody Welsh murderers," came a cry from across the way.

Out of it again the officers managed to acquire a gramophone: they had two records and Wyn had only to hear one of these tunes later in life to remind him of the people and scenes he lived with and through. There were also some Kirchner drawings of thin-legged girls in silk-stockings and arguments about the Tottenham Hotspur football team. This was interrupted by Wyn being ordered to run a cookery course by the Brigadier. Wyn didn't have a clue about cooking but the Sergeant cook turned out to be a treasure and with Wyn mugging up a book or two he actually ran a successful course from nothing!

The 15th Battalion had been in no open battle but the lack of proper protection meant a slow dwindling of their numbers – reduced by a half within three months. They were now replaced by Bantams, who turned out to be fine soldiers and very good Cockney company. The Germans immediately called out "Cock-a-doodle-do". The Tommies were ready to believe that the Germans had an enormous notebook with it all written down. They didn't have a clue what Germans they were facing were up to.

They were at 'cursed' Givenchy (Map 4), where conditions were even worse. Wyn mused on whether attrition was any good at all. He thought it just wasted men's lives just to please a Higher Command which believed that it had to be offensive. It was a blessed relief for Wyn to be called to an officers' course at Aire (April 10, 1916). A very kind town major gave him the best billet in town (putting him in front of a colonel) because Wyn had to come straight from the trench and was in a dreadful state. In many excerpts Wyn could remember the actual dialogue in which he engaged.

After ten days' ecstatic leave with his wife Wyn returned to be sent immediately on a 'show' at Laventie (Map 4) – a terrible awakening from bliss. 'What a plague have I to do with a buff jerkin,' – Wyn quoted Falstaff. He also wrote some good doggerel, good enough to get published in trench magazines. He was much sought after for good companionship – very popular with officers and men. He remembered the standard battalion report before any 'show'. 'Situation Normal. Wind south-west' – whatever way it was blowing.

A German deserter was found to have much better boots than the British. The C.O. was brusque but it was just his normal manner – they actually liked him. But the Brigadier was 'a daily plague', well-known as 'Jane'. He took a delight in exposing himself to fire: he had won the VC in the Boer War. He hated empty tins. He was in charge of 3,000 men yet in no way was a leader of them.

After six months at the front Wyn had not suffered as much as a scratch. Systematic, long-range shelling had not yet begun nor had bombing from the air in the back areas. He had not been engaged in open battle. He was on the look-out for any opportunity to move out of the line – and who can blame him? The position of temporary Adjutant of the battalion was a step in the right direction.

There was a new threat of mines. The Germans had exploded a big one at Givenchy – the 'Duck Bill Crater' which had luckily exploded in no man 's land – and there was a good chance they would try and detonate one under the Givenchy trenches. So when they thought they heard the sounds of mining under their trench the 15th officers were alarmed. But the noises they could hear were in fact wind rushing through empty rum jars!

Wyn's company held an impromptu concert and the Adjutant played the piano, entrancing these simple men with some classical music. "I thought they'd like it," he said afterwards.

Wyn's wish to be moved into staff work at a Brigade HQ came true in the summer of 1916. It was only a temporary post to learn more and perform general duties but he hoped to do well enough to rise up the ladder. He turned up at the big château but his dreams of grandeur were shattered when all he got was a tent in the garden! But he soon progressed in the work: by the time the brigade moved to the Somme he was Staff Captain and close to the General. At Mametz Wood it was his quick thinking which saved the lives of several hundred men. This gave him great satisfaction because it meant that he was using his talents to their best advantage on the Western Front.

GROOM, ARCHIE (born 1897)
Poor Bloody Infantry. The Truth Untold
A Memoir of the Great War
W. H. A. Groom
Picardy Publishing Ltd., 1983

This memoir was based on his 'original notes': these may well have been a full diary because he does include copies of actual entries for four days in 1917. He said that he did not include names of comrades in these 'original notes' so has put fictitious names in this memoir.

Archie enlisted in March 1916 into the London Rifle Brigade. There he learnt through hours and hours of training how to use a bayonet effectively but then never used it – like the vast majority of soldiers in this war. In fact, he had no strong urge to kill Germans or to be patriotic but he did want first-hand experience of the battle front beyond simple curiosity.

So he was on the Neuve Chapelle (Maps 1 & 4) front by October 1916. Archie wrote this memoir in the form of essays but the reader always gets a broad idea of time and place so this is further evidence of a diary. He disputed the notion of 'the glorious dead' and replaced it with a picture of very frightened men cursing their bad luck in being there, and suffering continuous mental anguish.

Archie was in the cold and wet Epinette breastworks. Death lurked at every corner. 'Rest' was every moment away from it, whatever work they had to do. He read a lot of poetry – he said that helped to ease his mind a little.

One wiring party (no date) was particularly hair-raising: a slight noise was made, the Very lights went up and the bullets started flying. He seized the chance to help stretcher-bearers carry away a pal of his. When he got back to the trench he drank too much rum and was later told that he had staggered out of the trench to avenge the death of a friend.

He became known as 'Fluffy' following a comment made by the C.O. (Archie only shaved once a week) during an inspection. This preceded a visit by Sir Douglas Haig during which they almost ran past him. Archie became a machine-gunner.

The front trenches east of Fauquisart (Map 4) were flooded with rain water so the Germans wisely decided to withdraw to their reserve line in order to celebrate Christmas. However Archie and his mates were kept in the wet in case there was an attempt at fraternisation.

Between January 9 and 28 advance posts were ordered into the abandoned and crumbling (because of 20 degrees of frost) German trenches. The idea was to prove to Higher Command that this front was trying to be offensive. The result was that the Germans were able to raid these highly vulnerable positions with impunity and cause heavy casualties (no officers were sent out). Archie spent several days out in these freezing shallow holes.

On March 1, 1917 they left this Laventie (Map 4) sector to go to the the Battle of Arras. Archie missed the opening of this as he went on a machine gun course. Neuville Vitasse and Wancourt (Arras – Map 1) were captured. His first job on return was to try to dig holes in solid chalk (May 2).

The assault on May 3 did not get far. The following rest in nice countryside in the rear of this front was sheer joy. It was this sort of interlude which gave journalists the impression that the Poor Bloody Infantry were cheerful souls when it was simply a case of 'mental relief'. Thus a talented pal described a chicken provided by a farmer's wife as having been born during the Crimean War.

In August the London Rifle Brigade lined up for the assault on Westhoek Ridge in the Salient (Maps 1 & 4), a futile operation as it was too well-defended. It was at this time that we discover that Archie had kept a detailed diary during this period. He copied out the entries for August 13 to 17. He now led a machine gun team. On the 15th he was buried up to armpits but otherwise unhurt. This was followed by an advance in Glencourse Wood through a hail of bullets.

He found himself alone with his Lewis gun, smashed it up to avoid the enemy capturing it and tried to shelter in a shallow shell hole, paralysed with fear. He managed to locate others and ran back with them – Glencourse and Polygon Woods were left to the Germans. He was relieved. Apparently a clerk at HQ had deserted to the enemy with the plan of attack.

Archie was promoted to Lance Corporal and there followed two months of quiet at Moevres near Cambrai (Map 1). He made the point that German trenches were generally superior to the British ones because they were always having to defend them. On November 20, 1917, the London Rifle Brigade followed in the wake of the advancing first wave and into the Hindenburg trenches. They remained there for a week as the British campaign stalled and retreated to their original positions following the massive German counter attacks. During the German offensive in March 1918 the brigade were near Vimy Ridge (Map 1) defending Arras. 'Nearly all the old faces had gone'. Archie was gassed and burnt in May and that was a Blighty One.

HAMILTON, RALPH (1888–1918)
The War Diary of the Master of Belhaven 1914–1918
John Murray, 1924

In August 1914 Lieutenant Colonel Hamilton was in command of the Essex Horse Artillery. This was a territorial unit and he was informed that it had no chance of going to the Western Front. So he managed to be sent to Belgium as an interpreter for the new 7th Division. This went to Zeebrugge on October 8.

The division was in great danger of being cornered by overwhelming German forces and quickly retreated south . But the decision was made to try to hold on to Ypres, which came under horrific artillery fire as the enemy tried to force out the defenders.

Lieutenant Colonel Hamilton was obliged to return to England because of an internal injury (October 27). Whilst he was in England he wrote up from memory his experiences to date and so this is the narrative he produced for 1914. From January 7, 1915, he wrote almost a daily diary until his death in 1918. He was an experienced regular officer and so his account was a detailed military one but he did write about other things – the environment, comrades, football matches etc. He liked a joke: on the topic of latrine rumours he recalled that Honolulu was about the only place in the world they were not going to!

He managed to obtain a commission in the 2nd Battalion of the Life Guards on December 9 and travelled to Havre on January 7, 1915. They went into the Ypres front line in February but Hamilton was left behind to look after 80 men and 160 horses. Eventually, he was sent in reserve to Windsor.

He eventually managed to get command of an artillery battery as a major in September and thus played a very important part in the British bombardments at the Battle of Loos (Lens – Map 1) where he was put in command of the guns of a whole Brigade – that is four batteries. He worked out the angles and ranges from a 1/10,000 scale map. His targets were in gun pits 2 miles away but he could put a shot within 25 yards of them. Infantry officers pointed out enemy positions such as a house containing a minenwerfer gun firing from inside of and a large periscope. He scored direct hits on both of them.

Another speciality of his was 'search and sweep' where all the guns of a battery fired 9 shots at three different ranges and three different angles.

After a week's firing at Loos the brigade artillery operated in the Ypres Salient at Dickebusch and Boeschepe. Hamilton reverted to command of a single battery. Within 2 months (October and November) all his guns were hit when German artillery managed to get a direct fix on their position. These were big shells and one which landed right next to Hamilton made a crater 10 feet deep and 20 feet wide.

Rest at Alquines until January 1916 was thus a welcome break but in February and March he was directing the battery by Ypres itself, then Kemmel Hill (Map 4) in April and Danoutre. He was often in charge of all 4 batteries but a permanent brigade command eluded him for the time being. In all, he lost three colonels and took over each time. It was a dangerous job commanding artillery; they had to move about a lot and were very much noticeable around the guns. Moreover, they often had to go to the trenches to confer with infantry commanders. On August 29 Major Hamilton was struck on the helmet by shrapnel and blown head first down a tunnel.

He had also been suffering for some time internally and was in England for an urgent operation in November and did not return until May, 1917. But finally he was given permanent command of a brigade's artillery, in time for the preparations for another big battle in the Ypres Salient. Hamilton was popular with the general staff because of his efficiency and lack of fussing – a very easy man with whom to work.

Because he was a good artillery commander he spent much time with maps and so his diary is full of them. Also, for each day there was a heading explaining where he was. But his luck finally ran out on March 31, 1918, when a shell exploded directly under his horse.

HERMON, EDWARD (1878–1917)
For Love & Courage
The Letters of Lieutenant Colonel E. W. Hermon
From the Western Front 1914–1917
Edited by Anne Nason
Preface, 2009

Lieutenant Colonel Edward William Hermon ('Robert' to his family) wrote almost every day (nearly 600 letters) to his wife. He was killed on the first day of the Battle of Arras (Map 1), April 9, 1917.

The letters remained in a family desk until inherited by Anne Nason, Hermon's granddaughter. The letters were usually dated but where not the editor was able to use postmarks for dates.

Major Hermon was in a Reserve Regiment at the outbreak of war – the King Edward's Horse. Months of training followed for these part-time soldiers until they were sent to France in April 1915 to near Béthune.

On Sunday May 2 Hermon was 'thoroughly enjoying' the front line and on the 3rd 'merry' and 'laughing' and on the 4th arranging a weekly box of food from Harrods. He took part in the BEF failure to capture Aubers Ridge (Map 4) in May. The Major described the action as 'liveliness'.

More than once Hermon remarked on a shortage of big guns and shells, which could result in defeat. But he remained 'most cheery' on this stalemate front. He suffered from an early enemy gas attack at the end of May. Deaths of other officers were mentioned in passing. He applauded Lloyd George's efforts to get more shells (June 5).

His 'C' Squadron took over some of the French front line at Headigend. On June 18 he became part-time Commandant and Chief Instructor at a divisional bomb school (he was an expert). He asked his wife to send over two lacrosse bats. Someone put a live bomb in his demonstration box and this blew up and also exploded more detonators.

Hermon was struck in the face with lumps of hot metal. A fellow instructor at another school was killed in a similar accident in July.

He left the school (it was only a temporary position) later in July, having invented 'Hermon's Hun Hustler' (it didn't work) and 'Bob's Boche Buster' (a bomb catapult). He obviously liked a little laugh. He rather liked saucy French postcards and sent a few of these home: they are shown in the book. He was a judge at the Divisional Horse Show (August 11).

The Battle of Loos (Lens sector – Map 1) came in late September. The King Edward's Horse were at Haillicourt carrying up cylinders of 'frightfulness'. It was a tough struggle fought amongst an industrial wasteland. Its main purpose was to relieve pressure on the Russians and failed miserably to do that. Even Hermon considered the fighting as 'desperate' so it must have been terrible – 50,000 British casualties. The Germans launched frequent violent counter attacks accompanied by heavy and persistent shelling.

He set out with a burying party on October 16 to inter men who had been killed on September 25. Hermon wrote that it made one 'perfectly callous to everything connected with life and death'.

Robert's fifth child was born in November and later in the month he felt able to take leave in England (he tried to make sure that he did not take leave until most of his men had been granted some). His wife was naturally very anxious about her beloved husband's safety and he did his best to play down how dangerous and horrible the fighting had become. Now and again she misread what he meant or jumped to conclusions. So he had to try and convince her that things were not too bad.

Promotion was now in the offing for Hermon, either as a staff officer at Divisional HQ (he spent some time there in April and May 1916) or in command of a Regiment. The King Edward's Horse was to be upgraded to Regimental status and he was quite keen on the job. The unit was being trained for this upgrade on the French coast but its general view was that this was a waste of time for a unit with considerable front line experience (anyway, it was a nice break by the sea). Hermon became temporary Lieutenant Colonel on June 7.

The destruction of much of Arras by shell damage (right and below) is all too apparent in these contemporary photographs.

As the Battle of the Somme got under way the King Edward's Horse was well away to the north at Valhoun whilst Hermon rather fretted about the delay in deciding who was to became its new commander. He was thus very interested in the chance to command an infantry battalion (and see more action). But he was extremely popular with the officers and men of the King Edward's Horse and they persuaded him to stay for the time being.

But finally he became too impatient to wait and took over command of the 27th Battalion of the Northumberland Fusiliers in August. Early in September he was part of the Battle of the Somme at Contalmaison (Maps 2 & 3), in heavy fighting with serious casualty rates. They were there for most of September.

There followed rest near Armentières (Maps 1 & 4). After home leave he assumed command of the 24th Battalion of the Northumberland Fusiliers late in October. He was in hospital for rest in January 1917 and was sent home for more rest after this. He returned to the Arras front in February to prepare for the coming battle. The language in his letters was a reflection of the growing strain of command on the Western Front for nearly two years. It was 'strenuous' and he was 'weary'. On April 9 at 5.30 a.m. the 24th Battalion went out over the bags and Lieutenant Colonel Hermon was shot in the heart. His wife Ethel was not informed of his death until April 13.

HISCOCK, ERIC (born 1900)
The Bells of Hell go Ting-a-Ling-a-Ling
An Autobiographical Fragment without Maps
Corgi, 1977

Eric joined the University and Public Schools Battalion of the Royal Fusiliers (29th Battalion) in 1915 when he was just 15 years old; he told the Adjutant he was 18. This unit consisted of 'mainly amateurs'. He had a brush with sex in Oxford (where he was billeted at home) and gambling in Dover where he was placed in the 5th Battalion along with other under-age recruits and 'odds and sods'. This is possibly why he uses some fictitious names.

He trained with the under-age men until March 1918 when it looked as though the Germans would break through to the Channel ports and there was a desperate need for reinforcements. Eric was transported to the 26th Battalion in a slimy rat-infested trench in the Ypres Salient and the Sergeant next to him was shot through the head.

He was then sent with a raiding party to secure an enemy prisoner from a pill box bristling with machine guns. They were led by a lieutenant whose face twitched with fear. Eric became tangled up in the barbed wire.

"Crawl like a fucking snake," he was advised.

As bullets zipped past him he lay there for England in the Passchendaele dawn. When the raiding party returned with a shaking prisoner Eric followed and fell on a decaying horse in a pit. He was awarded the Military Medal (but took the alternative of 100 francs and extra rum).

But the salient was evacuated and Eric returned to rest and 'Black Velvet' (champagne and Guinness). He became an acting lance corporal (unpaid) and they protected the line in front of Kemmel Hill (Map 4). He was trying to get mud off his rifle when he shot himself in the upper arm. After hospital he found himself at Étaples camp in a hut with other suspected cases of self-inflicted wounds.

He was tried by 4 officers who discovered that the twitching Lieutenant Clarke, who had reported Eric, was a homosexual bent on seducing a comrade of Eric's. With Eric out of the way he was hoping to get his wicked way. Eric was freed but lost ten days' pay.

He went to a RTO to find out where his battalion was. "No wonder we're losing the fucking war," said the officer, "they're sending out fucking babies now!" So Eric returned to carrying tons of equipment, little sleep, intolerable discipline and 'men gasping for breath as death enveloped them in evil-smelling mud-filled holes'. He now loathed the Army and totally regretted joining it. He watched men drown as they fell off the duckboard road into shell holes brimming with slimy water. His only joy was when a shell just missed Lieutenant Clarke and the officer shit himself. There was even more light relief when Eric discovered a path made entirely from full tins of Fray Bentos bully beef.

A stunt was ordained from HQ in August when 'those fools sitting on office stools' decided that the 26th Battalion were not doing enough in the final push. In this raid out of 20 men 2 were killed and 9 wounded. They hunted rats and the 'Yanks exuded francs' (Eric was later a well-known journalist). But the Americans did lift British morale. On September 14 Eric was part of the 'Misty Morning Stunt' and was hit in the neck, hand and mouth ("Just like a stupid fucker to go into battle with his mouth open," said a pal). Eric lost an enormous amount of blood but managed to crawl back to a casualty clearing station. Later he joined the Army of Occupation in Cologne.

HITCHCOCK F. C.
"Stand To"
A Diary of the Trench 1915–1918
Captain F. C. Hitchcock
The Naval & Military Press, 2009

Captain F. C. Hitchcock (FCH) maintained a notebook from which he wrote up a daily diary from May 16, 1915, until the Armistice (and beyond) apart from 2 long spells when he was away from the Western Front and in October 1918 when he grouped a batch of days together. He also consulted his 'Army Book 152' (correspondence).

He first arrived in France on May 20, 1915, when he led a draft of men to Havre. He was immediately posted to the 2nd Battalion of the Leinster Regiment (a Regular Army Regiment). FCH provided a solid factual military account, as befitted an officer of the Regular Army. But, especially in the diary after he had been back in Ireland on a long course, the account became more wide-ranging and expressive. For instance, he wrote more about his fellow officers and men, whom he regarded as unfailingly enterprising and brave ('real Hun-slayers'). But he was able to maintain a detailed account of the military action, along with excellent topographical sketches and maps.

FCH began life on the Western Front in the Armentières trenches (May 25 – Maps 1 & 4), moving to near Ypres (engulfed in flames and smoke) on June 2. It was extremely 'unhealthy' there because of relentless German artillery bombardment and resulting battered trenches. Moreover, later in June they had to labour around the lethal Menin Road (Maps 1 & 4 –Ypres).

But these resilient soldiers preserved their humour – officers dressed up in fancy civilian clothes they found and larked about in the Yser Canal. They acquired a dog and made a stylish gas mask for it (July 6). The Padre rode around on a splendid ex-Uhlan black horse.

But 8 officers were killed or wounded at Hooge in July and FCH was lucky to escape a similar fate; apart from a trench collapsing on him and burying him in sand he remained unscathed.

He included some material from a diary written by Friedrich Kressis of the German 132nd Regiment of the same battle at Hooge. FCH had a few days checking for Belgian spies in Ypres (aided by a 'BF of an interpreter'). Returning to the battalion he became a temporary company commander.

In October they switched south to the St. Eloi sector, a great relief after the horrors of the Salient. A bullet grazed FCH's arm (October 24). "Jammy one, sir," yelled his platoon. 'I had no such luck.' A special feature of this sector at this time was the detonation of several large mines and scrambles by both sides to occupy the craters – much better than crumbling trenches.

FCH's garb during this cold and wet winter was a balaclava helmet, a goat-skin inside out and waders. He was sent back to Ireland on a long course (November 6).

He returned in July 1916 as the battalion prepared to go to the Somme. Here, they fought in two notable battles – the one for Guillemont (Map 3) starting on August 18 and in Delville Wood at the end of the month. Twice they were near to capturing their objective only to be recalled by Brigade commanders. Because they were so brave in going forward they had a lot of casualties. From Guillemont the survivors returned 'sore-hearted and disgruntled'.

FCH used an extract from the book by Lieutenant E. Junger (73 Hanoverian Regiment) in order to compare British and German accounts of the action from August 23 to 26.

At Delville Wood (Map 3) 2nd Lieutenant Hitchcock led his platoon through unarmed and demoralised troops returning in disorder straight at German defences, losing 12 men (August 31). It was here that they witnessed an extraordinary action of the utmost bravery: right in front of them a soldier from another battalion stood right in front of the enemy hurling grenades at them as they tried to gun him down. Eventually, he fell for the last time. "Faith an he's took the count this time," muttered an 'old tough' with Celtic psychology. 'This unknown Irish warrior of a daring exploit was swallowed up in the weeping countryside of tortured Picardy.'

The Leinsters suffered all the horrors of the Somme – colossal fire from guns of every calibre, hunger and maddening thirst, lack of sleep and enormous blue-black flies.

FCH became a company commander (promoted to Captain in October). Their next assignment was at Vimy Ridge (September 23 – Map 1). Featured here were 'Bungalore torpedoes' (wire-busters), talkative German prisoners when plied with whisky. The General descended unexpectedly on FCH (October 20) and the latter conducted the General around with his pyjamas worn under his uniform.

Canadians relieved the battalion on October 26 and the Irish soldiers went to Loos (Lens sector – Map 1) where they were harassed by Minenwerfers strafes, aerial darts and persistent sniping. The Germans were also using spies to infiltrate British lines and a daily password was needed – another chore to remember that.

FCH gave a detailed military explanation and description of trench raids in January 1917. He enjoyed time off in the pleasant town of Béthune. But because of incoming senior officers he lost his company command. He had been awarded the Military Cross for his bravery on the Somme.

When home on leave he became very sick (February 1917) and after recovery and a period of home service he returned to Hazebrouck (Map 1) on August 8, 1918. The front line by this time was beginning to became fluid as the Germans retreated. There was a Fourth Battle of Ypres (September 28 to October 3) and FCH was back on the Menin Road in the midst of German bullets, two of which rested in his Burberry – another lucky escape.

HODGES, FREDERICK (born 1899)
Men of 18 in 1918
Arthur H. Stockwell Ltd., 1988

Frederick served in the 10th (Services) Battalion of the Lancashire Fusiliers on the Western Front from April to November 1918. He arrived in France on April 8 with a new draft of 18 year olds. They were eager to get fighting: they were the 'Byng Boys' (General Byng commanded the 3rd Army, but this was also the title of a popular show in London).

In the German onslaught of March 1918 the 10th Battalion had been driven out of the Flesquieres Salient (near Cambrai – Map 1) with heavy losses to a new line west of Albert (Map 2). They came out of that battle with just one Lewis gun left. Whilst passing through Calais Frederick saw a 'Continental Daily Mail' headline – 'FOCH SAYS AMIENS SHALL NOT FALL'. It is a marked feature of Frederick's narrative that he is always keen to discuss war situations outside his immediate involvement (along with any number of other military topics relevant to the Western Front).

The 'old sweats' who had survived their recent hammering had largely maintained their good morale. Indeed, many of them said they enjoyed shooting down Huns as a change from being shot at themselves. The new boys were at Toutencourt when Field Marshall Sir Douglas Haig's Special 'backs to the wall' order was read to them. Whereas the old sweats tended to ask, 'What wall?' the youngsters were 'thrilled' by the message although the lice had started biting them – 'a great trial' for the rest of the war.

Almost the first event in the trench for Frederick was a shell exploding a few yards away and cutting him off from the rest of the platoon. The platoon NCO wanted to know what he was doing behind a wall of earth and Frederick had to point out that he hadn't put it there (April 15). It was precarious in these trenches because the Germans had occupied Thiepval

Ridge and tended to be able to look down on the British positions. The question was, 'When would they resume their offensive?' But by the middle of April in this sector there were no clear signs that they would. Thus, the battalion was encouraged to send out more patrols to find out exactly where the Germans were and what they were doing. Frederick, with his wider view of the situation, appreciated this situation. But this entailed a very dangerous 12 nights and days for him and the rest of his platoon.

There followed the 3 Rs in May – rest, reorganisation and retraining – out at Talmas (Map 2). Here, Frederick found a way round censorship of place names in his letters home by answering his parents' knowledgeable questions with two kisses for 'Yes' and three for 'No'.

The battalion returned to a maze of criss-cross old and new trenches (other ranks relied completely on officers and NCOs for directions) at Auchonvillers (near Albert – Map 2). They added to the puzzle with new trenches. Frederick was glad to get away from it to go on a course on poison gas (May 29).

He achieved top marks in the end-of-course test (June 15) but returned to find that his whole platoon had been 'wiped out' in a surprise German trench raid. But the tide of war was beginning to change and there were detailed preparations for a British attack on Aveluy Wood (Map 3). These fit young 18 year olds were quite eager to get going on this although most of them realised that the real battle would be very different from practice.

Frederick increasingly included material on military organisation, for instance, on how a machine gun team operates and about the Stokes mortar. There was also much on food, drink and songs, and his mate 'Gonga', who could tell a good long tale.

Life in the trenches had 'a primitive quality... our world was stripped of inessentials: each man was complete in himself, his equipment, weapons and food was his responsibility... in spite of the passage of more than 70 years, I can have many enduring memories... haunting memories come unbidden...'

The attack would be near Albert (now in enemy hands) at Bouzaincourt (July 13 – Map 3). Their objective was achieved and the German advance looked to be at an end.

Work with the Royal Engineers at Englebelmer (north-west of Albert

– Map 2) gave them a relatively pleasant break from the rigours of no man's land.

Frederick had been given a stripe before the attack but now a second one was added as his good result on the gas course bore fruit and he was appointed Gas NCO for the battalion, organising gas sentries etc. This meant a blessed relief from platoon duties in the trench.

He did very well, being smart enough to dig out an unexploded German gas shell in order to allow research to take place on its technical make-up. In addition to this new job he was also appointed Orderly Sergeant of the HQ Company, a task requiring him to keep an account of how many different types of soldier there was in the battalion.

The Battle of Amiens (Map 2) was imminent in August, with the ANZACs and Canadians beside the British 4th Army poised to attack along a 40-mile front. The plan for the Lancashire Fusiliers was to mop up enemy positions left behind the general advance. The operation began on August 9 with a 5-mile penetration of enemy territory. Frederick came across a hoard of cigars in a German dug-out but also a lot of lice – trained to bite the British, according to Corporal Wilkinson.

They were withdrawn 30 miles, which they hard to march. When they arrived at Beauquesne (near Peronne – Map 2) they were immediately ordered to march back again to the front. Unfortunately, most of the NCOs had got drunk (they were demoted to the ranks). Corporal Hodges had to rush around trying to get the men back on the road, with the aid of the regimental police. He was also now in charge of them – as well as distributing the rations.

They followed in the wake of the ANZACs across the old Somme battlefield – Thiepval, Pozières etc. The assault on Thiepval Ridge took place on August 23 and the objective of Martinpuich (Maps 2 & 3) was secured. Frederick led the regimental police into this action trying to establish advanced posts as they pressed the Germans back – a very dangerous commitment, although the enemy was surrendering in droves.

They went on to attack Flers (Map 4 – it was a second Battle of the Somme) as German resistance became more determined. In their counter attack the battalion suffered heavy casualties. Because Frederick had to move around so much to perform his various responsibilities he became a special target for the German artillery. But organising and leading men seemed to take his mind off these dangers. By the end of

August the Germans were back on their Hindenburg Line. In September came the struggle for Gouzaincourt (Doullens – Map 2), then Neuvilly in September. In his narrative Frederick increasingly ranges around on general topics – 'inferior gas masks', 'guide to the Brigadier General', 'high-speed butchery at casualty clearing stations', etc.

HORTON, HERBERT (1895–1976)
Stretcher-bearer
Fighting for Life in the Trench
Compiled and Edited by Dale Le Vack
Lion, 2013

Charles Herbert Horton ('Bert') was a graduate in Commerce from Birmingham University. Dedicated to saving life rather than taking it Bert joined the Royal Army Medical Corps (RAMC) as a stretcher-bearer.

Bert served with a RAMC Field Ambulance (not a vehicle but a complete mobile medical unit), and his main job was to get wounded men back to advanced aid posts. This was extremely dangerous because waiting behind the line for orders they were in danger from enemy shelling; going out into no man's land they had to contend with machine gun and rifle fire.

But when Bert wrote his memoir in 1970 his motive was primarily to protest about the lack of recognition of the work of RAMC other ranks in the war. All VCs were awarded to officers and of 120,000 other ranks serving during the war only 2% won medals. The account thus seems rather subdued, not dwelling on the horrors Bert must have witnessed.

Bert joined the new 1st South Midlands Field Ambulance. They had their share of training and drilling in England before crossing to France in January 1916. They moved to ten miles behind the front line at Beauval (south of Doullens – Map 2), not yet on call because of the static condition of the front. So there was more training, plus chores like cleaning ambulances and looking after horses.

But 'The Big Push' (the Battle of the Somme) arrived and the stretcher-bearers were quite pleased in a way because now they could get on with the real job for which they were there. But it was still a shock for them on July 1 to see a very large field filled with line upon line of wounded men, the Padres wandering slowly amongst them.

On July 2 the South Midlands team went into real action at Beaumont Hamel (Map 2). Even on the way up to the front one of Bert's closest friends was killed by shrapnel. Out in no man's land at night they soon ran out of stretchers and Bert and a few others were left searching for more wounded. They had to carry them bodily to the nearest shelter, perhaps a deep shell hole. They had no dressings, no food nor water. It was a desperate situation as they waited for help for many hours, alone in the dark.

They were moved to Bus-en-Artois (Amiens – Map 2) on July 3. The C.O. praised their efforts at Beaumont Hamel whilst the Sergeant Major, who had not been there, harangued them for overlooking some litter. Bert and others waited in devastated no man's land in an ex-German dug-out. The difference here in going out to seek out the wounded was that the enemy maintained machine gun and sniper fire throughout the night in order to deter British raids.

It was arduous and hazardous work: four men were needed for each stretcher over the shell-holed terrain. Two carried it, using a shoulder sling to take off some of the weight. Every few minutes the other two men had to take over. All four were engaged when the stretcher needed to be held head high. When they reached the road to the aid station it was a lot easier and they could move more quickly. They needed to get these men to the station as soon as possible.

They could rest for a while but remained on call all night. Later, at La Boiselle (Map 3), there was a better time for Bert as he got a job on an ambulance. Then at Martinpuich (Maps 2 & 3) it was back straining through the thick, squelching mud. Up and down the Somme front they went where they were most needed until the campaign petered out towards the end of the year.

There was a variety of work, including being an orderly in a hospital ward. Life became safer and easier for the stretcher-bearers – parades and fatigues were more acceptable than no man's land at night. Then the Germans did their early 1917 retreat to the Hindenburg Line. Bert worked in sacked Peronne where enemy booby traps could be lethal. His duties were now with sick soldiers rather than wounded ones. The same duties continued near Bapaume (Map 2) although they were out digging a lot of ditches – Bert and his pals never found out what they were for.

On an unspecified date (Bert did not remember many dates) they went by train to the Ypres Salient to a Field Ambulance near Poperinghe (Maps 1 & 4). They joined the big battle in September and were again on call day and night, dodging between shell holes across the deep, liquid mud – 'cross-country treks, which seemed to engender a protective fatalism in us… 'in complete isolation'…

Back in a cramped pill box Bert found it impossible to sleep on top of a narrow cupboard and was then called out to follow a raiding party. But later there was rest in Poperinghe and blessed visits to Talbot House. What next? It was carrying 'busters' (very large concrete slabs for the roofs of aid stations).

Their stay in Flanders was cut short at the end of September with orders to move to the Italian Front.

JACK, JAMES (1880–1962)
General Jack's Diary
Edited by John Terraine
Cassell, 2000

For many days of the war when James Jack was fit for service he wrote cryptic notes in a tiny notebook from July 28, 1914, to November 11, 1918. Only he knew what the script meant. This was set down immediately after the events described. When Jack was out of the trenches, or in reserve, or hospital, he expanded on these minimal markings. After the war he provided additional observations; these were always clearly indicated in the volumes of typescript. The editor, John Terraine, used about a third of Jack's diary.

Jack wrote in the language of the mess or orderly-room reports, such as the use of the word 'commences' rather than 'begin', or 'assist' not 'help'. This style reflected his rather reserved demeanour. That is not to say that he did his job without emotion or passion. Indeed, James Jack considered some of his senior officers as 'reserved'.

The great esteem in which Jack was held by the officers and men of the battalions he commanded are very evident in the 'Foreword' by Sidney Rogerson, his adjutant in the 2nd Battalion of the West Yorkshire Regiment. Rogerson commended his C.O.'s strong leadership and his devoted sense of duty. Jack himself recorded for July 22, 1918, that a private ('whom I regarded unfavourably') stepped forward at parade and called for 'Three cheers for the Colonel'. Jack's feelings were 'too deep to reply'.

He actually thought that his soldiers were 'great-hearted fellows', who suffered great deprivation with stoicism. At the same time, he was often critical of HQ senior officers who did not seem to understand what these men had to endure.

Moreover, he thought they often wasted the time of their senior comrades at the front. 'While the battle blows up in front we have to ride out a gale of paper at our back'. He was of the view that much of army routine could be standardised and thus heavily reduced.

Jack was a rarity in the sense that he was a Regular soldier who survived the whole war and who also kept a diary for most of it. Throughout it all he continued to believe in ultimate victory even in the darkest days. "You may bet your shirt on it," he declared to a French landlady. He had total dedication to his job. He won the DSO and Bar and was twice mentioned in despatches. But to an officer who remarked to him, "I suppose you Regular Officers like this sort of life." He replied, 'As much as you do, I suppose.' He had a good sense of humour. When he spotted a London bus still advertising Dewar's Whisky he thought it 'rather callous'.

James Jack worked like a trojan, eating little in order to keep himself fit. He suffered much from wounds and illness. By August 29, 1914 in the frantic retreat from Mons he fainted twice from exhaustion. He was 34 years old at the start of the war. Then early in November 1914 he was in No. 7 Stationary Hospital in Boulogne with an acute feverish chill, later transferred to Miss Pollock's Hospital, London. In February 1915 he was again in hospital, in Torquay, with severe flu and out of action for 3 months. This was a recurring condition – surfacing badly again in 1917.

He was also wounded in the Third Battle of Ypres on July 31, 1917, and in hospital again till January 1918.

James Jack started the war as a junior Captain in the 1st Battalion of the Cameronian Highlanders in charge of a platoon of 55 men. They arrived in Havre on August 15, 1914. He was in the thick of the early retreat, the Battle of the Aisne and the First Battle of Ypres.

In May 1915 he became a company commander in the 2nd Battalion of the Cameronian Highlanders and then C.O. of the 2nd Battalion, West Yorkshire Regiment in August 1916. On his return to France in May 1918, after recovery from his wounds, he commanded the 1st Battalion of the Highlanders. By the end of the war he was in charge of the 28th Infantry Brigade.

'… only partial success…' Page from James Jack's miniature diary, September 27th and 28th, 1915, Bois Grenier sector.

JACKSON, JOHN (1891–1956)
Private 12768
Memoir of a Tommy
The History Press. 2009

John Jackson kept a diary throughout his service in France and Flanders from 1915 to 1918 and developed this account from it in 1926. It is thus a precise record in terms of dates. The 'beautifully handwritten' volume was bequeathed to his niece, Margaret Cameron, who transcribed it on to a computer. Later, through the good offices of Professor Huw Strachan, the work was published. He also has written a foreword for it.

John volunteered to serve his country in September 1914, joining the Queen's Own Cameron Highlanders. He was eventually part of the newly-formed 6th Battalion. They sailed to Havre on July 4 1915, arriving on a 'quiet' front near Noeux-les-Mines (Béthune – Maps 1 & 4) on the 22nd, enthusiastically firing at the enemy all night. John became a signaller (as well as a cyclist). They moved on to nearby Vermelles and suffered their first casualties. John was the cycling postman and thus always popular. On September 25th, as part of the 15th Scottish Division, the 6th Battalion had pride of place in the centre of the assault on Loos (Lens sector – Map 1).

A breeze blew back the British gas and the heavy mist in no man's land contributed to an inauspicious start to the attack, and the Germans raised a hail of bullets and shells down the slopes. The Camerons pressed on relentlessly and entered the German trenches and engaged the enemy at close quarters. But their machine guns continued to take a heavy toll of the Scots. Yet Loos was taken within 3 hours when the target was to take it in three days! The next objective was Hill 70.

The enemy fire power continued to be formidable, especially from by the Hohenzollern Reboubt on the Scots' left. No reinforcements came to their aid and they had pressed forward a long way and were thus heavily exposed on their flanks. But the Camerons 'never yielded' and continued to press on up the slope of Hill 70 (near Lens – Map 1). Four times they desperately drove for the summit, the C.O. at the forefront, bareheaded and armed only with a stick (he was killed and won the VC) but the desperate struggles finally failed and they had to dig in at the bottom of the hill.

Support belatedly arrived but these were men new to the front and many had to be kept fighting under threat of being shot by their officers. Of 950 Camerons who fought on Hill 70 only 250 were unscathed.

A few days later John and his fellow signallers were trapped in an ex-German dug-out which became registered by the enemy artillery but apart from having to dig themselves free they were unhurt. The Loos front remained unhealthy because the Germans continued to shell British positions heavily. The Camerons only got out of it at the end of 1915.

After a month out of the line they returned to the Vermelles sector. On January 28 the Germans exploded a mine under their front trenches. John had a very painful leg and had to be taken back to England for treatment in February and the Battle of the Somme was under way before he returned (with the 1st Battalion). He went to High Wood (Map 3), suffering yet another murderous enemy bombardment. After several spells in the front line they were taken to the French coast for recuperation in October. The recreation activities here were very welcome; John won the half mile race.

The 1st Battalion was at the Butte de Warlencourt (Map 3) in November, where John's main task was to try and salvage broken wires. Much of this work had to be done in no man's land, very dangerous with enemy guns firing from the fortress of the Butte (hill) constantly. Existence in the trenches was tough in heavy rain and thick mud. Ironically, however, it was whilst with a working party well behind the front line that a shell landed between John's feet; but it was a dud (November 27).

Happily, the battalion was in Albert (Map 2) for Christmas. John was now a lance corporal.

In 1917 he was on a quiet front at Assevilliers (near Peronne – Map 2) but had the tough role of orderly sergeant, which entailed going round in the dark trying to avoid dangerous holes etc. in order to deliver orders to the various sections of the battalion. On March 16 he had first-hand experience of the German withdrawal to the Hindenburg Line as he followed a telephone wire right into a deserted enemy trench. Even the village of Barleuz beyond had been wrecked and abandoned.

As the Battle of Arras (Map 1) began John was in quarantine because of an outbreak of measles. They were taken away well to the north to the Nieuport (Map 1) sector in Flanders as part of the plan to capture Ostend from the Germans and to provide a supporting front for the planned offensive out of the Ypres Salient. But the area was strongly defended by the Germans and nothing became of the venture. He went on leave to Carlisle at the end of October.

The Camerons were in position for the final assault on Passchendaele Ridge (Map 4) in November. The battleground was a sea of mud and the rain was relentless. John was now in charge of the signals section and he had a very difficult task mending broken wires and setting up new ones in 'a gruesome swamp' and in full view of the enemy (for this work he was awarded the Military Medal).

Up towards the ridge the Camerons suffered terribly like the adjacent Canadians as there was little shelter beyond shell holes. The subsequent roll call was as depressing as the one following the Battle of Loos.

After rest at Proven (Map 4) the battalion went to the front by Houthulst Forest, which also had no trenches, just holes. John had another nightmare time repairing and developing the signals system. He was at Langemarck in Flanders when the Germans attacked in March 1918 but soon moved to bolster the threatened sector at Cambrin (south-west of Cuinchy – Maps 3 & 4). The very arduous and trying work he had been doing now took its toll on his health and he became very sick (April 23). He only returned to the fray when the Allies (with the Americans) were preparing to launch their own broad offensive.

JONES, PAUL (1896–1917)
War letters of a Public School Boy
Henry Paul Mainwaring Jones
Cassell & Company, 1918

This collection of letters was drawn together by Paul's father – Harry Jones. He preluded the letters with a very long memoir and tribute to his son. Paul was keen to join an infantry regiment but due to his severe myopia he had to be reluctantly content with a commission in the Army Service Corps. In this, he was an efficient requisitioning officer. But he always retained hope of something in the front lined and was eventually accepted into the new Tank Corps in February 1917.

Paul crossed to France in July 1915, appointed Requisitioning Officer for the 9ᵗʰ Cavalry Brigade. Censorship prevented him from saying where he was and his father did not later add this information but it is certain he was in the Armentières (Maps 1 &4) sector, probably at Vermelles.

The cavalry at this time spent much time digging reserve trenches, so in supplying their needs Paul was only in danger of long-distance shelling and aerial warfare. But purchasing local goods and services to supplement official supplies kept him very busy all day because the cavalry moved about a lot and often needed local supplies.

He was much more involved near the front line during the Battle of Loos (Lens sector – Map 1). 'I am about to leave on an official mission' (September 23). He was often involved in local disputes with French citizens over compensation claims because he was fluent in French. For instance, there was an inquiry over the use of doors from an empty village in trenches. The decision was that this was a 'fait de guerre'. If they had been used on the roads, for instance, this would not have been the case.

Paul's letters cover a wide range of topics – politics, history, literature, science etc, as befitted a young man educated at Alleyn's School in Dulwich. From August 1914 he had kept a war diary. There is much in the letters about school friends and their fortunes on the Western Front. One of them won the VC. Another was Ged Garvin, featured in this book.

His father saw Paul for the last time in May 1916 when he was home on leave. He had been promoted to Lieutenant and was transferred to the Divisional Supply Column in June 1916 – in the Somme region. He disliked this move very much because work as a supply officer was far less varied and interesting. But he did love machines and so work involving a lot of motor transport was very welcome. 'M.T. Officers are a very efficient lot' (June 22). They dealt with vast quantities of supplies.

But he still wanted to apply for something more exciting because he was 'fed up with grocery work' (July 27). What he saw on the Somme convinced him he must move to 'the thick of it'. Of his old chum who had died winning the VC he wrote, 'What a glorious end!' (August 8).

He did get work supervising working parties near the battle zone, such as loading and unloading ammunition, and he felt that this at least gave him more responsibility. He experienced the 'frightful odour of mortality... such is the so-called ennobling influence of civilization' (September 14).

On September 21 he had a miraculous escape when a shell exploded next to him. He was just deafened and a piece of shrapnel went through the sleeve of his coat.

He became Requisitioning Officer for the 2nd Cavalry Brigade (September 27). Work in the ASC for officers could be exhausting – in November he was doing two big jobs apart from his own one – Brigade Supply Officer and Divisional Forage Purchasing Officer (trying to obtain a supplementary supply of hay from French farmers).

On December 8 he again applied for a transfer after being passed fit for general duties (apparently he now had much better spectacles). He was recommended for the Tank Corps, which he joined on February 13 – to his intense delight. He was soon 'up to my eyes in oil, grease and mud all day.' He passed his written examination.

He then took part in the Battle of Arras (Map 1) in April – now 'participating in the winning of the war – what more can the heart of man desire?' (April 29). His father complained of lack of detailed information in Paul's letters but Paul insisted on avoiding careless comments or clues to strategic information. He also did not see the need for sending photographs of himself.

He wrote that 'the war has given to everyone a chance to get out of himself'.

Paul was shot by a sniper's bullet through the tank porthole during the first day of the Third Battle of Ypres – July 31, 1917.

KELLY, FREDERICK (1881–1916)
Kelly's War: Great War Diary of Frederick Kelly 1914–1916
Edited by Jon Cooksey and Graham McKechnie
Blink Publishing, 2015

Frederick Kelly was famous in Edwardian England – as an Olympic rowing champion, music composer and concert pianist. He had been educated at Eton College and Oxford University. He maintained a daily diary from 1907 until the day he landed on a Gallipoli beach (April 30, 1915). The 'War Diary' of 1915 and 1916 covered the fighting in Gallipoli and the Western Front. This was written in a thick leather-bound volume and 7 pocket sketch books.

Both diaries were passed on by Kelly's family to his friend and comrade in the Hood battalion of the Royal Naval Division, Brigadier-General Arthur Asquith (son of the Prime Minister), who produced from it a 'War Chapter'. This was a much-reduced adaptation of Kelly's war diary. Asquith left out much of what Kelly wrote because the editor said it was too long and that, anyway, Kelly was often too critical of other units and individuals. Jon Cooksey and Graham McKechnie have done their own editing for this present book, including some historical notes.

Frederick Kelly was commissioned into the Hood Battalion in September, 1914. The Royal Naval Division was Winston Churchill's brainchild – using the many thousands of sailors for whom there was no room on the warships as a trained land force, adding eminent volunteers such as Kelly, Rupert Brooke, the poet, and Arthur Asquith, the Prime Minister's son.

The division travelled to Gallipoli in April, 1915. Kelly was on leave in England between March and May, 1915 following the privations of Gallipoli – stomach trouble, jaundice, fatigue and a wound.

However, in May 1916 he was temporarily second in command of a 2nd Hood Battalion. There was obviously uncertainty by those in high command where to deploy the Royal Naval Division after Gallipoli was over. It was still in the Mediterranean in May and Kelly was sent there. Then the decision was made to use the RND in France and so Kelly had to make his way to Abbéville.

They had no experience of Western Front trench warfare so needed specialist training in Rouen for a couple of weeks. There was more of the same back on the Somme, bayonet practice using sticks with pads as targets (June 20). But they were sent north to fight amongst the Lens coalfields just north of Vimy Ridge (Map 1 – June 29).

Before battle commenced the RND had to be expanded into a much larger force (army infantry was added), which spelt the end of the 2nd Hood Battalion and Kelly's temporary promotion. He spent time with the army units to gain trench experience. It was a tough baptism because the trenches in this sector (Souchez II) were in poor shape and thus vulnerable to German shelling and mortar fire. The British specialism was raids on enemy trenches, equally dangerous.

By the end of July Kelly was in command of a Hood Battalion in the Souchez I Sector, where rifle grenades and sniping was added to the enemy repertoire. The busy requirements of staff officers did not help – '… in France one seems to spend most of one's time writing reports of what one has not had time to observe…' He added that rats were quite useful in clearing up rubbish but the mosquitoes were 'tiresome'.

He sang Wagner's 'Siegfried' to a German sentry, who always continued the song if Kelly paused.

Kelly ran the battalion band, taught and played music whenever possible. A performance of Tchaikovsky's 12th was accompanied by a German bombardment (September 16), an event probably planned by Kelly.

They were at this front for months, under heavy shelling, mortar bombing (doing serious damage to British trenches), and sniping, with the British, although doing their own fair share of shelling, specialising in trench raids, during which the British infantry was often shelled by its own artillery.

The battalion travelled by train to Forceville (north-west of Albert – Map 2) on October 4, taking over trenches in front of Beaumont Hamel (Map 3) on October 16, in the usual knocked-about state. A broad offensive was planned astride the River Ancre. Kelly did not have a great deal of confidence in the work of higher command – '… we are in that state of preparation for big operations in which counter-orders come several times a day…' Generally, he had no time for pretentiousness, false modesty or rashness (he could be adventurous in no man's land but if he scented trouble he very quickly sought shelter).

He knew that more 'Big Push' was coming but found time to write his 'Elegy to Rupert Brooke' and compose a piano sonata. The assault was intended to capture three lines of German defences and then Beaucourt-sur-Ancre. His B Company would lead the right flank of the Hood's attack. Meanwhile, on November 3, he learnt that beards were to be banned (he sported a very large one).

Frederick Kelly wrote no more after November 11. A 'Postcript' was provided by Lieutenant Colonel Bernard Freyburg VC, C.O. of the Hood Battalion from July 1915 to April 1917. He recorded that Kelly worked hard on the 12th ('… with that meticulous accuracy and conscientiousness which was well known to all of us…').

The offensive took place on an 8-mile front and the Hood was in the centre of it, on the north bank of the Ancre. Kelly advanced to the third line of German defences, amongst their strongpoint dug-outs, but in full view of enemy machine gunners from the flanks. He was shot in the back of the head.

LEONARD, PAT (1889–1963)
The Fighting Padre
Letters from the Trenches 1915–1918 of Pat Leonard DSO
Edited by John Leonard and Philip Leonard-Johnson
Pen and Sword, 2010

Pat Leonard was Chaplain to the 8th Battalion of the King's Own Royal
Lancashire Regiment (KORL) from 1915 to 1917, when he transferred to
the Royal Flying Corps. He sent home hundreds of letters to his parents
covering the great majority of days. In a letter of November 12, 1915, he
did muse over the notion of writing a diary. In a letter of November 25,
1917 he wrote, 'I see from my diary that I played chess with the General
and beat him for the first and only time.' Some letters were in diary form
as he had to catch up with several days.

Pat Leonard was an extremely active padre – counsellor, comforter,
caterer, censor, entertainments officer and sports officer (he was a boxer
himself). He rescued wounded men from no man's land and smoked
with the soldiers in the trenches. He was awarded the DSO for bravery.
His letters are crammed with close detail and represent a vast and vivid
description of the role of religion on the Western Front.

On October 12, 1915 Pat arrived in Flanders in the notorious
Ploegsteert ('Plugstreet') Wood (Map 4) near 'The City of the Dead'
(Ypres) and rats promptly ate his tobacco. He led services whenever
and wherever he could. He said that the more uncomfortable the
surroundings were the more real was the spirit of worship. For a
celebration in December 1915 in a vaulted cellar he and his congregation
could not stand upright.

He was in great danger: on Boxing Day 1915 enemy artillery followed
him along a road – but luckily it was registered at a distance of thirty yards
from him.

In January 1916 he started up a coffee stall for his battalion and arranged a concert for it. He could not, however, locate a piano but the performers managed cheerfully without one. In his spare time he did the accounts for the beer canteen and the hairdressing salon.

In the battle around the Bluff near St. Eloi (south of Ypres – Map 1 – where another Chaplain, Captain Mellish, won the VC) in March and April 1916 Pat spent many hours around the aid post and the field ambulance, where he could tend to the dying and wounded. Actually, he found it safer in the front line because further back was subjected to 'incessant and murderous shelling'.

The battalion's losses at this time were terrible: Pat recorded that there were not words to convey the courage of the Tommies. He wrote hundreds more letters to bereaved relatives, a depressing task. A 'Quiet Day' for chaplains at Talbot House in Poperinghe (Maps 1 & 4) was a welcome relief (after the war he was heavily involved in the growth of Toc H).

The King's Own were on the Somme in July 1916 and in the centre of the Guillemont (Map 3) action during the following month. Lieutenant Colonel Kentish wrote to Pat later 'You have proved yourself a born leader or men. I can never forget your splendid example of gallantry and cheerfulness…'

In November he was at the attack on Serre (near Beaumont Hamel – Map 3) and was mentioned in despatches (although that was not mentioned in his despatches). He did write about the paradox of the war – 'danger and pay, discomfort and recompense go in inverse ratio… the nearer you are to the Hun the less you get' (February 9, 1917).

Just after this the King's Own were involved in the Arras campaign, and it took Pat a whole week to write to bereaved relatives. Then to the Third Battle of Ypres: like all letter-writers he could not mention where he was and had to resort to cryptic clues, such as the classic 'Blank to Dash' (the Ypres–Menin road). They still had time for a laugh: replacing a fellow officer's hair oil with lime juice caused much merriment, and crystallised hair.

In November 1917 Pat moved to the Royal Flying Corps as chaplain to six squadrons, a transfer which Neville Talbot influenced. The King's Own tried to get him back, but in vain. Pat enjoyed the accommodation for a non-flying officer in the RFC. There were days and days of services, visits to the different squadrons – and lots of football and rugby, which he enjoyed very much. Occasionally, he flew over the war zone as a passenger. He moved to other squadrons in May and at one of them he enjoyed an enormous fireworks display with Very lights on November 11, 1918.

LLOYD, R. A. (born 1892)
A Trooper in the Tins
Autobiography of a Lifeguard
The Naval and Military Press, 2009

R. A. Lloyd joined the 1st Life Guards Battalion (cavalry) in 1911. It went to the Ypres Salient in October, 1914, by which time Lloyd was an acting sergeant. He had received a good secondary education and passed more educational qualifications in the Life Guards before the war (after the war he took a university degree in London).

His narrative at this period appears to be based on a diary, probably the battalion's 'War Diary', which he helped to compile, although he felt that his recall was 'blurred', unable to establish any clear sequence of events. The First Battle of Ypres was about to begin but by October 19 it had settled into a primitive form of trench warfare – the trenches being little more than joined-up shell holes. The Life Guards were deployed to 'plug holes' which appeared in the front line, and thus became known as 'Kavanagh's Fire Brigade'.

The battalion remained billeted around Ebblinghem (west of Hazebrouck – Map 1) until May, 1915 with frequent excursions to the front line where emergencies arose, so Lloyd spent short periods in the trenches. He seemed to be used for all sorts of jobs – delivering rations and mail etc. He had a 'rollicking Christmas' and later supervised the work of the transport wagons – in charge of the care of 60 horses.

At Herzeele in April Lloyd's Squadron discovered lice for the first time but an old soldier exclaimed, "Och, mon, it's a puir body that canna keep out a few 'o they wee beasties." Late in May Acting Sergeant Lloyd became Corporal Lloyd again, in charge of sanitation at Campiegne (near Peronne – Map 2) and later Quiestede (July – near St Omer).

At Delette (near St Omer) in August life was 'free and easy' in very nice weather. Lloyd made friends with the squadron cook, Richard Brockwell, who was able to make fags 'with a kick'. In September Lloyd had leave in Ireland and on his return he was not sure whether his horse 'Herbert' had missed him or not.

Corporal Lloyd's account has a wealth of detail about the men with whom he served, such as Percy Scott, who later volunteered for a Pigeon Squad although he 'didn't know a pigeon from an emu'.

Early in 1916, in Verchocq (west of Béthune – Maps 1 & 4), Lloyd became an acting sergeant once more (squadron quartermaster). He found this a tedious job and was glad to return to general troop duties. They went to Corbie on the Somme in June. Cavalry, during the Battle of the Somme, was initially set to 'plug gaps' in the front line again but in the event most of their casualties were hit by shell fire 'in lousy bivouacs just behind the line' or working in no man's land at night. Weeks were spent now (there are no dates) moving up and down back areas doing fatigues.

The battalion moved out in September and moved to near Montreuil on the coast, still on working parties – and later the same at Beaumont Hamel (Map 3) and Engelbelmer (November – north-west of Albert – Map 2) where Lloyd managed the canteen and hunted wild boar.

The battalion entered the Battle of Arras (April 9, 1917 – Map 1). On the 11th the sergeant major, the quarterbloke and the farrier were killed by a shell. The battalion's main occupation after this was trying to seek shelter from the snow and ice.

In the Summer the battalion (in fact, the whole of the 6th Cavalry Brigade) took over 'The Birdcage', a part of the devastated Somme front line near Épehy (south-west of Cambrai – Map 1), for two periods. Sergeant Lloyd was in charge of drawing and delivering rations. The Battle of Cambrai (Map 1) in November appeared to provide an opportunity for the cavalry to shine at last but it was the Canadian cavalry which went in with the tanks.

At Christmas Lloyd went into Auxi-le-Chateau (north-west of Abbéville) to get some fruit and vegetables but was confronted by two Cockney WACs demanding a bite out of his apples –"Garn, give us a bite!" Lloyd's driver exclaimed, "What the hell were those flappers doing out here?"

In the New Year, 1918, the cavalry were turned into machine gunners to meet the new German threat. Sergeant Lloyd became part of the 1ˢᵗ Battalion the Guards' Machine-Gun Regiment.

He was in camp at Étaples on May 19 when a bomb from a German plane hit his marquee, killing 9 of 11 guards sleeping in it. Lloyd's left leg was smashed (and a hand badly wounded). It was not until October that he could walk again. After service in the new Army Education Corps he became a graduate in German and became a schoolmaster. His book ended with, 'I would gladly go through it all again for the sake of the good times in camp spent in company of the great fellows of all ranks who were my comrades'.

LUCY, JOHN (1895–1962)
There's a Devil in the Drum
J. F. Lucy
Introduced by Terry Cave
The Naval and Military Press, 1993

John Lucy served in the 2nd Battalion of the Royal Irish Rifles as a regular soldier from 1912. By the time the battalion sailed to France on August 14, 1914, he was an established corporal, like his younger brother, Denis. The citizens of Rouen gave them a tremendous welcome, and it was the same in every town and village through which they travelled.

John wrote in intricate detail on the early stages of the war as they searched for the enemy and then engaged him at Mons and Le Cateau. There were trenches in August 1914 – 'kneeling' trenches, designed for very temporary occupation. In fact, the Germans found them first and shelled them, a sign of events to come.

"Send for the police!" cried an Irish wag.

The German officers blew trumpets and bugles and the British whistles. The Irish marksmen shot down the German infantry in hordes with rapid fire. But the BEF was driven back pell-mell by sheer weight of soldiers and guns, leaving their packs and greatcoats. –'distasteful' was how it felt at the time. They did get a laugh when a young soldier started to count his used cartridge cases, a good peace-time practice.

They dug more shallow trenches at Le Cateau but the enemy steadily pressed them back but not getting too near as they had learnt the lessons of rapid fire at Mons. A shell struck John's section with fearful consequences. He got one man into a small Red Cross hospital but then had to leg it fast to get back to the wagons he was running as the Germans swarmed through the town. A single corps faced a whole army. There followed the 'sleep march' where the BEF had to keep moving in fear of being outflanked.

'The pained look in the troubled eyes of the men who fell by the way will not easily be forgotten...'

Then the Germans appeared to go crazy, disastrously changing their strategy – and paid the price on the Marne and the Aisne. Now the Royal Irish Rifles began to chase them and expected to go on doing so. But then came the stiff resistance of massed artillery and machine guns at Vailly in the Aisne valley (September 15). By the 19th German shelling had transformed into a prolonged bombardment.

After rest the battalion did resume northward movement (October 6), joining the action north of La Bassée (Map 4 – October 12), still very wary of the big German guns, now seemingly getting even bigger. They were glad to get into deeper and longer trenches. And whenever the German infantry approached it was still shot down in great numbers (Neuve Chapelle October 23 – Maps 1 & 4) but on the 24th at last began to find gaps in the British lines as their fire power declined with the loss of so many experienced riflemen. Desperate close-at-hand fighting failed to save Neuve Chapelle and John's section was reduced to two men and of the 32 corporals who had left for France two months previously only 4 had survived. On the 27th even the British artillery fired at them.

They could not re-take Neuve Chapelle and what was left of the battalion only escaped by fleeing across open ground.

John saw a whole cartful of officers' swords, the sign of a type of warfare gone for ever. Highly depressed, Sergeant Lucy burnt his diary (November 1 at Locre – Map 4) but the writing of it did help him to write this later memoir (in 1936, published by Faber and Faber in 1938) although he pointed out himself that because of the absence of the diary he might have got some facts wrong. He seemed to remember the precise words of conversations spoken at critical moments, such as the ticking off he gave a man who had left his observation post and the subsequent cover-up he afforded him.

The battalion joined the First Battle of Ypres: only 40 out of a whole battalion (much of it already replaced before the battle) walked away from it. John then became the battalion clerk. The few Regulars left closed ranks, noting with disfavour that some of a new class of officers even called their men by their Christian names –'the old army was finished'.

John compensated a little for the loss of the diary by collecting together copies of all the battalion messages since August 1914 in order to supplement the sparse battalion war diary. In this memoir he used fictitious names for some reason.

'My chief asset was that I was alive, young and hopeful, but I could not enjoy life'. He could not sleep without hearing the noises of war and the voices of his dead comrades. At the end of 1915 he was diagnosed with 'neurasthenia' and had an operation to cure a digestive system ruined by army food. He returned to light duties in Britain in the Summer of 1916 and was commissioned in his battalion in May 1917. He was in action at Westhoek Ridge on August 10 and his description of this is vivid and terrible (later in life John Lucy worked for Irish radio). He was badly wounded by a grenade in December – hit in the knee, buttock, thigh, abdomen, back and forearm.

LYNCH, EDWARD
Somme Mud
The Experiences of an Infantryman in France 1916–1919
Edited by Will Davies
Bantam, 2008

Young Australian Private Edward Lynch left for France in August 1916 and went straight on to the Somme battlefield at Pozières (Map 3) with the Australian Imperial Force (AIF).

Edward wrote up his experiences in 1921 in pencil in 20 exercise books. About ten years later he typed it into a tome 9 inches deep. Initially, just a few excerpts of it appeared in the magazine 'Reveille' whilst the manuscript as a whole lay idle at his home.

Edward's grandson, Mike Lynch, eventually loaned it to Will Davies, who was a battlefield guide. Will considered it be a record which should reach the public domain. He edited this abridged version. Will was fascinated by the rich detail of the story in Edward's straightforward and honest style – the experience of a young man, like all these diarists and authors of memoirs, thrown into a very extraordinary situation. Writing at the beginning of the book Professor Bill Gammage thinks the text is 'magnificent, written on a par with the more famous 'All Quiet on the Western Front'. Gammage described the text as 'fast and close – Somme Mud puts you in the trenches'.

The memoir has a great deal of precisely worded dialogue. This will have an historical base – it was written quite soon after the event. It is a narrative in the present tense. There are few precise dates but the reader will roughly work out when particular events were happening. There is a clear indication of place names.

The text is also sustained by a rich sense of humour and humorous writing, due, to some extent, to the fact that the AIF had its fair share of comedians, such as the one who greeted the young Lynch on his first patrol in no man's land and tried to convince him that the Germans were firing electrocuting arrows.

Lynch acquired many colourful friends – 'Darkie', 'Longun', 'Snow', 'Prof', 'Jacko' etc. Lynch was 'Nulla'. They helped him to endure the harsh conditions and tensions of the front line. He was quickly advised to 'give up thinking too much or this war will get you down'. The book deals with all the trials and tribulations of the poor bloody infantry. They had little idea of how the war was going on the grand scale but just got on with it – 'in a world of Somme Mud'.

It was not only Fritz Edward had to worry about as the weather became colder and colder and wetter and wetter. He 'shivers himself to sleep when he can'.

He had two spells in casualty clearing stations as some of 'Fritz's ironmongery' acquired in Delville Wood (Map 3) and Neuve Chapelle (Maps 1 & 4) had to be removed. Orders in the AIF were often received with 'Goodo!' rather than 'Yes, sir!' and there was one occasion when Nulla and his mates told a Tommy officer more about himself and his parentage than the 'Genealogical Society could have told him in a year'. They tended to have a similar opinion of British tanks, which also often let them down.

In the Summer of 1917 they moved into Messines (Map 4) and they were shelled by the British artillery. Lynch described a terrifying encounter, bayonet to bayonet, between Longun and a crazy German officer. In the battle Lynch and some of his friends were wounded. He emerged from a casualty clearing station with 'seven open wounds' covered with adhesive tape.

They were then up in the Ypres Salient at the famous 'Plugstreet Wood' (Map 4) and then Passchendaele (Map 4), where he was blown into the air by a shell which landed between his feet shattering one of them. It was a Blighty One but he would have preferred an Australian hospital. It was 'half a year' before he was in action – in the thick of the German offensive of 1918 – at Dernancourt (near Albert – Map 2). His description of the capture of a German trench is exhilarating.

The going was hard in April and May, back on the Somme. But by August the great push forward was under way – a 'leap-frog'. At this time Lynch changed his mind about tanks, which he now considered very useful in a broad and quick offensive 'following Fritz'. He celebrated the end of the war in freezing weather without a blanket – typical!

MACGILL, PATRICK
The Great Push
Birlinn, 2000

'The Great Push' is a unique document in that it was a book about the battle of Loos (1915) mostly written whilst the battle was still in progress (completed afterwards in hospital). It thus stands out as a 'super diary'.

Patrick, already a very popular writer, joined the 2nd Battalion of the London Irish Rifles but by the time he went to the Western Front he was in the 1st Battalion. When this account opens just before the battle he had become a stretcher-bearer.

His draft marched towards the slag heaps and chimney stacks of Cuinchy to join a Battalion which had suffered cruelly at Cuinchy, Givenchy and Vermelles (Maps 3 & 4). The first job of the new men was a dangerous one for men with no experience in the trenches. They had to dig a new sap trench out towards the German line. Through this Patrick leaves us a beautiful description of no man's land at night and the chat of the Irish as they did the work. It is highly amusing, especially the contribution of Gilhooley, the mad Irish bomber. They mixed well with a few Cockneys, who had a different way of talking –"I can't eat 'ardly nuffink".

Rumours were rife about a 'big push'; even the Germans put up a notice – 'When is the big push coming off? We are waiting'. This survived all of ten minutes before being shot to pieces.

Les Brebis (Loos – Lens sector – Map 1) was the temporary home of the London Irish – '… they knew every brick in the place, every French villager, especially 'Joan of Arc', who watched over them like a loving mother. A few villagers were killed or injured but the rest carried on with fatalistic phlegm.

On September 24 they were given instructions for the action the next day. Their objective was to be the second German line of defence in the village of Loos. Patrick tried to console them by introducing them to champagne whilst Bill the Cockney was attempting his latest female conquest: she threw a bucket of water over him.

A football was provided for them to kick to the German trenches (a game later used by Billie Nevill). The dawn of the 25th was grey, hazy and moist. Patrick slung his stretcher over the parapet and a German appeared imploring "Kamerad! Kamerad!". 'The moment had come when it was unwise to think'.

'The air was vicious with bullets' but the football was being dribbled in the opposite direction. Patrick's hat was blown off and shell splinters twanged past his face. Men were dying around him and he was treading on bits of men. Gas was coming over. He saw a man completely naked shot down (British or German?).

They reached the German wire in Loos; the Germans scrambled for safety but still tossed over petrol bombs and grenades. The football had been shot and lay forlorn on the wire. Patrick's pal had bayoneted five Germans but his Mum forbade him to smoke. These were the first enemy soldiers Patrick had seen in the seven months he had been in France.

German officers' dugouts were sumptuously furnished. In one was a dying officer and Patrick gave him morphine. Wounded men 'cried out like drowning puppies'. He had nothing but pity for the mutilated enemy and dressed their wounds.

These trenches were right in the centre of Loos village. They waited in trepidation for a German counter attack: shelling and machine gun fire were getting worse.

Patrick established a dressing station in an estaminet so that wounded men who could walk could come to it. To collect those who could not walk he had to get together three other men to carry them to safety. He kept going for hours and hours without sleep, making occasional trips through the thick mud to the first aid post in Maroc. As he crossed the fields he saw the corpses of hundred upon hundred of the Highlanders who had been shot down in droves attacking the German first line. Patrick's minute-by-minute story is harrowing in the extreme. Its immediacy gives it a quality above any other narrative about a full-scale battle.

Also, the dialogue sounds more authentic than anything elsewhere because the reader is induced to imagine the men speaking – in their myriad accents. Cockney Bill located a hen in the ruins of the village and, risking life and limb, stalked it.

"Yook! Yook!" he called to the bird as the bullets flew around him (he wasn't going to miss a chicken meal for anything), trying to coax it nearer. They thought he had gone mad. "Yook! Yook! It's my own 'en." Patrick handed him an unloaded rifle to shoot it and Bill did not think this was funny and warned Patrick that he would not be getting any fried chicken. Bill reckoned the army was not an honourable occupation and that no one should join it.

The expected German counter attack began east of Hill 70 and British troops who had gone beyond the German second line now came crowding back calling "Retire!" It was a false alarm: they were merely being asked to move aside for reinforcements. There ensued a furious and ear-splitting encounter. 'Surely a little atom as myself would be untouched'. The desperate defence held back the enemy. Patrick had not slept for 48 hours.

But he still went out on to the scene of the recent struggle confronted by dozen upon dozen men who needed urgent medical attention. He asked around for help and after a refusal an understanding Captain provided 20 men to help him.

The account demonstrates well the confusion which arose in these major confrontations: a relieving force just arrived in France had little idea of its whereabouts and started arresting British working parties, ration fatigues and stretcher-bearers (including Patrick). Out there Father Lane – Fox – was trying to bury the dead, surrounded by enemy bullets.

Rations failed to arrive and they were ravenous by the time a fresh fatigue arrived with food. The bread was soaked in deep red blood but they were too famished to care. The battle was over by Michaelmas Eve. Patrick's body was very weary but his mind was content. He slept on a door and was about to be buried when he woke up.

After rest at Les Brebis they had to go back to Loos and Patrick was shot in the wrist. 3008 Rifleman P. MacGill was on his way to Victoria Station. It was pouring with rain but he did not care any more.

MARTIN, 'JACK' (1884–1970)
Sapper Martin
The Secret War Diary of Jack Martin
Edited by Richard Van Emden
Bloomsbury, 2009

'Jack' Martin served in the Royal Engineers from 1916 to the end of the war. He wrote 12 diaries in all but kept them secret to himself. His grandson discovered Jack's first post-war transcription of some of the original diaries in 1999. It was a great surprise because Jack had never spoken about his war experiences.

Why did Jack write so profusely about his war? Perhaps it was due to his mature age – he was 32 when he arrived in France in 1916. Perhaps, as in so many other cases, it was so that his family would know in some detail what had happened to him. If so, he must have changed his mind about this because he decided on secrecy.

Jack left school at 14 but went on to teach himself law and accountancy and also acquired a wide knowledge of literature. His diaries are thus well-written, clear, sometimes elegant, often humorous. Every entry is precisely dated.

Richard Van Emden used about two thirds of Jack's transcribed material for this volume. There is intense detail about Jack's officers, comrades and events. As a sapper he possibly had more opportunity to write and also to up-date the material.

As diaries were officially banned Jack's efforts were the cause of friction with his C.O., Lieutenant (later Captain) Buchan. This may have been part of Buchan's tendency to criticise Jack's work generally or just about the diaries (Jack was not sure of this himself). He was upset by Buchan's attitude. When later their relationship improved Jack was obviously pleased. He did tend to get on the wrong side of officers, perhaps because of his age, as in the case of Alfred Burrage. Anyway, Jack agonises at some length about Buchan and there is also much detail about work with officers behind the lines – in parades, inspections, marches etc.

Jack served in the 122nd Infantry Brigade Signals Corps. Engineers played an increasingly crucial role on the Western Front as defensive fortifications became larger and more and more intricate. There was only 25,000 of them in 1914 but 298,000 by the end of the war.

He arrived on the Somme battleground in September 1916 but moved north to Flanders in October. In the support trenches near Dickebusch (Map 4) in the Ypres Salient on January 6, 1917 a shell landed by his feet but quite remarkably he was not hurt. But his hands trembled so much in after-shock that he couldn't write for several days. Jack's job in the front line was dangerous because he had to go out into no man's land to lay communication cables.

At the outset of the Third Battle of Ypres Jack's section spent much time underground in 'Hedge Street Tunnel' (also dangerous because of the proximity of enemy miners) in support of their own miners. He was moved to the Italian front in November with the whole 41st Division. The division returned to France in March 1918 to meet the new German threat.

MASEFIELD, JOHN (1878–1967)
John Masefield's Letters from the Front 1915–1917
Edited by Peter Vansittart
Franklin Watts, 1985

By 1914 John Masefield was an established author (and a copious letter writer). He was determined to do some type of war service, so he went to France in February 1915 as a Red Cross orderly.

On leave in April he was planning to create a mobile field hospital nearer the front line (an Authors' and Artists' hospital). This did not work out because he was unable to raise adequate funds. So he went to Gallipoli with the Red Cross, later writing his acclaimed book 'Gallipoli'.

He travelled in the USA on a lecture tour from January to July 1916, also to drum up more support for the Allies from the Americans. Pursuing this aim further he was back in France in August 1916 working for the Propaganda and Intelligence Service (at the instigation of Sir Gilbert Parker, MP for Gravesend, and also a writer). He was to study and report on American voluntary medical services – field ambulances, relief units and hospitals. He later toured the Somme battlefield (August – he wrote 'The Battle of the Somme' in 1919).

The collected letters are to his wife. He worked 'hard and continuously' all day in a French hospital at Arc en Barrois behind the Argonne front line. He was a very gifted French speaker with a vast knowledge of French literature. He thought well of the nurses – some of them American – but took a poor view of French women helpers ('catty young mixens').

He devised and ran a fire service for the hospital – non-existent before. He performed all manner all tasks – carrying wounded men about, helping at operations (at one he assisted in taking skin off a man's thigh and pressing it down on his shoulder), serve meals and clear up and

185

generally tidying up etc. Every day they took in hundreds more wounded men, transported there in filthy stinking railway trucks. No wonder some of them lost their minds.

After his tour of the USA he returned to France in August 1916, based first in the American voluntary hospital at Neuilly to begin his research into American voluntary medical aid. Neuilly was something of a show piece – 'a brand new fine French lycee' (September 3). The wards here were 'charming'. There was much specialist work in 'face-making' – new noses, mouths, tongues etc. The faces of a few men were cut down diagonally and had to be re-aligned.

There were in all 11 annexes – a dental clinic (supporting the face-making repairs), pathological laboratory etc. He watched germs under a microscope so they were conducting research into infections. The staff worked very hard but were not all that helpful to Masefield.

He travelled to Verdun in September to see the American Field Sections (Ambulances). There were also advanced aid posts.

In total, he discovered that the Americans ran 29 hospitals and 54 'other works', far more than he had been led to expect so the trip took him much longer than he anticipated (he was for ever apologising to his wife for not being with her and their young children). He had to go to Limoges, Lyons, Aix les Bains, Nice and Sens. He saw no less than 5 hospitals in one afternoon (September 29) –these were French establishments but supplied by the American distribution system.

Ordinary Americans he met in France believed that their nation's neutrality was 'despicable' (dud shells were called 'yanks') whilst their diplomats there considered they had kept the Allies going with their 'sympathy'. Masefield wrote on October 6 that 'the Americans have done very little… the nation at large has done nothing'. Many individual volunteers had done their best, kept going with a struggle until the money ran out. He came across many services which had been closed down.

The Foreign Office paid him just about enough to cover his expenses. He had 'seen nearly every kind of wound, including some which it took a stout heart to look at but the burns easily surpassed anything I've ever seen…' (October 12).

He toured American charities in Paris but the lists provided him were inexact, out-of-date and misleading. There were some nice surprises, like the elderly American lady who made customised splints and supports.

Later in the month he was invited to visit the Somme in preparation to write an officially-backed history of the battle. He returned in February 1917 to range over the battleground (as a 2nd Lieutenant) in order to get a grasp of its topography before consulting brigade and battalion diaries. The landscape was hideously scarred – 'Can you imagine a landscape in the moon, made of filth instead of beauty' (March 6). Officers and men were very helpful – wonderfully kind, gentle men'. He sometimes walked 15 miles a day over mud-encrusted terrain when a car or lift on a lorry were not available. He said the Y.M.C.A. was his saviour.

'My days are crowded and tiring' (March 30). His letters contain much comment on the general war situation and the hundreds of people he met. Some French officials were surprised how quietly spoken, unaffected and self-effacing he was but mightily impressed by his knowledge of France and its language and literature. But he had a very low opinion of Germans and he was equally critical of the British tactics in the Battle of the Somme – 'supine, stupid, inadequate thought'. Later in the year he published his book 'The Old Front Line'.

MAULTSHEAD, JIM
Star Shell Reflections 1914–1916
The Illustrated Great War Diaries of Jim Maultshead
Edited by Barbara McClune
Pen and Sword, 2015

Living in Donegal (although an American citizen) at the beginning of the war Jim joined the Young Citizen Volunteers of the Royal Irish Rifles. He was badly wounded on the first day of the Somme but later joined the Chinese Labour Corps (1917).

Jim's platoon officer, Lieutenant Monach, went looking for Jim's diary and sketchbooks after Jim was hurt. He found them in an abandoned rucksack in Martinsart (north-west of Aveluy – Map 3) and returned them to a very delighted Jim. The Lieutenant knew Jim was keeping the little black book with notes against the rules but knew how important it would be to return the documents. They were really close friends by July 1916.

Jim drew 'anywhere, anytime' – in dirty dug-outs, trenches, open spaces of the Somme, forests of Picardy, farmhouses, barns etc. This book has simply hundreds and hundreds of tiny black and white and coloured sketches (with some larger ones). It is much like Len Smith's exotic collection and is remarkable mainly for this reason.

'Hats off to the boys,' declared Jim. They fought and they laughed, 'a mystery to the sombre foreigner'. In the present book Jim re-wrote notes but used some original drawings and re-drew others. Also available were various newspaper cuttings, postcards and photographs. At the start of the book there is a selection of diary entries for many days from September 14, 1914, the day he joined the 14th Battalion of the Royal Irish Rifles, to October 4, 1915, when he arrived in France.

For instance, he became a Lance Corporal on April 20, 1914. On

May 8, 1915, there was a large and proud parade (20,000 men) in Belfast of the Ulster volunteers. Jim won all the sprint races at a sports day on May 25. He was a great athlete, very proud of his physical fitness.

In October 1915, he was promoted to Corporal. After October 4 there are very few dates and place names. Perhaps he did not keep this information any more or he chose not to transfer it from his notes. There appears to be a very loose narrative flow, determined by the order of his notes. This is conveyed by several side headings on each page. He was able to add a lot more information from his personal recollection.

They were soon near Amiens (Map 2) and Jim was sliding into a wet hole which apparently was a trench. His mouth filled with muddy water and someone started firing bullets at him. He saw a notice proclaiming 'Beware' and out of curiosity went to look at it and a bullet smacked into it.

Out of the line they found an orchard full of apples (Auchonvillers – north of Albert – Map 2) and swarmed up the trees, inciting a hail of enemy artillery of all sorts. They were learning fast. He became lousy and reckoned that 'bloodless' men escaped this trial. He tried burying his shirts but couldn't find them afterwards. He sniped rats. There was a spell cutting down trees and he was in his element – he loved this work.

They sent him on a bombing course ('Suicide Club') and he quite enjoyed this role but not being out in the snow at night without shelter. His body actually froze solid and they had to beat him back to life. On another night he was buried alive, luckily along with a spade.

Christmas 1915 was not bad, billeted with a nice old lady (although his drawing of her makes her look of young middle age and not unattractive). She was very hospitable but refused to take any money and they had to practically force a 50 franc on her. Not so nice was the next lady who complained about the disappearance of a large, fat hen. She asked for exorbitant compensation: someone slipped her 10 francs and the soup was delicious.

These enterprising boys worked out all sorts of dodges in the trench, such as having a rifle fixed at a set point and firing it if anything moved. Another trick was to connect up 5 rifles with a cord and fire them all at once.

The platoon had great characters, perhaps notably above all, Ginger

McMullen. The book finishes with him described as a hero on the first day of the Somme (when Jim was wounded). He was a fearless rough diamond who could swear and drink like the rest, be late on parade and grouse perpetually. But he loved his God and read his little bible under the light of a candle.

Sam the cook was another fearless personality: if you approached him and asked if there was any 'duff'' you were taking your life in your hands. Jim loved Sergeant Billy Kelly.

This platoon building a railway was a sight to behold because heavy sleepers tended to slip from hands and approach feet. Sundry sources of firewood are illustrated – some of it Jim wondered whether some poor French citizen had been using it quite recently. A sergeant fell down a well, the source of great hilarity. No. 14 'knew no more of him'.

A great favourite with the boys was the Stokes gun squads, who fired their weapon and cleared off fast before the enemy replied with 'half of Krupps foundry'. The platoon had marvellous skills such as smelling a fatigue squad a hundred yards away and promptly 'drying in' (disappearing): it was an art. But they were ready to make up a parcel for a comrade who never received any from home. No one in No. 14 got any leave whilst other platoons and Companies seemed to do quite well on this score.

Jim was made up to Sergeant (a proud mate sewed on his stripes for him) and he made friends with a rat. The hands on the village clock whirled round at intervals followed by an enemy bombardment. Someone scaled up the tower and removed them because it was obviously a spy signalling to the German artillery. They were taken home to Ireland but returned ceremoniously after the war.

The village shop did a roaring trade because of the presence of a very attractive blonde (Jim's picture does her justice) but she suddenly disappeared and they reckoned she was en enemy spy and was really a man – a big talking point for ages. Jim slept in a kennel with a dog – the best night's sleep he'd had for weeks.

Willie Reid was blown to bits (April 6, 1916) – it was the sort of date it was easy to remember. Jim helped to produce a trench magazine with Lieutenant Monach (who was from London but loved these Irish boys). The battalion had a mascot goat from England and it joined in everything. The platoon swam in the Ancre with shells popping around them and had a nice spell in Aveluy Wood when Jim went went for walks in the sunlit countryside.

They built another light railway in Thiepval Wood but a shell hit it. The 'most awful night our boys ever experienced' came on May 6, 1916. The pre-Somme raids were frightening experiences because the enemy fought back fiercely in anticipation of the 'Great Push'. So many pals in the platoon were lost. "Can we go out there at those b******, Captain?!" screamed Jim. Ginger McMullen was the hero in this wild warfare east of Thiepval.

MAY, CHARLIE (1888–1916)
To Fight Alongside Friends
The First World War Diary of Charlie May
Edited by Gerry Harrison
William Collins, 2015

Captain Charlie May was from New Zealand but served in the Manchester (7th City) Pals' Battalion. He wrote a daily diary from November 7, 1915 until the early morning of the first day of the Battle of the Somme – July 1, 1916, the day upon which he lost his life along with so many other British soldiers. The diary consists of 7 wallet-sized pocket books, which were sent home to his wife. They were discovered around 1980 in a suitcase in an attic, and typed up by a family friend. He had to use a magnifying glass to decipher the tiny handwriting.

They were edited by Charlie's grand nephew with researched footnotes. There is also a foreword about Charlie's life by David Crane.

Charlie May wrote with gusto and style – jolly, full of humour and a great flow of detail about the men he served with, events and environments – ugly and beautiful. Before the war he had written many short stories and poems (listed at the end of the book).

The battalion arrived in France on November 11, 1915. Captain May was in charge of B Company. He sorely missed his wife and new baby and wrote hundreds of letters to her, and she to him (they provide some of the material for his diary entries). 'Dear old, tax-ridden, law-abiding England! How I would delight to see one of your wolf-nosed sanitary inspectors turned loose in this, our Brucamps!'

They marched south towards the Arras front – '… whither I know not' – but there was time for a nice day in Amiens (Map 1) on November 20. There were adventures – stealthily trying to get wood for fires from under the noses of watchful citizens, rats running over their inert bodies at night. They were eventually in trenches at Mesnil – Martinsart (east of Albert – Map 2) on November 28 in a 'quiet' front with the occasional shell, mortar and machine gun fire and sniping.

There was a move to Candas (Map 2) early in December. The battalion shifted about so much it became known as 'Whetlands Flying Circus'.

The diaries are not short of opinions. He bemoaned the lack of encouragement of the initiative ('brains') of lower ranks.

'When you are right up alongside sudden death… you see what a man really is' (December 18). Around Christmas and the New Year the 7th moved further south to Le Quesnoy (east of Béthune – Maps 1 & 4).

The diary had become 'a tyrant that would ere long rule me, and here I am reduced to impotence when evening comes, unable to refuse the call' (December 22').

Charlie loved his Tommies with all their funny ways; they could get drunk and fall into stinking duck ponds but they were a continual source of delight and frustration for The captain.

Higher command was also a source of frustration – 'why not treat generals as admirals are treated when they make a mess of things?' (January 15, 1916). In the same entry he also complained that the previous professional experience of officers of the New Army was not being used. The opinions (his C.O. was 'an ass') were joined by lots of anecdotes and jokes.

Out of the front line the battalion engaged in all sorts of competitions – for marching, cross country runs, lots of football. It was obviously a very enterprising unit, a fact often remarked upon by other battalions. Later in January it was in the town of Corbie (Map 2) and to the trenches at Fricourt, with the River Somme glistening in the valley below. They were there to protect a British salient.

Charlie had ten days' leave with his family in February. Back at Fricourt (Map 3) there was a constant battle to maintain the trenches because of the vast amount of water in them – continuously exhausting work. 'What a life! What a war! What a game it is!' (March 4).

Not all the battalion's officers were popular – all the NCOs in one major's company asked to be reduced to the rank of Private because they no longer wanted to serve under this officer (March 16). But Charlie had great praise for French liaison officers, who acted as interpreters and often as peacemakers between the military and French citizens.

Charlie found the war 'peculiar' because it was a long continuous battle against an almost invisible enemy but one who inflict devastating damage.

'The chief reason for patrols is that the staff like them' (March 22). Charlie believed that a good diary should offer a wide range of information as well as an account of personal experience, such as the fact that a shell just missed him on March 28 and he worked from 4.30 a.m. to 11 p.m. On the same day an officer and the Sergeant Major were arrested for being drunk.

There were frequent rumours about something big happening on the Somme front but in April and May there were just days of hard work, patrolling and suffering the odd enemy shell or continued with not much of a sign of anything more significant.

Then in the early days of June more and more raids on the enemy were ordered, for instance, on June 3, and now the battalion casualty rate started to rise sharply and friends were lost. A big battle obviously loomed as reams and reams of orders were issued – 'till one's head is in a whirl'. Fresh ammunition supplies poured in and the British bombardment over Fricourt, La Boiselle and Mametz (Map 3) hotted up.

The Manchester Pals moved up to their positions on June 28 and the 29th was a long day of waiting. There was no diary entry for the 30th and on July 1st, that fateful day, in the early morning Captain Charlie May indicated that the diary was closing down for a few days, after which he would write up 'The Battle of Mametz'.

Three of Charlie May's seven pocket books, in which his diaries were meticulously written each day.

'Our camp in the Bois', a 'vile' sketch by Charlie May. 'Its only excuse for existence is that it will serve as a slight record of four happy days.' (19 May 1916)

MAZE, PAUL (1887–1979)
A Frenchman in Khaki
Paul Maze
The Naval & Military Press, 2013

On his own initiative, Paul Maze, who had been turned down for French military service on medical grounds, presented himself to the Colonel of the Royal Scots Greys in Havre and asked for a job as an interpreter. After some deliberation they got him into khaki (August 1914).

Paul wrote 'A Frenchman in Khaki' in the early 1930s, by which time he was one of the most famous artists in France. In an introduction Winston Churchill confirmed that Paul was 'the friend of generals'. Paul Maze kept a diary because he sometimes refers to important specific days.

He travelled to the Battle of Mons with the Scots Greys and was immediately involved in the action, seeking out information during his own movements as well as taking and delivering messages between Generals. On August 26 the village where he was billeting was entered by Uhlans and he had to make a desperate escape to the British lines. But here he was arrested by General Munro on suspicion of being a spy. Luckily he was rescued by a major in the Royal Scots Greys (August 27). He went to Paris, which was in state of turmoil.

But then began a long association with General Gough, in command of a cavalry division on the Aisne. They trekked north in early October, chasing Germans out of Bailleul (Maps 1 & 4) and entering Flanders (October 12). He saved a German deserter from being executed as a spy. Around Ypres the Germans stopped retreating. The First Battle of Ypres commenced as the cavalry was pulled into reserve and Paul spent three months in Vieux Berquin (north of Béthune – Maps 1 & 4).

He made himself generally useful, helping the maps department at HQ, and escorted staff officers to see the front line at Ypres. He also had to settle 'everlasting' claims for compensation from French peasants.

But in April he was back with General Gough in Ypres into the storm of renewed German bombardment He became ill and went to his sister in Normandy for a break. But he was back for the British attack on Aubers Ridge (Map 4) in May, where he made landscape drawings of German defences using a periscope although he needed the occasional (and risky) glance over the parapet.

General Gough was put in command of the 1ˢᵗ Corps and he commissioned Paul to draw the German lines in preparation for the Battle of Loos (Lens – Map 1). During the battle he also began to take a close look at the battle plans and then moved around the front line to assess progress. The confusion following the attacks meant he had to take his own initiative, often following just behind advancing British troops and assessing how they fared. He just 'longed to be in touch with things'.

In the winter, however, there was just 'dull routine' at Corps HQ (Bailleul – Maps 1 & 4). But in March 1916 General Gough ordered Paul to draw the Messines-Wytschaete front (Map 4), another very intricate and dangerous task. After that, a new (4ᵗʰ) army was formed under General Gough to prepare for battle on the Somme and Paul once more did the landscape pictures – the Bazentin, Contalmaison, Pozières area (Somme – Maps 3 & 4). At Ovillers on July 2 he was terrified to be caught on his motor bike in the middle of an enormous German bombardment. He used motor bikes a lot but often he had to get off and walk because of the devastated ground.

He worked with the Australians at Pozières, where he was able to actually follow on the heels of a battalion as it went over the top, which enabled him to send back a continuous stream of first-hand information with runners (July 22). Staff officers never got near the action like this. He was invited to do the same at Thiepval.

Constant exposure to gas made him ill and he was in hospital in Amiens for 5 weeks until October. In November he was back on the Somme front at Beaumont Hamel (Map 3). He stayed on the Somme for the winter – at Toutencourt. He joined in the pursuit of the Germans as they retired to the Hindenburg Line in the spring of 1917. But they left strongpoints and made lightning raids on approaching Allied troops. Paul's task as usual was to check on progress, 'thrilled' to be abreast of situations and make recommendations about further action.

He went with the 5ᵗʰ Army to Flanders in June and again he was set to make sketches of the landscape up to Passchendaele Ridge (Map 4). Dissatisfied with having to go back to HQ every night he sheltered in a dug-out at St. Jean right in front of the enemy lines.

Of course, he remained a great puzzle to guards and sentries. He had no insignia of rank and yet there he was conversing with generals. Brigadiers reckoned he brought them good luck. As the day for attack approached (July 31) he stayed in the front line trenches with three motor bikes placed at strategic points. Again, he kept just behind the advancing infantry, moving from sector to sector to assess progress.

But one day he was knocked out and wounded in the buttock and he had crawl back to HQ. He was in hospital until September. The 5th Army then moved from Poperinghe to Amiens (Maps 1 & 4) and he rode down on a horse. Again he drew the front as there was accumulating evidence of a big German offensive in the spring of 1918. General Gough knew in March that he faced 40 enemy Divisions. Paul was brought into his usual role but this time he was reporting on the progress or otherwise of safe retreat, not advance. He included his diary entries for these critical days of March 1918.

Once more, he took terrible risks in order to do his job, sometimes riding on roads in view of moving German troops. He became a go-between for British and French generals, the latter very critical of General Gough's headlong retreat. Paul was often able to supply an opinion even to sceptical French generals. But Gough was withdrawn to England. He had said to Paul that if he had stood his ground and fought the Germans the casualty lists would have been disastrous.

In the Allied summer offensives Paul worked for General Rawlinson and later the American 27th Division. But Paul's war was ended by a bullet in the wrist on September 29 as the Americans were storming the Hindenburg Line.

MEERES, CHARLES (1894–1962)
I Survived the Somme
The Secret Diary of a Tommy
Charles Meeres
Edited by Frank Meeres
Amberley Publishing, 2013

Charles's son, Frank, edited this selection of his father's diaries, wonderful sketches and paintings. Charles had written up his memoir from his diaries (sometimes he just puts in the original diary entry). When he wrote the memoir is not indicated.

He was a subaltern in the Royal Artillery from 1915 to the end of the war, and after. He was in the C/96 Battery of the Royal Field Artillery (The Royal Horse Artillery worked with the cavalry and the Royal Garrison Artillery fired much heavier guns that the RFA). Charles was commissioned in November 1914 and arrived at Havre in September 1915 after many months of training in England.

On September 13 the C/96 were at Tournehem, a scruffy village near St Omer, grooming horses and training the signallers. They moved on to St. Jans Cappel where the gunners dammed a stream to provide water for the horses: if the horses were not fit the Battery could go nowhere. Near Lillers they could hear the big guns firing on the other side of Béthune (Maps 1 & 4).

British artillery was being clustered together for a great bombardment and offensive at Loos (Lens sector – Map 1). But the roads were jam-packed with vehicles, supplies and men in pouring rain. C/96 moved at the rate of about a mile a day.

They eventually found their battle position. Each 18-pounder gun needed to be slid into a shallow pit, a task which took all night. Having completed this they then discovered that the supply wagons and the ammunition column were actually in front of the guns and they had to be hurriedly moved back out of harm's way.

The news in the morning was that enemy infantry was likely to engulf them at any moment (along with a gas cloud). Charles had the 'wind right up'. Yet nothing came their way. Then he was ordered forward to establish a post where he could see the British infantry so that their guns could try to miss them. He had no map but just came across an ex-German trench opposite Hill 70 suitable for an observation post.

Telephone wires were run back to the battery by signallers. The air stank of chlorine gas. The British guns proceeded to plaster Hill 70 and the infantry advanced. Having done his job Charles returned to his Battery only to find it had moved and it took him hours to find it.

Now the area stank of rotting flesh. The attack on Hill 70 (Lens – Map 1) had failed miserably and the corpses of Scots Guards littered the ground and the enemy artillery began to fire on the British guns. Charles closely escaped being hit and the battery was very glad to be relieved.

The Battle of Loos was a disaster. There were all sorts of mistakes, for instance, failure to cut the German wire by the La Bassée Canal (Map 4). The troops who did break the German line proceeded on too far and were decimated in counter attacks. Reserves trying to get up to the front were caught up in traffic jams. Enemy positions were almost completely unknown. Charles's C.O. was one of many to be removed from command.

After resting and recuperation nearer Armentières (Map 1) the next action was a prolonged bombardment on German positions to soften them up for a further offensive (December). But the unheralded sequel to this was a heavier onslaught from the German artillery which wrecked the town and made the BEF extremely unpopular with its citizens.

At least there was goose for Christmas. In January there were spasmodic exchanges of fire from the big guns of both armies but the balance of fire power was changed with the arrival of powerful enemy howitzers. The result of this was severe damage to the British 18-pounders. Charles had to take all his battery guns for urgent repairs.

They left this front to go to the Somme on April 1, taking up a position on the wet plain of the River Ancre (Charles gives his account a good spine of specific dates). They stole a lot of timber from the Royal Engineers and there was one hell of a row.

The bombardment which began on June 24 was the biggest ever

from the BEF C/96 (now 97) fired about 1,000 rounds a day; Charles was busy managing the supply of shells. They attacked the enemy wire and communications and thus supplies. When Charles had a later look around Fricourt (Map 3) he found that the countryside was completely devastated; but this had obviously not been enough to put the enemy out of action. C/97 was back in action on July 10, against Contalmaison (Maps 2 & 3) which was captured. They later fired on Longueval (Map 2) and the Bazentins (Map 3) but the infantry did not make progress and general breakthrough became more and more a remote possibility. C/97 came out of the line on July 24.

The appearance of tanks raised hopes but they soon evaporated in the mud, along with villages and vegetation. Losses of experienced artillery officers had become a big concern: they were not easy to replace.

The bombardment at Arras (Map 1) in April 1917 proved too much for the battery's weary and emaciated horses; 120 were lost out of 173, seriously damaging the effectiveness of the unit. The gunners themselves were living on two thirds of iron rations. By May the whole operation had ground to a halt. Charles himself was invalided to England for several months.

His story is picked up again in December 1917 at Longavesnes. The New Year brought more and more rumours of an enormous enemy offensive to come in the Spring. Charles was on leave when it opened up on March 21. He was detained at base and finally sent up to Flanders on April 13 (at Mons des Cats – Map 4) to the north side of the huge German salient which had engulfed Armentières (and Bailleul from April 15 –Map 1).

But the German advance faded away, and Charles was not bothered at Mons des Cats. He was now a Captain. The battery went south to replace French artillery at Bouvaincourt (near Abbéville). But they came out of the front rapidly following a fierce enemy attack on May 28. The unit was effectively put out of action and passed their guns over to another Battery and became an ammunition supply column. New guns arrived on June 10. They rested on the French coast and caught Spanish flu. But the German thrust had evaporated and ' the tide had turned' (July).

MELLERSH, H. E. L.
Schoolboy into War
William Kimber, 1978

H.E.L. Mellersh became a 2nd Lieutenant in the East Lancashire Regiment in 1915. He reached the front line in the Summer of 1916 in the 2nd Battalion. He experienced 'disgust' at the ever-pervading sickly-sweet smell of human decay – a grim relic of the earlier struggles here of the French (around Armentières – Map 1) '…one grew used to it, more or less'. At least it was a quiet sector, a situation thankfully not yet discouraged by Higher Command. A few desultory rifle grenades came over and the occasional burst of machine gun fire and shells.

When he went on patrol in no man's land he was accused of being a 'fire-eater', after suggesting a 'rush' on an enemy trench. To remind him of the perils here a grenade landed on the parapet in front of him. But it did not explode and it had a message attached informing them that Kitchener was dead.

As the most junior officer his 'bed' was a hole for his hip in the hard ground. He thought well of the Sergeants – self-assured with 'clipped talk' and sporting the 'pointed wax moustache'. The men were cheerful and always jesting.

They walked to the Somme, rolling country like Sussex. They had Field Days, mock battles in open manoevres. At night the more extrovert officers talked about the lack of sex. Mellersh considered them outrageous, even nasty. He was 'well-meaning and uncertain', bearing the talk with as much grace as he could muster. They were personally rude about a parcel he had received from a lady. They certainly knew little about the general state of the war and didn't want to know.

On July 1, 1916 they were in billets near Albert (Map 2). The battalion were scheduled to 'nibble away' at the Germans in preparation for a further big assault later in July. For this they approached Fricourt (Map 3). Mellersh remembered his tin hat bobbing up and down on the top of his head uncomfortably as his horse jogged along. He saw his first German at Contalmaison (Maps 2 & 3).

In the shelling which followed Mellersh was thrilled because he realised he was not afraid – '... a sort of self-drugging'. He found that he had even taken out his revolver and was ragged about it by one of these loud officers. But the Germans were too far away for an effective rush, at least one in which they would not be shot down by machine gun fire. Mellersh found the casualty toll rising and was glad when the call came to get out as quickly as possible.

Then he was shot – his 'arms flopped uselessly at his side'. But he was able to walk back to a field dressing station. He really had a tremendous emotion of relief: he had done 'his bit' and he was still alive!

He returned from Blighty early in 1917 as the Germans prepared to retreat to their Hindenburg Line. He was in the vicinity of Buchavesnes (near Peronne – Map 2). Like many of these memoirs written from recall 60 or more years after the war Mellersh has few dates and place names, relying on the narrative to convey his story. He soon went out with a night patrol but they made too much noise and an alert sentry started taking pot shots at them in the dark. Accordingly, he was shot in the back; he had only been back on the Western Front for seven weeks and now he was on his way back to England.

His second return came in September 1917 to Warneton near Armentières (Map 4). The C.O. was young, fiercely efficient and a total pain to all his subordinates. They tried to rag him in the Mess by continually making the comment, 'It makes the grass grow greener' (i.e. bull-shit). He didn't notice.

Mellersh was sent on a horse course despite being extremely 'unhorsy'. At least he could wear his puttees upside down. Only senior officers were allowed to wear long, shiny boots. The puttees stopped the legs rubbing against the horse's flanks

He was promoted to Lieutenant and they were then at Passchendaele (Map 4) – a 'dim greyness of mud below and a pall of cloud above.' It was November but there was still enough shelling to make it unhealthy: neither side was going to walk away from it – how would this war end? Their food ran out (and Mellersh was Mess President!) and porridge was served at 5.30 p.m. In celebration his servant became helplessly drunk on rum.

Leave came early in 1918 but he had a strange feeling of disappointment as he felt he would have preferred to be with his war companions (without the war). But he did enjoy the theatres, especially the comedians.

Back to meet the new German threat he was next to the River Somme at Béthencourt, in a wide valley. They searched in vain for 'marauding' Germans. There were no maps and The company commander was not inspiring.

Then quite suddenly the 3-inch whizz-bangs flew about them. But there was still no sign of enemy infantry so Mellersh took two lance Corporals with him to find them. They couldn't locate any Huns but there was vin blanc in a cellar in the village. Mellersh thought they were 'muddling through' in true British fashion whilst the Germans were about to accelerate a highly efficient campaign.

On March 24 there was panic as the enemy infantry was reported to be advancing. Companies retreated because other companies were retreating. This made Mellersh very annoyed and he ordered his half company back to where it had been. A 5.9 shell landed right next to him and he was dazed and bleeding profusely. He was awarded the Military Cross for his bravery in this action. After treatment in England he prepared to leave again for the Western Front on November 12, 1918.

NEVILL, BILLIE (1894–1916)
Billie The Nevill Letters 1914–1916
Ruth Elwin Harris
The Naval and Military Press Ltd., 2003

Wilfred Percy Nevill, known as 'Billie' to his family, wrote to his mother on August 28, 1915 from 'I wonder. Try to guess. Hard to Say'. 'Ici nous somme', he added. This was the sort of jolly, bubbly personality that was Billie Nevill of the 8ᵗʰ Battalion of the East Surrey Regiment. He kept a diary – for one day. The first entry was also the last (July 25). He preferred to communicate immediately – by letter.

He had his own code consisting of dots and other devices, such as describing 'Albert' as' the name of one of Mrs. Bull's sons. Not Fred' (July 30). 'Dear People, nations and languages. Hail! I've such a lot of interesting (I think) odds and ends to tell you.' He kept assuring them it was not really dangerous where he was. He told them not to worry about snipers because British ones were better shots.

The battalion went to Dernancourt (near Albert – Map 2). 'We're simply dying to see these curious blighters (the Bosche)'. The star shells were 'awfully pretty'. 'The trenches are the greatest fun' (Fricourt – Map 3). But the enemy trenches were sometimes only 30 yards away so they had to keep a 'cute look out' and if they shelled the Hun he gave it back tenfold. The parapet was held up with bedsteads, sideboards, table legs, cart-wheels, bricks etc.

They billeted at Ribemont (south of Albert – Map 2), later Ville-sur-Ancre in the Somme region. On September of Billie penned one of his funny little rhymes – 'Hop it, for Peachy with the water he comes / His ghastly hobnails titulate my drums'.

Billie continued to assert that he was quite safe despite indications in his letters that he was venturesome. 'I will have the sentries at night looking over the parapet <u>the whole time</u>'. He loved underlining some words or phrases. There was a chance he would get the Military Cross and when that did not transpire he was really disappointed.

Early in October he was depressed by the loss of a young subaltern, Thorne, when he was on patrol trying to bomb snipers and see if Germans were occupying some of the mine craters. 'It has been an unpleasant tour'. With the Battle of Loos raging 40 miles to the north the German artillery was generally active ('reliable', as Billie put it) with retaliation from the British artillery limited by lack of shells. There was also the constant fear of enemy mining and the 'sausage' (aerial torpedoes).

But there was a 'sporting crowd of Huns opposite' (October 2) putting up targets for the East Surreys to fire at and then indicating their relative success with different flags. Billie reckoned they were 'at the end of their tether'. He got his mother to send his servant, Private Miller, a very nice parcel. Miller wrote a thankyou letter on November 18 saying how cool and collected Billie was. He was always genial and a great comfort to every man he came into contact with. He could not ' be beaten for courage' and he was 'respected and admired by every man in his company'.

He was at 'UP' (the front line) on November 27 and was still 'having a ripping time' in deep freezing frost. He was made temporary Adjutant after leave in December. Fraternisation was not allowed at Christmas: the Germans even sent over a present of poison gas. Meanwhile, Billie was taking lessons in French and horse riding – 'Great fun, you ought to see me on an 'orse'. He admitted to submitting some material for a trench magazine but in truth he was writing almost all of it – 'bawdy, full of local jokes and the men loved it'.

The letters are obviously crammed with allusions to family and friends and to fellow officers. He was a keen photographer and got many orders for his pictures. But on January 22, 1916, he wrote, 'I know I am not writing these rambling letters… but somehow I just can't… you know I am permanently alright'. But the letter of January 27 was back to his old form. He was out in no man's land on the 29th with the odd enemy machine gun firing off. 'Things were humming', he reported in a letter full of code indicating that the neighbourhood was simply crawling with troops and guns and that he was getting into the front line between La Boiselle and Fricourt (Maps 3 & 4).

The East Surreys Charging Towards the German Trenches
'The Surreys Play the Game!' by R. Caton Woodville, which appeared in
The Illustrated London News, 27th July, 1916.
"The Game" was published in the *Daily Mail* on 12th July, 1916.

He was on a course at the Infantry School at Flixecourt (Map 3) in February and like Siegfried Sassoon, who was there a little later, thought that the idea of the course was to give some officers a rest. They had some nice days in Abbéville and Amiens (Map 2). He also did some drawing and dined at Godbert's.

He was in command of a company (March), a temporary Captain (paid as a 2nd Lieutenant). He had now given up trying to convince his family he was safe. He found it difficult to attend a church service through lack of padres in the front line; he complained, like Robert Graves, that they stayed mostly in the back areas.

Leave beckoned in April. 'P. S. I've still a good week to get hit' (April 26) – pessimistic for him (perhaps ironic). At the beginning of May the whole (18th) Division was withdrawn for intensive training – mock battles etc. The Germans, of course, had wind of the 'Great Push' and indulged in raids and hurricane bombardments.

The battalion was in place when the Somme bombardment began on June 24. 'UP, UP, UP. Dear All. Still alive. Why? Ask me another' (June 26). His last letter was on June 28 and it concluded, 'I'm as happy as ever, yrs ever Bill'.

Billie Nevill was killed on the first day of the Battle of the Somme on July 1, 1916. Before his company went over the top he distributed some footballs amongst them, challenging them to kick them all the way to the German trenches, with a prize for the first one there. On one of the balls he scribbled 'The Great European Cup – The Final, East Surreys v. Bavarians, Kick-off at zero'. On another ball he wrote 'NO REFEREE'. The balls were later found in captured enemy trenches. Billie lasted only a few second after leading his company over the top.

OGLE, HENRY (born 1887)
The Fateful Battle Line
The Great War Journals and Sketches of
Captain Henry Ogle, MC
Edited and introduced by Michael Glover
Leo Cooper, 1993

Henry Ogle was educated at Chester Teacher Training College and the Leamington Spa College of Art. He volunteered for service in September 1914 and went to France with the 7th Royal Warwickshire Regiment (Territorials) in March 1915, taking with him his miniature paint box – he was a highly competent draughtsman. His book is full of his clear landscapes and portraits.

Henry wrote these memoirs between 1937 and several years after the Second World War, which Michael Glover converted to this narrative. Henry had added historical notes to his chapters.

The Warwickshire Terriers went to the sector between Ypres and Armentières (Houplines – Map 1) but did not take part in any serious action – the tendency was to send Terriers to 'cushy places'. However, there were plenty of fatigues and lessons about surviving in the salient (from the Durham Light Infantry).

Details are clear in Henry's mind after 30 years – the baths, the notices by the roadside – 'The pump must NOT be used for drinking'. He also appeared able to remember conversations. Private Gulliver Giles shouted, "Rotten square-headed German bastards have smashed our signboard." The shells came over, not many, but enough to keep the Terriers hopping about. They moved, like so many other units, to 'Plugstreet' Wood (Map 4).

On July 13, 1915 – 'one of my very few dates combined with places' – he recalled travelling south to Arras (Map 1) and contemplating an intricate maze of German trenches. He was sent out with another graduate of Leamington Spa School of Art to survey and draw it all, developing his scouting skills, later to come in very handy. The Germans took occasional pot-shots at them.

But they did hit him whilst out on patrol on August 13, 1915. After an operation he was sent to Rouen Convalescent Camp – 'designed to make soldiers desire fervently to get away'. They had to work hard shifting stuff like rolls of barbed wire.

When he returned to his unit they were south-west of Arras at Foncquvillers (Map 2), in time for Christmas. It was so wet here that it was impossible to wear greatcoats or capes and they had to turn to enormous ground sheets. Then Henry caught trench fever in January 1916.

They prepared for 'The Great Push', including bombing practice (they knew how to throw bombs but not how to evade them). They also learnt bayonet-fighting but the instructor, trying to look very fierce, just reduced the onlookers to helpless mirth. A Stokes gun demonstration ended in tragedy when men were killed or badly wounded.

For the Battle of the Somme Henry was chosen to be a runner (of messages) in the Hébuterne sector. However, during the pre-battle bombardment he became orderly escort to a new and active C.O. Henry was promoted to Lance Corporal.

'Entangled in or sprawling across the barbed wire, slumped over the remains of trench parapets, or half buried in the ruined trenches, were corpses ' (July 11). Henry was in the thick of the action near Pozières and Ovillers Ridges (Map 3) in the shattered and littered terrain. He became a Corporal: he does not write about fear in these two weeks in July in the heat and dust, stench and surrounded by swarms of large flies.

He was relieved and on ration delivery for the next spell in the front line when the Regiment was in Authille Wood (north of Albert – Map 2). But such 'details' could come under murderous artillery fire (he remembered dreadful August 17 because it was his birthday). He also recalled trying to analyse the cacophony of sounds made by the various big guns – 'a continuous pulsation' which shook the ground. It was impossible to hear anyone speak. When they returned to camp they were bombed from the air.

Lady Egerton's Coffee House in Rouen. Drawing by Henry Ogle.

'To this day if I hear the sound of footsteps on wooden boards or on a plank bridge, I see the awful landscape around Courcelette' (Maps 2 & 3). It was so wet they learnt to wrap sandbags around their legs.

Christmas was spent in Albert, alongside carefree and generous Australians (Henry was born in Australia) but the Terriers found difficulty in keeping up with them when it came to the consumption of alcohol. They actually saw the River Somme for the first time in 1917.

Henry Ogle went away for nine months to learn how to become an officer. On his return he was despatched to near Armentières (Map 1) to the 2/5 Royal North Lancs Regiment (Territorials) to learn the trench routines of a quiet front. But it was not a happy unit: the C.O. was hostile and very keen on digging more and more trenches. He appointed Henry O/C Baths until he was rescued by a brigadier and transferred in May 1918 to a Regular Battalion – 1/King's Own Royal Lancasters near Lillers (west of Béthune – Maps 1 & 4), where the C.O. was much more friendly.

Eventually he was appointed to be the battalion Scouting Officer, a skill he had been developing for years. The work he did here during the early days of the Allied summer offensive earned him the Military Cross. They moved beyond Arras (Map 1) to the Scarpe and Henry's battleground skills became invaluable. Towards the end of September he was wounded and that was a Blighty One.

PARKER, ERNEST (born 1896)
Into Battle 1914–1918
Longmans and Green, 1964

This was a memoir written by Ernest in the 1930s. Before the Great War and after (until 1962) he worked for Longmans & Green as a publisher of literature and poetry (except for further service for his country in the Second World War). Considering that he was employed in a publishing house it is surprising that his work was not produced earlier. It was actually 'disinterred' by his son.

Ernest knew in the 1930s that he had 'forgotten so much of the detail' of his war experience. He enlisted on September 1, 1914, saying he was 19 years old when he was only 17. By the time he was trained for the Western Front he was in the 10th Battalion of the Durham Light Infantry, which went to the Ypres Salient in August, 1915 (Ernest has few specific dates).

The Durham talk was something of a puzzle for Ernest. What did 'cracken' mean? They were in the West Lane communication trench where stretcher-bearers carried 'blanketed forms aloft' past them. They quickly learnt to freeze still when German flares went up, as West Lane was very shallow.

They were forced to turn back because of the heavy damage to the dug-outs for which they were heading. Instead, they switched to an area north of the Menin Road. They tried to cook breakfast until officers screamed at them because of the smoke. Ernest got into a dug-out with three others, muddy boots each side of his head.

'Alertness' (and 'tension') were the orders of the day. They had been ducking when anything landed within hundreds of yards but soon learnt when this was really necessary. A dud landed a yard from Ernest as they walked back to rest in Watou (Map 4).

The hour of 'rest' in the front trench was mostly taken up with collecting rations or going out via a sap trench to a listening post. A lance corporal ate most of their rations and later absconded and was eventually apprehended disguised as a peasant, trying to bomb pigs.

There were baths at Poperinghe (Map 4) to remove 'a month's dust' but the 'deloused shirts in fact had dormant lice in their seams'. As winter progressed pants fell apart.

The battalion had some involvement in the disastrous attack at Loos (Lens – Map 1) in September. The battalion runner (of messages) reported that he had spotted a comrade spread-eagled on the enemy wire and he went to his aid. A German officer popped his head above his parapet and the runner simply sprang to attention and saluted. He then safely retrieved his pal.

Ernest groomed mules in the battalion transport lines, a tricky job, and was later put into the bombing (grenades) section, which had the advantage of getting him out of parades and drills. In order to be accepted as a bomber you had to be able to handle a lighted grenade without fumbling it (before the invention of the Mills Bomb they had to use the 'Newton Pippin', a primitive device, and thus unreliable).

At the end of 1915 the 10/ Durhams were near St. Julien and later Elverdinghe (Map 4), more in the north of the Salient. Bombers had to occupy outposts, and staggering across the holed, squelchy terrain was hazardous. Ernest did eventually fall down a hole and had to be hauled out by his mates, minus his thigh boots (size 10 – he took size 8). It was at Elverdinghe, too, early in 1916, that he brought back an oversize ration of rum and the bombers got very drunk. However, 'the dear old bombing officer' (Captain Pumphrey) did not report the incident. They received their first shrapnel helmets – nice but adding to their 'Christmas Tree' of stuff they had to carry around.

As spring approached the 10/ Durhams undertook a long march south to the Arras sector (Map 1) to take over trenches from the French (who were off to Verdun) and Ernest became sick with exhaustion. But he kept going and was rewarded with a well-earned stripe. He also burnt his leg and was slightly injured by shrapnel.

In the early Summer of 1916 the battalion helped New Zealand miners to dig tunnels near Arras, a task enjoyed by the many miners in the ranks of the Durhams. Later, in a another Arras area, Ernest joined his company commander in night patrols in no man's land. He actually took charge of a party trying to take a German prisoner but they made too much noise in cutting the enemy wire and were then subjected to a hail of rifle bullets. They lay as still as statues as the bullets whizzed around them – in fact, they fell asleep and crawled back to safety before dawn.

In July they marched to Albert, then to the front line in Delville Wood (Map 3), still littered with corpses from earlier struggles. The trenches were shallow, vulnerable to whizz bombs. Ernest's foot turned septic and he missed a successful raid which captured a trench and all its contents. But the Germans still held another trench in the wood, from which they fired destructive stick bombs ('potato mashers').

Getting beyond Delville Wood in September proved very costly in casualties due to a prolonged onslaught of high explosives, so intense that at one point Ernest wondered if he would better off dead. But he managed to dive into a shell hole as bullets zipped around him. He was also shelled later by the the British artillery. He and a companion were around 400 yards in front of the rest of their Battalion. They managed to struggle back but all the C.O. wanted to know was why they were so far away. Ernest's tunic was ripped to pieces by passing bullets. He was not asked, for instance, what he had learnt from the experience.

Back near Arras he was called to England to train as an officer, returning to Flanders in June, 1917, as a 2nd Lieutenant in the 2nd Battalion of the Royal Fusiliers. He enjoyed leading raids on enemy positions from the banks of the Yser Canal (he was asked to report back, contrary to the earlier reactions of senior officers). Light relief was provided by a mock naval battle on the Canal in converted cardboard boxes.

Ernest participated in follow-up patrols following the first waves of Allied attacks early in August, 1917 (Third Battle of Ypres) beyond the Steenbeke stream. In a later offensive on the edge of Houlthulst Forest he was shot in the wrist. His active war was over but the King did pin a Military Cross on his chest.

PATCH, HARRY (1897–2009)
The Last Fighting Tommy
The Life of Harry Patch: Last Veteran of the Trenches
Harry Patch with Richard Van Emden
Bloomsbury, 2004

This book is based on recorded interviews between Harry Patch and Richard van Emden. Harry was conscripted in June 1916. A year later he was on a paddle steamer from Folkestone. In Boulogne he was drafted into the 7th Battalion of the Duke of Cornwall's Light Infantry (conscripted men had no choice of regiment), sadly depleted by losses at Arras.

Lance Corporal Patch became a Number 2 in a Lewis machine gun team. They had an agreement that they would not shoot to kill unless their own lives were in danger.

Then the 7/DCLI was at 'rest' – refitting, training, drilling, rifle practice and lectures plus instruction on map reading, patrolling and bayonet fighting. But they were soon in the front line near Ypres. Harry was determined not to show how frightened he was, and that he would not let down his mates on the Lewis gun, who had already been in the trenches. Harry's job was to carry spare parts for the gun and to put them on the gun if required.

The team found a spot in the trench. Harry soon had his baptism of fire – shells, bombs, enemy planes flying overhead. No amount of training could prepare men for this fearful experience – the deafening noises, the filth and the uncertainty – the calls for stretcher-bearers. They had to stand on used ammunition boxes to get out of the water in the bottom of the trench.

Lewis gunners were excused fatigues (working parties) but they had to make really sure that their gun was in good working order, clean and dry. An officer came round for a daily inspection, which even included a look at their Webley pistols (they had no rifles).

The nights were cold, even in the Summer of 1917. The 'stand to' order at dawn meant that everybody had to stand on the firestep to check that the Germans were not preparing to raid. Then the rum came round followed by breakfast and, best of all, a letter or a parcel from home. Clean water was very scarce and washing was an infrequent luxury. Harry was in Flanders from June to September but he did not have a single bath or change of clothes during that period.

Harry and his pals slept when they could – an hour here, an hour there, cramped up on the firestep. There was hour upon hour of complete inactivity until there was a turn to look out for the enemy. If any movement was detected a star shell was exploded and the area was brightly lit up. If Germans were spotted in no man's land they had to be fired on, including from the machine gun. Once the team fired they then had to move quickly to another part of the trench to avoid being targeted by enemy fire. 'You were scared all the time', said Harry. Sometimes he started shaking uncontrollably. They smoked as much as they could, hoping to survive, fearing the worst.

At rest Harry managed a few visits to Poperinghe (Map 4) and the delightful Talbot House, where exhausted and battered soldiers could enjoy real rest and something resembling civilisation. Harry described the place in loving detail.

The Third Battle of Ypres was launched on July 31 and Harry went over the top with his machine gun team near Langemarck on August 16. The night preparation for the attack did not go according to plan as the DCLI lost its bearings coming up to the Steenbeke stream. They eventually managed to get across a rickety pontoon bridge with enemy positions nearby. In these situations Tommy had little idea of where he was – a nearby pile of rubble was Langemarck and that low slope was Pilckem Ridge, but to him it was a pile of rubble and a little slope.

An RE officer laid white tape from crater to crater indicating the way forward. Harry carried his heavy store of spare parts etc., stumbling past corpses and wounded men crying out. German prisoners scrambled the other way. A lad died crying out "Mother!" and Harry always remembered this as a greeting to a mother in 'the next world'. A German came at them with a fixed bayonet and Harry shot him low down with his pistol to save his life – that cry of "Mother!' still ringing in his ears.

They reached their objective – an enemy trench; everyone helped to move the defences to the other side of the trench. Afterwards, when relieved, the team were walking back towards the reserve line when a shell landed amongst them. Returning to consciousness, Harry saw that his tunic was torn and blood was pouring from his body.

By the time they got him to hospital the shrapnel lodged in him had cooled and he was in excruciating pain. But the anaesthetic was being reserved for more seriously wounded men and Harry had to endure his operation without it. It was a small piece of shrapnel but it was a Blighty One. The three other members of his team had been blown to bits.

Harry never returned to the Western Front due to a later chest injury.

PLOWMAN, MARK
A Subaltern on the Somme
Mark VII
E.P. Dutton & Company, 1928

The Naval and Military Press have re-printed this 1920s memoir. Mark Plowman (usually called Mark - 'Mark VII' was a pseudonym for the book) was a journalist and poet who objected to war but did volunteer on Christmas Eve 1914 to join the Territorial Army Royal Army Medical Corps, 4th Field Ambulance. However, he later transferred with a commission to the 10th Battalion of the Yorkshire Regiment.

The memoir covers the period July to December, 1916, with a chapter for each month (without specific dates). It was written in the present tense. In July he went to Belancourt to meet the Yorkshires. It was not a pleasant introduction, with subalterns indulging in obscene exchanges and the C.O. reprimanding all the officers for inefficiency when most of them had only just arrived.

Mark Plowman objected to barbed wire, censoring letters, field punishment No. 1, and pack drill. His platoon sergeant had 'a criminal look'. They occupied trenches near Longueval (Maps 2 & 3) in August when enemy shelling was 'incessant': two big guns 'flash a pair of devilish eyes' directly at them. Would it ever stop? When it did this provided 'acute pleasure'.

The MO smothered himself with bully beef fat in order to avoid washing, and to keep out the lice. Sick men were to him 'damned scrimshankers'. 'Stick it' (out) was the watchword as the machine guns opened up.

They marched north for 36 miles to Hébuterne, over 2 days in sweltering weather carrying 40-pound packs. But here there was at least little of the cursed shelling – just hour-long bursts from machine guns.

Plowman found his platoon sergeant asleep when his men were working hard to push forward to a bombing post in no man's land. What was the use of doing anything about it? But discovering yet another sleeping sentry was too much so Mark hid the man's rifle and fired a revolver shot over his head, and the man awoke 'gibbering with fear'.

Corporal Side's kit was destroyed by a direct shell hit when he went to the toilet and he complained bitterly about the loss. Second-in-command Major Smythe made a rare tour of the trench at a rattling speed. He was excellent on parades and drill. The C.O. strolled around up, too, and may have been very drunk. He later sent Plowman out with a raiding party on a bright moonlit night. But it all made going back to billets such a delight. He 'actually fell in love with a lamp post' at Doullens (Map 2). He turned down the chance of 'hired feminine company' in Abbéville (October).

'Rest' consisted of – 8 p.m.–11.30 p.m., a night march on a compass bearing, next day 6.30 a.m.–8 a.m., adjutant's parade, 9.30–10.30, close-order drill, 10. 30 walking out to brigade bayonet course, 11–2.30 p.m., bayonet fighting and returning, 3.30–5, assisting at pay parade, 7.30–9.30, walk to Brigade HQ for lecture on tanks and back again (the lecturer tended to say that tanks were useless).

It was raining nearly all the time so there was an attempt to cheer up everybody with a concert. There was no piano but lots of speeches from the officers. However, there was a barrel of beer and lots of fags.

A mother wrote to the C.O. pleading that following the death of two of her sons on the Somme could her remaining son be given less dangerous duties. They returned to more water-filled trenches near Lesboeufs (Map 2). Sliding mud threatened to invade dug-outs. They needed more sandbags, and there was a trek in knee-deep mud to get them in pitch darkness: they became lost for hours. Getting back, hungry and exhausted, they then had to fill the bags with oozing mud. But throughout it all, praised 2nd Lieutenant Plowman, Corporal Jackson was marvellous.

The downpour in November was almost ceaseless: it took half an hour to move 50 yards in the Le Transloy line (north-east of Albert – Map 2). Plowman's Company now had 52 men fit out of the 200 a month before. The mother's third son was blown to pieces.

Mark went on a sniping course in Amiens and on his return was given temporary command of his Company. Despite his reservations about what he was doing he was pleased it was done to the satisfaction of his superior officers. There were courses in December – care of horses (he had never been on one) and 'general'. He would have preferred some leave: when the C.O. was short of officers to send on courses he tended to select those due for some leave.

In January, 1917 Mark plucked a still-warm shell out of the mud and it exploded in his arms. When he recovered consciousness (they thought he was dead) he found it difficult to remember anything. He was sent to a special hospital in Craiglockhart for shell-shock cases (Wilfred Owen and Siegfried Sassoon also went there but Plowman did not meet them).

A year later he asked to be relieved of his commission on the grounds of religious objection to all war. He was then arrested and tried at a court martial (April, 1918) for not returning to his battalion. He was dismissed from the Army but not otherwise punished. On June 29 he received a call-up as a conscript but successfully appealed against this, again because of conscientious objection to war.

QUIGLEY, HUGH
Paschendaele and the Somme
A Diary of 1917
The Naval & Military Press, 2009

When he wrote a preface to this work in 1918 Hugh described the entries as 'letters' but in 1928 when they were published he refers to them as a diary. As he wrote them during 1917 he sent them home obviously to be used in a later publication. He pointed out in 1928 that he had not changed the wording of any of the entries or letters but used them some of them in a different sequence in order to create a better narrative.

This work is a prolonged venture into prose-poetry and only towards the end (when he was wounded in the Ypres Salient) does it conform to the more normal account. It is exquisitely literate, rather effete as the author is very conscious of the effect of his words. He clearly wanted to create a new way of viewing being in the midst of a terrible conflict. But when he was in serious trouble in the Salient the account began to take on a more prosaic tone.

He was in France with the 12th Battalion of the Royal Scots Regiment on June 22, 1917. His mood was up and down, like a ploughed field ('like Laocoon in the toils' – the text is full of literary, classical and artistic allusions). The country had dreary, poverty-stricken villages. 'Machonochie does improve with intimacy'.

They went to billets near Arras (Map 1). Parkson was witty and optimistic company. Flynn could easily ingratiate himself with the peasantry because he made them laugh with pidgin French. Many of these poor people were utterly sick of war, and there was a 'dim kind of socialistic unrest'. Hugh wrote about the state of French life, society and economy (he could speak fluent French).

He saw much beauty in this countryside, however, especially at night under moonlight. But they found the Somme landscape very different despite 'Nature beginning to cover up her wounds' (Bertincourt, August 3 – south-east of Arras – Map 1). Bapaume (Map 2) was a 'gaping wreck'.

They took over quiet trenches at Royalcourt (August 15). During the day there was just a few whistling shells but at night it was silent and still: even the movement of troops could not be detected because of a maze of sunken roads and communication trenches in this flat country.

He took an interest in insect life in the trench – beetles, glow-worms, caterpillars, earwigs and huge spiders. There were also swarms of green flies and bluebottles. Grasshoppers stayed up on the parapet, and beyond it the crickets rattled.

He looked forward to reading the 'Literary Supplement'. 'Stand to' was a good idea because it enabled him to watch the beautiful dawns. On August 19 he was beneath a serious bombardment for the first time (Havrincourt-Arras sector) – mainly minenwerfers and whizz-bangs (faster than sound so the bang of the gun coincided with the explosion). They did not hit anything worth hitting.

Then it intensified and a great billowing wave of fumes swept over Cambrai (Map 1) – gas shells, trench mortars, 'flying pigs', minenwerfers, G2s, 18 pounders, whizz-bangs, machine gun fire came crashing over in a rising crescendo of noise converting into a general humming.

Back in the billets a singing Highlander performed – clan-songs and pibrochs – delicious melodies. He could also tell them Highland folk stories. Hugh saw his own sort of beauty in the battle zone – a succession of word pictures. 'The night was a lyric in itself'.

He found the diary of a German soldier in an orchard in Velu (August 24 – south-east of Béthune – Maps 1 & 4). This man was or had been a loving son and a fine husband, just married. Addresses and names were included and Hugh included them in his book.

The entry for August 27 looked just like a letter. It opened, 'I am inclined to think you are causing yourself too much discomfort about me'. There was no use for him to keep saying he was 'in the pink'.

He was beating the lice and the flu (September 2). The French were starting to plough over the Somme devastation, which had been made worse during the German planned retreat to the Hindenburg Line. They even drilled holes in the trees, placed explosives inside and blew them up.

Indigestion became a problem for the battalion after the discovery of masses of crab apples (September 8 at Courcelles-le-Comte – Maps 2 & 3). Washing was done with green water in shell holes, washing up with wet grass, and razors were sharpened on rifle slings.

The colonel announced several weeks of training – bombing, assault formation etc. He tried to improve motivation by reminding them of the past successes of the regiment and the way Germans treated prisoners. He reckoned they had the Germans by 'the short hairs'. Hugh was impressed – 'this was the real thing at last' (was he being ironic?).

They moved north to Vlamertinghe (September 17 – Map 4). Flanders resembled a 'sewage heap' and was very difficult to traverse. Whilst struggling across this with a working party they were spotted by enemy artillery and were very lucky to escape unscathed. But the worst moment came when shelled whilst sheltering in an ex-charnel house which had been converted into a strongpoint. The stench of the bones was overpowering and Hugh was terrified as the shells crashed around them. It went beyond fear, beyond conscience, a grovelling of the soul itself.

The very next day a shell fell amongst the battalion killing or wounding 60. The cries of dying men would live for a long time in his ears. The survivors struggled to find their way as the shattered terrain bore no resemblance to maps. An artillery officer mis-directed them and they stole food and drink from his dug-out.

At Winizeele, on September 25, the British artillery was out-gunning the German guns. There was growing belief that the enemy was on the down-grade and suffering the hell he had promised the Allies. Anyway, according to Hugh, the way to survive was to get the maximum enjoyment from the smallest detail. On the canal bank at Ypres (October 6) this was not easy. He remained in great danger.

Thus he was in hospital on October at Le Treport with a 'comfortable wound'. He wrote (to someone) that he would be in England in two days. He provided a detailed description of the action which led to his wound. Four RAMC stretcher-bearers carried him for 10 kilometres over this shredded landscape. The 'diary' takes on a familiar look.

He concluded by condemning war as a desecration of life and suggested that the 'ruddy generals find a new occupation other than that of spreading an aereole round hell'. The final pages have a moving poem entitled 'A Death in Hospital'.

READ, 'DICK'
Of Those We Loved
I. L. Read
Pentland Press, 1994

The first page of 'Dick's' book announced 'A Narrative 1914–1919, remembered and illustrated by I. L. Read, sometime No. 12819, Sergeant, 17th Leicestershire Regiment, and later Lieutenant, 35th the Royal Sussex regiment, for my grandchildren'.

Dick's book is clearly written (occasionally with profound historical insights) and with a most delightful and evocative collection of line and wash sketches. 'Of those We Loved' is a memoir – Dick 'delved into the long ago – already I have forgotten much'. Indeed, the fear of forgetting more drove him on to set it all down as soon as he could.

Private Read actually began his service in the 8/Leicesters as a machine gunner. He arrived in the front line at Wulverghem in July 1915. In September they went south by train to France. The account then is of special interest because of the highly detailed (and beautifully illustrated) account of the splendid hospitality of the local French people at Berles-au-Bois (south-west of Arras – Map 1), especially Dick's beloved 'Tante', given generously despite the proximity of the front line.

In October 1915 Dick was hit on the thigh by a grenade splinter and was out of action for two months in hospital in Rouen. On his return to Berles-au-Bois the periods of rest continued to be a joy because of good times in the estaminet ran by the sisters Emilienne and 'Skinny Liz'.

The coming of Christmas 1915 evoked strong emotions in the pleasures of this domestic environment. Indeed, there was an attempt at another Christmas 'Truce', but scotched quickly by the officers. On Christmas Eve Dick was at the wrong sort of 'party', out in the Arras no man's land on his stomach in the thick mud repairing barbed wire defences.

SUPPER WITH THE FAMILY IN OUR BILLET. XMAS EVE 1916. AUCHEL, P. de CALAIS.

Billet, Xmas Eve, 1916 (drawing by Les Read)

(drawing by Les Read)

The first big event of 1916 was the acquisition of Dick's first tin hat, its main use being to keep out the bitter snow and winds. But the Christmas spirit stayed with them as the main collective thought was that this war could not last for ever. But fear re-surfaced: how long would it take?

By April the Leicesters were in the Somme battle zone. They took part in the assault on Bazentin Ridge from Mametz Wood (Maps 2 & 3) on July 14, suffering heavy casualties, especially amongst the officers. Dick lost several close friends. Could it possibly get worse?

Later in July the Leicesters moved to the Arras sector (Map 1) but they were back on the Somme in the middle of September, near Delville Wood (Map 3). In the Battle of Gueudecourt (Maps 2 & 3) Dick and his fellow machine gunners were stranded out in no man's land in a shell hole and expected to be taken prisoners. But still they fought on vigorously, delivering withering fire at the surrounding Germans, killing dozens of them. Shrapnel hit Dick in the back but a nice bulky haversack saved him, and the Germans withdrew and they had saved themselves.

They were retired to Vermelles (south-east of Béthune – Maps 1 & 4) on October 2. Dick was now a sergeant and he was also invited to apply for a commission. He had leave in Eastbourne (where he had been educated at the grammar school) and returned to more great friendship from the local French at Christmas 1916 – superbly illustrated by Dick's detailed sketches.

The New Year, 1917, was seen in by severe snow storms, ice and cold gales of the Flemish winter. Dick's description of the horrors of trying to wash and shave in these conditions is truly chilling.

The Ypres Salient had been reinforced in case the Germans tried yet once more to breach it as the weather improved.

As his regiment fought at Arras in April 1917 Dick was plucked away for officer training in England. He returned to the continent as a 2nd Lieutenant in the Royal Sussex Regiment in March 1918 but went straight through France by train to Tarranto in southern Italy, and then later to Egypt.

He came back to France with the 4/ Sussex in time for a new Battle of the Marne as the enemy was driven back in July and August 1918. The battalion went on to become part of the drive east beyond the former Ypres Salient, reaching Courtrois by November.

REID, ERNEST (1897–1917)
Arras, 1917
The Journey to Railway Triangle
Walter Reid
Birlinn, 2005

This memoir dedicated to Captain Thomas Ernest Reid of the 9th Battalion of the Black Watch was written by his nephew. There was no diary to consult and a suitcase of letters had disappeared. Walter built up his uncle's story from a long narrative written by Captain Reid's servant, a letter from his C.O., and a scrapbook of cuttings which Walter managed to save.

Walter Reid traced the history of his family, a highly-educated lineage of Paisley – hard-working, religious people. Ernest entered Glasgow University to study law in 1914 but managed only one session before the war claimed him. From a population only a tenth of Englands' Scotland produced a seventh of the British Army. 'The glamour of the kilt is irresistible', wrote an officer at the time. Patriotism and a sense of duty was strong north of the border.

Ernest joined the OTC at university and subsequently joined the 3rd Battalion of the Black Watch in 1915 and was at the depot at Nigg for nearly a year, being commissioned during this period. This was a Kitchener Second New Army Battalion (the Second was reckoned to be better than the First New Army because of the length and rigour of the training). It reached France a year after the war had started.

Its first real blooding was at the Battle of Loos (Lens sector – Map 1), where it was tested to the limit in an assault over open ground. Despite a successful advance the losses were terrible – 701 officers and men out of 940, worse than the Somme or Arras.

In the first half of 1916 the 9th Battalions was in and out of the front line. On July 23 2nd Lieutenant T. E. Reid reported for duty. He arrived with 2nd Lieutenant D.W. Cuthbert (he became Ernest's best friend according to a letter written by the C.O.). Lieutenant Cuthbert was fatally wounded on the same day as Ernest.

The battalion was in reserve at Martinpuich (Maps 2 & 3) on the Somme at this time, in open country vulnerable to the enemy artillery. It was heavily involved at the front on August 17 and lost 157, and it fought as hard at High Wood (Map 3) in September.

They returned to Martinpuich on September 17 fighting in badly damaged trenches on ground turned to a quagmire by heavy rain. In a letter to Walter's father on October 28 Ernest wrote that he was thinking of joining the RFC, where the casualty rate was worse than the infantry's.

Because ground conditions were so bad the C.O. decided Battalions should stay only two days in the line but this entailed a lot of work and marching (and thus sickness). Ernest was in Scotland for the last time in January 1917.

He left the Somme for Arras (Map 1) in February, arriving at Buneville on the 18th. At that time he was the battalion Adjutant but he became a company commander in March with the rank of Acting Captain.

The 9th Battalion took a direct part in the campaign against Vimy Ridge and Monchy (Arras – Map 1) on April 9. The objective was to capture the Third (Brown) Line of enemy defences. They advanced over ground soaked by rain (it later turned to snow) at 5.30 a.m.

Private Alexander Black, Ernest's servant, recorded that his Captain led the way from the trenches. 2nd Lieutenant Cuthbert was killed almost instantly. The plan was to keep just behind a creeping barrage, walking at 50 yards a minute. It worked well on this occasion, clearing the way for the infantry. Ernest did get a slight wound in the leg but Private Black dressed it and Ernest was able to continue.

Ernest walked along a railway track and reached the first line of German defences ('Black Line'). They had to secure and consolidate in this area – a position which included Fred's Wood. Ernest was locating snipers, putting his machine gunners in position and letting HQ know that the first objective had been attained (it was in sight of Monchy). Indeed, the 'First Wave' was behind the Second, which had been hampered by the shell craters.

Ernest Reid, 1897-1917.

They resumed their advance at 7.10 a.m., aiming at the 'Blue Line' of defence ('Railway Triangle'). But they met stiff resistance and Ernest was shot in the leg and an artery was punctured. Private Black bound this, using a shilling to twist a tourniquet (and making beef tea to lessen the trauma). Meanwhile, the Blue Line had been captured and the Black Watch was relieved. For his conduct under fire (he carried his officer through a hail of bullets) Private Black was awarded the Distinguished Conduct Medal.

Ernest was taken to casualty clearing stations, first to Arras and later further west to Duisans. He had an operation on April 12 and was then taken by train to hospital in Le Touquet, a very painful journey. They discovered there that his leg bone was smashed. On April 13 the artery was re-tied under chloroform.

His parents received War Office telegrams and they flew to Le Touquet, arriving on April 14. Ernest made light of his wound but it had been infected before reaching the CCS and this was before the days of antibiotics. He died on April 18.

REITH, JOHN (1889–1971)
Wearing Spurs
Hutchinson & Co., 1966

Lord Reith maintained a war diary during his service in France in 1914 and 1915, and based this memoir (written in the 1930s) on it. At the outbreak of war he was a lieutenant in a Territorial Battalion – the 5th Scottish Rifles.

They arrived in France early in November, 1914 with Lieutenant Reith as its transport officer. They were in the Armentières sector (Map 1). No offensive seemed likely here but both sets of artillery were active. The battalion took over trenches in front of Houplines from December 11. Shelling got worse and Armentières came under more intense fire (before the Scottish Rifles went up to the line two of them were killed in the town on the 8th and 9th). Reith had to worry about moving the horses and wagons to a safer spot.

The Lieutenant was having a haircut in the town on the 17th when shells started falling outside the shop and the barber disappeared rapidly down to the cellar with Reith's hair half cut. He refused to return and the Lieutenant got a free half haircut.

He took his job as transport officer very seriously and in the New Year set about improving the quality of the horses and the wagons. For the latter he needed vehicles designed for military purposes. He also foraged around for better fodder. He worked very closely with Army Service Corps personnel, able to give him expert advice.

For a while he was the brigade's transport officer and also made improvements here, such as getting supplies of better barbed wire brought up to the trenches along with steel loophole plates for snipers, very handy in these breastwork trenches. He did more than his fair share of trench duty whereas the C.O. and the Adjutant never came near the trenches.

He was a teetotaller, which had the disadvantage that he had to drink a lot of water, some of which was of dubious quality. This caused him to have diarrhoea: castor oil and Number 9 pills brought no relief. More pain was delivered by the Adjutant, who did not like the outspoken young lieutenant. Reith stood up for himself and the transport needs of the battalion (he had reverted to battalion transport officer).

"You've no right to talk to me like that and accuse me of not being on the job in the middle of a battle," he said (on January 4, 1916) when he had been as efficient as ever under enemy shelling, retaliation for British artillery activity between Ploegsteert and La Bassée (Map 4).

Lord Reith's account is a highly personal one – about relationships with senior officers, fellow subalterns and other ranks, and about family (especially his parents) and friends. He wrote home nearly every day (sometimes 16-page letters) and conducted a voluminous correspondence with others. On Easter Saturday 1915 he received 7 letters and 3 parcels.

Lieutenant Reith was highly enterprising; for instance, he was not satisfied with his horse and went off in search of a much better one. It was something of a triumph to return with a beast which had been earmarked for a Brass Hat. He named it 'Sailaway'. He kept above the quota of horses for the battalion, hiding the surplus ones during inspections. He 'thoroughly enjoyed the war'.

Eventually, the Adjutant took him away from his job as transport officer, sending him to a different company for more ordinary trench duties. He missed the horses but there was 'at least a chance of something happening'.

He obviously became devil-may-care in the trenches, walking about without stooping when sniper's bullets were hitting the parapet etc. He was apparently fearless.

He began to investigate the possibility of transferring to the Royal Engineers (he had envisaged an engineering career in civvy street).

He watched as his C.O. ran away from shelling (May 1). There was now the prospect of the Germans using gas and 'primitive' respirators were issued. Lieutenant Reith was keen to get patrols going right up to the German trenches to try and find out what they were up to. He crawled up alone through the enemy barbed wire, almost up to their parapet in order to investigate.

On May 9 he had a high temperature but still attended an interview with the local RE commander. There was a bureaucratic delay at the War Office which held up his application for a transfer. Meanwhile, the Armentières front was becoming distinctly unhealthy. On June 16 he was showered by earth and sand as a shell fell a few yards away.

One day he goaded the hated Adjutant to crawl up a sap trench towards the German line whilst he walked in bravado up on top in full view of the snipers. He did not like his new company commander either.

Reith wanted to write up his diary every night. Sometimes this was obviously difficult but even if it was only a few notes he did it. He sent it home with trusted comrades by 'instalments' for safekeeping. One day in July it was sent by mistake by ordinary post, and he was in danger of being in trouble for keeping a diary but he heard no more about it.

German snipers were lethal – 2 or 3 men a night were lost in this way in these Bois Grenoir (Map 4) breastworks. The battalion left for Steenwerck (Map 4) on July 18 but Reith became quite ill and was in a casualty clearing station until the end of the month and was then sent home. By the time he returned to France in September he was a sapper. But this lasted only 3 weeks before he was badly wounded in the face and back in a London hospital. He never returned to France during the war.

RICHARDS, FRANK
Old Soldiers Never Die
Anthony Mott Limited, 1983

Frank ('Dick') Richards had been in the Royal Welch Fusiliers for 13 years when the war started. By August 10 he was in Rouen with the 2nd Battalion. Here, a formidable old comrade, Billy, ordered wine in a mixture of English, Hindustani and Chinese (like Dick he had served overseas) and when he failed to make himself understood he reckoned that all foreigners needed a good hiding.

Dick's account of his war was first published by Faber & Faber in 1933. He probably wrote it some years after the war but he could remember his part in it in detail, with some precise dates. He wrote well – to the credit of a Welsh elementary education.

Dick was part of the wild retreat from Mons and the fight back on the Marne and the Aisne and was already in a trench (at Fromelles – Map 4) in October ('little did we think… we were building our future homes'). They had one strand of barbed wire in front of them.

His company commander sought to maintain control by threatening his men with his revolver, and thus became known as 'Buffalo Bill'. The Germans were still hoping to advance and the Fusiliers had to beat off raids. By the time they got back in reserve on November 15 they 'were lousy as rooks'. Their next experience of a trench was knee-deep in water at Houplines (in front of Armentières – Map 1). The survivors of the 'Old Contemptibles' were learning the art of trench warfare. 'During the whole of the 1914-15 Winter we endured enough of physical hardship… but we suffered most in our morale'.

The Fusiliers had a Christmas truce with the friendly Saxons opposite them despite Buffalo Bill's attempts to stop it (he finished up with a barrel of beer from them). Dick exchanged his lousy pants for a pair of lady's bloomers giving the lice even more room to breed and inviting ribald comments at bath time.

They were at Bois Grenoir (Map 4) in January 1915. All trenches in this zone were by now in a decrepit state and most of their hard work was reserved for trying to repair and strengthen them. They had to build communication trenches, until they did approaching and leaving the line was hazardous. In February they got periscopes; previously looking over the parapet had been very dangerous. Buffalo Bill now threatened his company that he would stick men on the barbed wire if they stepped out of line. He also had the idea of using a dog cart to bring up supplies. But 'Dog' was uselessly crazy and the cart was destroyed by a direct hit. The company became very fond of 'Dog' as a pet and it stayed with them until killed later in the war.

The 2nd Battalion moved to Laventie (Map 4) in July, where the trenches were even worse (only breast-high in places). Dick became a signaller amongst the Cuinchy brickworks (Map 4). German shelling by now had become distinctly unpleasant ('hate'). The shells were getting bigger and more explosive. Trying to mend telephone wires in the face of this onslaught was precarious. Very often all wires were out of action and signallers (or 'runners') had to dash back through the barrage to deliver messages by hand.

They were at Cambrin (south-west of Cuinchy – Map 4) when the Battle of Loos came late in September. With a second wave of infantry Dick found it difficult to move forward over the dead and dying of the first wave whilst clouds of poison gas floated by. Daily 'stunts' from September 23 to 26 were all miserable failures and the one for the 27th was abandoned.

The battalion stayed in this sector through to 1916. On February 4 Dick was part of a raiding party which captured a very large crater (it became known as the 'R.W.F. Crater') only 60 yards from the Germans. He won the DCM for his bravery in this action. But there were 60 casualties.

A back area genius had invented the 'Bangalore Torpedo'. This would be placed on the enemy wire and when detonated was intended to destroy large sections of it. It was dangerous enough for volunteers to get it across no man's land and on to the wire but when it failed to explode they had to go out again and rescue it in order to prevent the Germans from learning its secrets. They found it much lighter: the Germans had taken out its innards and put it back on the wire.

The Western Front was stagnant, officers were ordered to be more 'offensive' and a 'Great Push' was planned. So Dick found himself in Mametz Wood (Maps 2 & 3) on July 15 under intense and prolonged shelling from High Wood (Map 3). One of his old comrades was badly wounded. In the attack on High Wood Dick was one of the signalling group on a prominent position to observe the battle and report back. However, they were also in full view from enemy positions. Trying to signal by heliograph or flags became impossible and they had to run back with messages. They were rewarded with dead men's parcels.

By now only 50 men out of 200 of the original BEF Battalion remained (the casualty rates in 1917 and 1918 were even worse – surviving the whole war as Dick did was quite miraculous).

In August he went into High Wood, still under severe German shelling. They had a spell near Arras (Map 1) but were back on the Somme in September at Lesboefs (Map 2), and Le Transloy (in October – north-east of Albert – Map 2) as they tried to drive towards Bapaume (Map 2). But as hope of a breakthrough faded rain and cold set in they were in the Crombles (south of Bapaume) swamps. The next major offensive was going to be in front of Arras and the 2nd Battalion moved up for it in March, 1917.

It was at Basseux as part of the attempted and abortive attacks on the massive Hindenburg Line that an officer of the battalion distinguished himself – it was Siegfried Sassoon. Such assaults became more and more costly, and the battalion lost half its strength over the Whitsun of 1917. The casualties amongst signallers were particularly heavy because all messages had to be taken by runners. The hero of this weekend was the MO, Dr. Dunn, out in no man's land tending to the wounded (see also Dr. Dunn's 'The Infantry I Knew').

Up at Polygon Wood in the Third Battle of Ypres the brave MO armed himself when many senior officers were killed and someone had to lead the men. Dick needed medical aid in hospital for five weeks (his leg kept bruising up). Even when he went back to Ypres late in 1917 the leg was still very painful but he chose not to report it.

And he continued to fight in 1918, in the Albert sector (Map 2) against the German offensive. He was in reserve by the time the Allies were on the attack but he was there towards the end, advancing ten miles in a day to Le Cateau – where he had started the war.

ROGERSON, SIDNEY (born 1894)
Twelve Days on the Somme
A Memoir of the Trench 1916
Frontline Books, 2009

Lieutenant Sidney Rogerson was part of a draft of reinforcements sent to the Somme battlefield at the end of July 1916 to replace the losses suffered by the 2nd Battalion of the West Yorkshire Regiment. He had been commissioned in August 1914 after a degree course at Cambridge.

This memoir was first published in 1933. As it was based on just 12 days the day-to-day details are intense but there is no indication that he kept a diary. Perhaps after 17 years the memories were still vividly in his mind.

The memoir begins on November 7 with Sidney near Fricourt (Map 3) in charge of B Company; under his charge there were two subalterns who had been on the Western Front since 1914. One was 'Mac', who possessed 'astonishing personal courage' and a cynical sense of humour. He also hated drilling men.

Although the battle had lasted 4 months it still offered 'nerve-wracking strains' from shelling and raiding and 'an air of putrefaction'. On the 7th they were warned that they had go to the front line on the 10th, opposite Le Transloy (north-east of Albert – Map 2).

They moved on the 8th in torrential rain, still exuding cheerfulness and companionship. But some Brass Hat had screwed up and when they arrived at the camp behind the line it still had its previous occupants, who pointed out they had another hour to go before they had to go and refused to budge, emphasising that 'orders is orders'. At a much inferior site the West Yorkshires enthusiastically set about making it more comfortable with gusto – although tired and soaked to the skin.

On November 9/10th they stumbled through the thick mud of

a sunken road to the left of Lesboeufs Wood (Map 2). The men they were relieving tried to show them what to do. But this position was 'precarious'; the Germans could easily have overpowered them if they really stirred themselves in the rain and thick mud (apparently they were in an even worse state, sheltering and suffering in shell craters). Brass Hats didn't have a clue about situations in these wastelands (it was like 'Earth before the appearance of life'). Trying to move around was hell, especially at night.

But under Sidney's energetic direction they set about improving their defences, enlivened by eccentrics such as 'Buggy' (mad) Robinson, expert fire-lighter, scrounger and souvenir-hunter. There was not a lot to eat apart from bully beef and a little water for drinking – not enough for washing. Tea tasted of petrol (it was brewed in ex-petrol cans). Sidney preferred rum.

The artillery fired at the Germans with the result they fired back just after Sidney, having worked all night, had fallen asleep. Unfortunately for Buggy he was out scrounging at that time. A gunner came over to see if they had any Very lights. There was some abandoned German lights in the trench and they let them off. Incredibly, they must have represented a signal to cease firing, which the Germans obligingly did.

Rogerson wrote '… we were comrades, brothers, dwelling together in unity… pals… filial devotion (demonstrated in letters home from 'tough, drunken characters)'. They were kind to French children, dogs and German wounded and prisoners.

The war stopped for breakfast – bacon and 'gunfire tea' – ah! Buggy rigged up a stove from a whale-oil tin. Their primitive trench was now looking almost homely. A ration party brought up letters and parcels. Sidney was blessed with the ability to make them all laugh, describing German shells as 'flying commodes'. But they were all pretty disinterested in praise from the Brass Hats.

On the night of the 13th he spent the night as usual keeping the men at work and cheerful. A few hundred yards to the north the Battle of Beaumont Hamel (Map 3) was about to start and Sidney's Company were warned of a 'Chinese attack' (false) barrage before the big assault. This duly passed over their heads but the Germans could not be bothered to fire back. Heavy mist now protected the battalion and the rain had stopped.

They were now relieved by the Worcesters, and Sidney, making his way to report to HQ, lost his way in the pitch blackness (exploding shells gave off surprisingly little light). He had slept for 6 hours in 3 days. He stumbled fortuitously on to the right path. From here he had to lead the company to another camp miles away but in the end they all collapsed with fatigue. Forcing them on they found the camp just a few yards further on.

The officers of the battalion all now cheerfully gathered for a whisky and soda with the C.O. (see James Jack). Sidney had grown an enormous beard. The big topic of conversation was the complete disappearance of one officer. Was he a German spy? The men worked hard all day to clean up (when they passed a Guards Regiment the next day they didn't look bad in comparison – Colonel Jack was very proud of them).

They now had to return to the back camp (Citadel Camp) several more miles away. Packing up a whole battalion was a massive job (November 15). So the stew for dinner tasted very good. Sidney found that dishing out the rum himself meant that the men were very cheerful as he was doing it, and it provided a marvellous opportunity to converse with them as individuals.

At Citadel Camp 'rest' resulted in some officers and men having to go back into the danger zone and work all day (November 16). The remainder had a bath – no benches nor chairs! It was becoming extremely cold.

Next day at 5 a.m. they got orders to move, where to they did not know. Sidney had a day in Amiens (Map 2). New regulations were received from the Divisional Commander adding even more to the chores of the P.B.I.

They marched to the rail station in heavy rain. The train was 4 hours late but they used the time productively, scrounging about the area for food and equipment. Buggy got a fire going in the pouring rain, to the wonder of the whole Battalion, but only his Company were invited to use it.

They rumbled on all night and disembarked at 'Oisemont'. Where the hell was that? But – wonder of wonders – there was GRASS!

SAMBROOK, ARTHUR (born 1897)
With the Rank and Pay of a Sapper
The 216th (Nuneaton) Army Troops Company
James Sambrook
Paddy Griffiths Associates, 1998

Army Troops Companies of the Royal Engineers were composed of skilled tradesmen expected to perform specialist engineering tasks. But until the growth of Labour Companies they also had to complete much menial work, such as digging trenches. The Army Troops Companies were raised under a Lord Kitchener scheme of early 1915–48 of them eventually. To provide for a war which became one gigantic siege operation this type of soldier became more and more crucial to the drive for victory.

Professor James Sambrook, an editor and biographer of 18th and 19th Centuries literary figures, has produced this account from his father's own writing (and excellent little sketches) completed in the 1970s (written for his grandson), and that of a comrade, Arthur Dolman, plus a war diary of 1915–1919 kept by another comrade, Frank Hextall. Professor Sambrook was also able to gain access to other accounts and letters written by other men who served in the 216th Company.

After extensive training the 216th arrived in Havre on January 28, 1916. They began work in the area of Mazingarbe (south-east of Béthune – Maps 1 & 4) about 3 miles behind the front line (which did not prevent them from becoming lousy), establishing reserve trenches and extra strong points.

They were always in danger from enemy shelling and one of their billets – a barn, was hit on February 6, killing 5 sappers and wounding 21 others. Sometimes the company split into sections according to work demands. In February one group went to Minz near Béthune whilst another travelled to Havre for a course on heavy steel girder bridging. In March more reserve trenches were prepared at Bouvigny (west of Lens – Map 1). They also improved their skills at shooting or clubbing rats. Professor Sambrook admitted that 'my father's recollections are more of food and drink than of fighting'.

The next big job was to improve the defences on Vimy Ridge (May – Map 1). German shelling became heavier, including the use of tear gas. 'Pretty hot show: rotten place to go… seven days working all day and until 3 a.m: got fairly done up,' remembered Frank Hextall.

Half of the company went to Ribemont on the Somme (south-east of Albert – Map 2) in June to join the preparations for the coming battle – a variety of tasks on defensive features and others such as howitzer pits. The rest of the company was at Corbie (Map 2) providing water supplies for a casualty clearing station.

Most of the 216th were sent to the Ypres Salient in July to provide a fresh water supply, developing the large reservoir at Dickebusch (Map 4). There was an increasing demand for specialist skills but much of the work remained menial, such as filling thousands of sandbags.

They went on to construct a reservoir on Kemmel Hill (Map 4), also developing a taste for riotous evenings in estaminets. They liked a drink. A few of them were still down on the Somme engaged on minor building work, such as carpentry, plumbing, decorating etc.

Later in the summer nearly all the company were near the Nieppe Forest at Clairmorais (north-east of St Omer). They now had 'Berna' lorries for transport but they still relied much on mules. Skilled German POWs helped with the work. Near Hazebrouck (Map 1) in October the company built a bridge over a waterway as well as building railheads for ammunition dumps – not popular with the local populace (along with the lively off-duty life styles of the sappers). They were there for months until January, 1917, when they moved to Reminghelst (Map 4) near Ypres.

Here they were extending a reservoir, contending with months of icy conditions. As summer approached they supported the preparations for the assault on Messines Ridge (Map 4), putting down 'corduroy tracks' at night (and camouflaging them before dawn), water pipes and taped lines to guide back wounded troops. The sappers continued to get casualties, for instance, one killed and another wounded on June 5. 216 had to move the water supply forward as the advance at Messines proceeded.

They switched to the Ypres sector in September for the coming battle there, building dams, sluice gates, pump lines, fencing, pipes and water tanks. The German artillery continued to register their positions as they became increasingly adept at targeting logistical operations. Trying to work at night was hindered by the thick mud, also by frost and ice as the weather grew colder.

In January 1918, the company was sent down to Peronne (Map 2) to work on bridges. After a short spell back north they were on the Somme as the Germans attacked in March. New and repaired bridges had to be blown up by other engineers so that the enemy could not use them. Both Arthur Sambrook and Arthur Daulman were wounded in the arm, and others lost their lives or were seriously wounded by shrapnel and even the stray bullet in the wild retreat. Luckily, they were able to get to safer work near Arras (Map 1) in April. By now the Army Troop Companies were beginning to get the support they needed from the evolving Labour Corps. My own father was in a Labour Company (see 'Weeks, George') and worked with engineers in Flanders. This is where 216 was in April, 1918 now working almost exclusively on bridges and under less danger from enemy action. They were back on the Somme in August for bridge construction as the supply of steel girders increased. This kept them going up to the Armistice.

SHEERWOOD, ELMER W. (1896–1979)
A Soldier in World War 1
The Diary of Elmer W. Sheerwood
Edited by Robert H. Ferrell
Indiana Historical Society Press, 2004

Elmer was from Indiana and served in the 1st Indiana Regiment of Field Artillery (later Battery D, 150th Field Artillery). This was part of the 42nd ('Rainbow') Division. He enlisted in April 1917 and kept a diary which he subsequently lost. But in 1919 he wrote a book entitled 'Rainbow Hoosier', a narrative covering the period of the lost diary (April 1917 to February 1918).

He sent home a shipboard diary of his journey over to France (October 18–30, 1917) and this was published in his home-town newspaper 'The Linton Citizen' and used in this current volume.

When the battery moved from training in Brittany (at Coetquidan, an old French artillery school) to the front line in Lorraine he began a new daily diary, also published in its original form in the 2004 book. This ran from February 21, 1918 to the end of the war and beyond. They got new guns and learnt how to fire them (and how to use their gas masks). At Christmas there was a box of candy for each man from the Rainbow Cheer Association of Indiana – plus a very good dinner, of course. 'Chow,' wrote Elmer, 'is a soldier's obsession'. But as the 1918 campaign developed they seemed to get less and less (as supply lines lengthened). In Brittany they got on very well with the 'congenial' French.

In Lorraine they were near the front line at Luneville in the Vosges where they had to dig hard to construct dug-outs, ammunition and gun pits. General Pershing visited on March 12. On March 15 they began firing at Vailly. Elmer was part of artillery observing, getting telephone information from an observer plane sending information to to him at

'Radio' (HQ). Elmer was obviously very skilled in installing phones and signalling wires.

Because Elmer's diary is really daily most of the entries are short – just a few lines, but altogether presents a mass of information about how the American artillery operated in the 1918 campaign. Now and again he was able to put in a longer entry.

On March 17 they suffered their first casualties as a German shell hit one of their guns and three fellow gunners were seriously wounded. Horses arrived – just nine of them at first. Elmer got a small one but he loved it and called it 'Rabbits'. Gunners had to spend a lot of time looking after their horses. An artillery battery depended completely on these animals to transport everything.

The German offensives starting on March 21 were delivered a to the north of Lorraine and the 42nd Division. But Elmer and the boys kept in touch on the phone as the situation in early April seemed to be very serious. But the arrival of a lot more horses cheered up the battery.

In Lorraine the battle hotted up in May as the 42nd Division prepared to make its own move forward. Elmer's guns fired ten shells to every German one. He got very busy – one word only for the June 7 entry – 'Inspection'. His main task once more was to observe the effect of their shelling from information received by telephone. But for a while he was the gas NCO because of his university course in Chemistry (until May 28).

Still much of his time was taking up caring for his horse – even when at rest 'Rabbits' had to be in good shape. When the horse of an NCO was out of action he lost his stripes. He wrote that he did not want to go to heaven unless there were horses there.

In July the 42nd Division moved east of Rheims behind two French Divisions. General Pershing had refused to hand over command of the US Expeditionary Force to the French or British and it steadily began to play a major part in a major advance. To the north German offensives were petering out – on July 15 they suffered a serious defeat in the Second Battle of the Marne.

Later in July the 42nd Division moved north to take part in the giant American push, ejecting the remaining Germans from the Marne Salient. The US forces now took over their own large section of front. As the doughboys progressed in front of them the gunners also pressed forward and Elmer described a devastated battlefield strewn with mutilated corpses. He spoke to some 'doughs' – they were winning but thousands of them were being killed or wounded.

The effective part eventually played by the massed American howitzers was in smashing out the dangerous German machine gun nests.

Maintaining communication and observation was a dangerous job for Elmer, often exposed to enemy shelling, and especially operating OPs in the open valley of the River Orgue. But by August the daily advance had reached 3 miles. On August 13 they began rest and The captain read orders telling men to stay in camp, but Elmer and his mates suddenly went deaf. 'Meals are worse than ever' (August 24) so they needed to get out to augment a meagre diet. Even at rest they had to do a lot of hiking (marching) to keep in touch with the front line.

The Germans were easily pushed out of the Mihiel Salient (southeast of Verdun) in September and October. Elmer was back in the thick of the action on September 15. They were firing so much they were getting short of shells (September 21). By then Elmer had fleas, cooties and hives and itched all over at night. Stray German shells could also be lethal. He was digging potatoes out of a field when they targeted him with whizz bangs.

The Meuse – Argonne campaign of October and November was altogether more difficult than St. Mihiel. The battery was north-east of Mont Facon (place names are often omitted because of the fear of censorship). On October 8 they heard about an offer of peace from Berlin but incoming whizz bang 'didn't sound like peace terms'. One of them struck Elmer's tent when he went to get breakfast, killing and wounding some of his comrades (October 8).

So the battery gave the Hun hell for the next few days around Exermont – October 23 – Battery tore up a wood occupied by the Hun'. They fired over a hundred gas shells. But -'October 30 – Last night he gave us hell and I didn't see how any of us are alive…'

Elmer reckoned that the howitzer barrage of November 1 was the biggest ever. They actually fired from in front of their own machine guns, thus creating a mayhem of destruction in the enemy front. Over went the 'doughs' and there was nothing left to stop them. 'November 3 – Doughs are chasing the Hun who ran like rabbits' (Burzany).

SLACK, CECIL
Grandfather's Adventures in the Great War 1914–1918
Cecil Moorhouse Slack
Arthur H.Stockwell, 1977

Cecil Slack kept war diaries and press cuttings and wrote and received hundreds of letters during the war, and later recalled additional details in order to develop this memoir. He said that he had written it for his children and grandchildren. In turn they were keen to add some background historical notes to this narrative.

After service as a private in a Hull Commercial Battalion Cecil obtained a commission in the 1/4th Battalion of the East Yorkshire Regiment (he forgot to inform the Hull battalion of this move and a squad of soldiers turned up at his home to arrest him for desertion!).

The East Yorkshires sailed to France on April 20, 1915, and were greeted in the Ypres Salient 4 days later by enemy tear gas. Another five days and Cecil was in no man's land enduring machine gun fire in a counter-attack following enemy raids. He described his trench as a 'scratch' in the earth. It was no wonder he didn't last long – shot through the scapula and in hospital in London early in May.

He did not return to France until January, 1916. He attended a sniper's course. The Ypres Front was much quieter now but jobs such as setting up barbed wire defences in no man's land still had their dangers, not to mention German shells, mortar bombs and rifle fire (his platoon Sergeant was shot dead standing next to him – late in February).

'I sniped three Huns yesterday', (March 18) but he was hit on the helmet three times on April 4. Thus although the Battle of the Somme had commenced the Salient was still unhealthy (in a letter of June 10, 1917 he remembered 'my little raid' and sticking 'a Boche in the neck with my pocket knife'). Lieutenant Slack led many raids into enemy trenches and for the one on June 26, 1916, he won the Military Cross.

The battalion eventually moved to the Somme. The narrative is largely carried verbatim by letters, which means that place names were not mentioned and also they were not provided in Cecil's 'Postwar Notes'. However, the place name 'Martinpuich' (Maps 2 & 3) was referred to in a letter of September 17 (and in another missive dated June 6, 1917, Cecil did mention that he had re-visited the Somme trench where 'the Boche had pinched my British Warm and field glasses…').

When on the Somme he became a company commander (but he was 'simply awful' with lice, sending for 'Boots Vermin in the trench cream'). He was definitely in High Wood (Map 3) on November 4, when the rain seemed endless and his 'company were standing in mud over their knees for 18 hours with absolutely no shelter'. January 1917 brought the hardest frost ever, according to local people, and the milk froze.

The battalion moved in March – south, apparently because they were with French troops and a letter of March 24 mentions Amiens (Map 2). Around this time he was trying in vain to get into the Royal Flying Corps. Heavy casualties in early April (17 officers) suggest that the East Yorkshires were in the Battle of Arras (Map 1).

Cecil was able to reveal that in July he was at Le Touquet on a Lewis gun course ('as a parasite… trying to make a football pitch out of shell holes'). On the 22nd he was Battalion Assistant Adjutant, Intelligence Officer and Lewis gun officer. But he was still waiting for the investiture for his Military Cross.

Auntie Bertha wrote to Cecil on August 16 '… where are you in all this terrible fighting?' A letter from Cecil to his old school chum, Dora, gives the answer – 'I have been to Arras today'. He was home in Hull in September and obviously very pleased to see Dora (he wrote to her all the time). Whilst he was in England the King pinned the Military Cross on Cecil's chest at Buckingham Palace. Many letters from comrades reveal that Cecil was held in high esteem.

He was in the 49th casualty clearing station in October and November after he injured his knee playing hockey (his brother Bob was also in hospital in Rouen after suffering a serious wound to his ear). When Cecil came out of the CCS it took him three days to find his Battalion.

He was clearly part of the Third Battle of Ypres eventually because he bought Dora a Christmas present in Poperinghe (Maps 1 & 4). But he spent Christmas frozen stiff in a pill box by Passchendaele (Map 4).

In January, 1917 Cecil's pay rose to 12/ 6d. a day, up from 9/ 6d (he was now the adjutant, acting captain on a lieutenant's pay).

On the dramatic events of late March and April, 1918 Cecil used notes directly from his war diaries which he 'wrote later whilst the related events were still vividly in mind'. The battalion retreated with the rest of the Allied armies. The (ostensibly, secret) diary could reveal they were at Vraignes (near Peronne – Map 2) on the Somme. Cecil was in the thick of desperate situations, often separated from his men and almost surrounded by enemy troops. By March 23 two thirds of the officers and half of other ranks were lost. Each day they retreated about ten miles – to Rosieres (March 26), Louvrechy (near Amiens – Map 2 – on the 28th).

They temporarily recovered on March 30, capturing 50 prisoners and 8 or 10 machine guns. But on the 31st the Germans came back again formidably, their heavy artillery blazing away and their planes bombing furiously. The East Yorkshires were driven back almost to Amiens, and they had so many killed or wounded or missing that Cecil was the sole surviving officer and thus senior officer. The whole brigade was just a remnant of its original strength and had to come out of the firing line. Cecil had 'two dents in his helmet and umpteen chat bites' (April 3).

But he was back in action a few days later with some reinforcements on the River Lys by Nouveau – Monde – Map 1). As Sir Douglas Haig issued his 'Backs to the Wall' message Captain Cecil Slack was captured by the enemy.

251

SMITH, AUBREY
Four Years on the Western Front
By A Rifleman
The Naval and Military Press, 2016

This soldier served in the London Rifle Brigade. His narrative memoir is based on letters he wrote home. It was first published in 1922 by Odhams Press. Thus material added to the content of the letters was still very fresh in his mind.

Aubrey reached France on January 25, 1915. He won the Military Medal in August 1917 and a bar to that in November 1918 but he does not mention these awards. He wrote very clearly and with some style. This is a very long book with an amazing amount of detail about the work of the London Rifle Brigade, through which the fortitude and humour of the rifleman and the transport section shine through. Aubrey was a talented young man who could play the piano and who was considered to have officer potential.

He joined the 1st Battalion in Ploegsteert (February and March 1915 – Map 4) with billets in Armentières (Map 1). Here, his French landlady was unable to make roly-poly pudding. The front was quiet but carrying sandbags full of wet mud 150 yards was hard enough not to mention the squashed turnips they had to slide over. The German snipers were an occasional menace. 'Plug Street' Wood reminded him of Pembury Wood in Kent.

He was in hospital in April with poisoned hands. By the time of his return the battalion was busy with sport, concerts etc. But then came the Second Battle of Ypres and the battalion went to the Salient as the BEF struggled to hold back the German onslaught and Aubrey was horrified by the masses of wounded men laying around the battleground. Ypres was engulfed in flames.

They fought around St. Julien, pounded by big enemy guns which easily overwhelmed the depleted Anglo-French artillery. The battalion were in sketchy trenches which tended to get enfiladed by German machine guns and snipers. The battalion suffered 170 casualties between April 22 and 24 and the situation looked desperate and the Salient in serious danger of collapsing.

The German infantry surged forward again on May 2 but the response from the British artillery was better this time. But during these bombardments Aubrey and his pals were terrified by prospects of immediate death or mutilation. Shrapnel wounds were suffered by one in three of his company during this period – 'nine days and nights in hell!' They fell back towards Ypres, resting for a time in Elverdinghe (Map 4). They still thought the Germans would break through but the impetus went out of their onslaught and by May 20 the salient was saved.

The LRB moved to near St Omer and Aubrey had to return to hospital with his sceptic fingers (June). There were diversions when at rest (fatigues on improving defences were still hard) not least a beer-spitting fight between two local French citizens (July 26). Rifleman were liable for any sort of work – there were 'navvies on telephone work and clerks picking up sardine tins off railway lines'. But anything was better than the terror at St. Julien. Aubrey'a mates, Chrisp and Cox. bet each other on anything all day long. 'Bet you five francs…' etc.

Kitchener's 'tough-looking' New Army was now arriving in train loads, cheering up the battered Regulars. Aubrey gave a lovely description of how he scrounged food from a French family by being nice to their little daughter.

He managed to get into the transport section of the battalion at Blendecques (south-east of St Omer) on September 14. He had to train to ride a horse and drive a wagon. The men of this section were mostly 'white collar' – clerks, merchants, solicitors etc.

They moved to near Poperinghe (Maps 1 & 4) in November (this town in 1915 obviously had not not acquired the magic qualities so loved by the troops in later years). Transport had to deliver food, water, fuel,post, ammunition, tools, machine guns and ordnance no matter where the infantry was so this often led the drivers into dangerous territory. His two horses – 'Jack' and 'Tar' – gave him endless grief. Otherwise his main enemies were the mud, the rain and traffic jams. At least, in 1915 and 1916 back areas were not targeted by the German artillery (they were in 1917). But driving through Ypres at night remained risky.

There was an 'excessively convivial' Christmas evening in an estaminet apart from British reactions to a Belgian singer who reached verse 19 in a patriotic Belgian song before being suppressed.

The hard work continued – the transport lines (accommodation, stables etc.) needed improvement and constant cleaning. Pulling these heavy loads with two temperamental horses for several miles in poor conditions was exhausting. They had to help ration parties to unload and load the wagons although the transport men, tending to be older and white-collar, managed to be considered superior to ordinary infantry. For instance, on sick parades the medics would always call them forward first.

In February 1916 the battalion moved to the Somme and at last Aubrey got rid of Jack and Tar, replaced by the more amiable 'Jumbo' and 'Ginger'. Another delight at this time was strolling through Doullens (Map 2) with a pretty, well-dressed young lady 'of the highest class'. This impressed passing soldiers but actually she was only showing him the way to a piano. He also got a cushy job at HQ in St. Pol (March) but it was only for a few weeks.

Aubrey and two pals produced a magazine –'The Old Doings' –which remained very popular in the transport section. Ginger went elsewhere to be replaced by the willing and lovable 'The Grey', who remained with Aubrey until September 1918. At Hally in June preparation for the coming campaign accelerated and a vast dump grew at Hèbuterne (between the Somme and Arras – Map 1). So vital was this that a special track was constructed to it, and Aubrey drove along this countless times.

Aubrey included many snatches of precise conversation in his memoir, and considering he wrote this memoir so soon after the war ended they are probably accurate (he may have written this into his letters, of course). Their 'unnatural lives', like the infantry, were dominated by thoughts of food and drink, repose and safety. 'Going mad with delight over a cracked harmonium in the middle of a wilderness' was a typical high spot of existence. Meanwhile, promising careers were 'being borne away on the wings of Time'.

At least the Somme and incessant toil with water carts ended in November as the battalion moved to the Neuve Chapelle sector (Maps 1 & 4). There was some 'fascinating females' in La Gorque (north-west of Neuve Chapelle) but around Arras in 1917 the peasants were more hostile. On April 7 a shell fell directly on to their convoy of wagons and they lost men and horses – 'their incredible luck had run out'. It made Aubrey doubly nervous about taking a limber piled up with grenades through a 'hot spot'. Indeed, at Arras there were many 'exciting ration trips'.

In June he developed trouble in an eye and went to hospital again. He observed that generally men who had been on the Western Front for three years were beginning to develop all sorts of ailments.

There was transport work at the Third Battle of Ypres and the Menin Road was a 'nightmare… to make your hair stand on end'. On at the Battle of Cambrai (Map 1) the ration trips were 'extraordinary'. He lost another old pal – Jumbo. He had to bid goodbye to his faithful horse, who had lost a foreleg.

As in the case of the men of the Labour Corps (including my father) the labours of the transport men were crucial in maintaining supply to the men in the trenches. Aubrey was obviously often in hot spots and the fact that he won the Military Medal and Bar gives you a sound idea of his 'bit' on the Western Front.

SMITH, LEN (1892–1974)
Drawing Fire
Private Len Smith
Edited by David Mason
Collins, 2009

Len Smith's diary is perhaps the most exotic of them all, crammed with around 350 of his attractive, whimsical pencil and colour wash sketches and cartoons. This is an extraordinary production from an ordinary soldier but a very gifted artist.

The book also has facsimile reproductions from the original diary, plus pictures of Len's many souvenirs and contemporary postcards, and other photographs. There is also a long Appendix of Len's numerous letters to his family.

Len Smith wrote notes on nearly every day he was at war on tiny scraps of paper torn from notebooks which he hid away in his pockets. Len did not alter these 'scrawls' later because he wanted his highly detailed account of what happened to him 'to ring true'. They are thus, in his own admission, a 'ramble' – a strung-together, rather miscellaneous collection of observations and reflections. He was not writing a book but trying to set down what he and his comrades were enduring.

He or they did not know whether they would have a 'tomorrow' but his writing became more and more like a compelling daily duty. He could not rest until he had completed this task.

Not long after the war Len transcribed his scrawls into a lovingly crafted diary which he called 'My Written Diary of the 'Great Adventure''. Yet when he tried to get it published in the 1970s he could find no takers and this beautiful work was stuck away in a box. It was eventually discovered by an incredulous great nephew, David Mason.

Len joined the 7th City of London Battalion in September 1914 and served for the whole war. The first action in which he was involved was at 'The Valley of Death' at Festubert (Map 4) in May 1915. He later fought at Loos (1915), Vimy (May 1916), High Wood, Somme (September 1916), Butte de Warlencourt (October 1916), Messines (June 1917) and Cambrai (November 1917).

During 1916 he was assigned to sniping, a job he 'hated' ('but 'orders is orders'). He was later recognised as an accredited war artist, giving him freedom to work across a whole brigade sector. This was not a cushy job because he had to do a lot of work in no man's land in order to get the necessary detail into his drawings.

By 1918, after a long bout of trench fever, Len was transferred to the Royal Engineers Special Branch, a unit which designed camouflage cover for positions and weapons. For instance, he was able to design his own version of the hollow steel 'tree', a disguised observation post. He had to crawl out into no man's land to copy a German 'tree' (my father tried to hack some 'firewood' off one – see 'Weeks, George'.)

Len finished the war in Lille (Map 1), newly re-captured from the Germans. The population of this city had suffered greatly at the hands of the invader and they welcomed their saviours with open arms. Len, like Dick Read, enjoyed some absolutely marvellous hospitality.

Len Smith's art reminds one strongly of that of Bruce Bairnsfather's – light-hearted and whimsical (like 'The Wipers Times', too). Len's cartoons raise many a smile, such as 'Fritz at the Ritz'. In another a keen officer is trying to interest the men in pictures of wild life; the caption reads 'The Wrong Sort of Birds, Mate'. He had a way with words: trench foot was 'elephantite arse'.

There is a copy of Len's panoramic view of Vimy Ridge (Map 1) in 1916. Len actually ran through a heavy enemy bombardment to get a message to his C.O. here. The Colonel said he deserved a VC Len would have preferred a W.C. That was Len Smith.

SPICER, LANCELOT (born 1893)
Letters from France 1915–1918
Robert York, 1979

Lancelot Dykes Spicer was commissioned in the 9th Battalion of the King's Own Yorkshire Light Infantry in 1914 and arrived in France in time for the Battle of Loos in September 1915. Collecting them together was the work of his mother, and the book was edited by his sisters.

His letter of September 30 alluded to a big battle ('THE SHOW') but he could not reveal where it took place (newspapers at home would have told the family this). He told them he had no coherent idea of what took place: additional information in italics was added later. His terse judgement of the Battle of Loos was that it was 'a fiasco', resulting in an enormous casualty rate and half a mile of territory gained around Hill 70.

He was billeted in Armentières (Map 1). At times he felt very sympathetic with French citizens but they could be 'beastly'. One told him he preferred the Germans! He was grateful for the Gillette razor (October 15) – much better then the 5-franc effort from Hazebrouck.

The Germans were so close he could hear them cleaning their teeth. He went into no man's land with a sergeant and was amazed when the NCO started talking loudly. The episode finished up with a chat with a German who had been living in Euston Road. Sir John French sent round a communique blaming divisional commanders for 'the fiasco'. Lancelot added that no one knew where they were going, where the enemy was and what the British soldiers were supposed to do.

2nd Lieutenant Spicer's platoon were a 'helpless lot of babes' (November 2) and he was 'perfectly sick of making out foolish and fatuous returns to Battalion or Brigade office' (November 9). It was taking about £5 to kill a German. However, he had become 'a drainage expert' (November 22). 'We never stop pumping' (December 3) so there were lots of reasons for not writing often enough.

He thanked his father (Sir A. Spicer, M.P.) for a nice warm waistcoat.

He was on the Somme near Albert (Map 2) in February 1916 (he was now a lieutenant) and always apologising for not writing sooner. To see a live German was a rare experience. The Attorney General came for a visit and was arrested for straying out of his allotted zone (he was in Winston Churchill's dug-out!).

If they fired a trench mortar the Germans fired back a massive aerial torpedo which created a crater 14 feet deep by 30 feet wide – so much for armchair critics at home who campaigned for a bigger employment of trench mortars. Lancelot's letter of March 2 was chewed by mice. This didn't help at all because he often professed to not knowing what to write about. He hated his deceitful C.O. and wanted a transfer (March 15).

He was inspected by Field Marshal Haig on March 25, who said to Lancelot, "Well, this is a great responsibility on your young shoulders, isn't it?" and chatted on for half a minute. Lancelot kept muttering, "Yes, sir."

Some batches of his letters never turned up, at all. He was one of those enterprising officers trying to get battalion canteens going – 'dry' ones, at first. French shopkeepers were charging high prices. Also, by soldiers using their shops it meant that French citizens could not get food and drink.

There was a 'colossal' row between the C.O. and his officers (Lancelot was frequently a stand-in company commander) after some of them applied to go balloon observing just to get away from him. He accused them of being cowards.

Lancelot wrote much about fellow officers – good and bad. Captain Walker was nice but 'a perfect maniac for missing the essential' (May 15). Lieutenant Oldershaw was 'heavy as a lump of lead'. 2nd Lieutenant Ellenberger was 'loquacious and argumentative' (later to become a brigadier and a long-standing friend).

An attempt to get going on a 'wet' canteen failed when no beer was available from breweries over a 10-mile radius. Lancelot also reported that he could do with some feminine company (June 20).

A letter of July 5, 1916 reported the death of the the C.O. and Captain Walker amongst other battalion officers. For three days Lieutenant Spicer was in command of the depleted battalion. Some incoming officers were 'useless – quaint things'. He was promoted to Captain.

Then he had to go into hospital (apparently with trench fever) and then to an officer rest station (August). A War Office telegram fell on the front door mat at the Spicer residence on September 21 informing them of a severe bomb wound to Lancelot's left arm and chest, inflicted during the attack on Guillemont (September 16 – Map 3).

He was not back in France until April 1917. He soon became Adjutant of the KOYLI 10th Battalion (July). Because of censorship it is often difficult to work out where he was and this stayed largely uncorrected when the book was edited. He was 'possibly' in Hendeghem (north-west of Hazebrouck – Map 1) in September (and thus probably in Flanders). The Third Battle of Ypres, like the Somme, was 'A GREAT SHOW'. But he certainly did not like fighting and told his parents that he would get out of the Army as soon as possible. He was simply doing his patriotic duty.

Lancelot continued to assess his senior officers – his C.O. at the 10th Battalion was scared of his superiors. In December Captain Spicer went on to the Divisional HQ staff; he would rather have been in the front line. He was embarrassed at eating luxurious food in Amiens (Map 2) when people were starving but when his mother told how depressed people were with the war he wrote a long letter explaining why they must keep going to the end. But he was obviously sensitive to the anxieties of his parents – 'you probably picture me hurrying along the road… followed by a large fat Hun with a very long bayonet'. At least he got a job more to his liking in April – as a Brigade Major, flung into the Fourth Battle of Ypres. On May 28, between the Marne and the Aisne it looked at one time as if the whole Brigade staff would be captured. For his efforts there a Bar was added to his Military Cross.

General McCulloch was shot by one of his own men (not seriously but nevertheless painfully) at Miraumont (north-east of Albert – Map 2) as he got himself and his brigade staff in front of his advancing troops – so much for the legendary cowardice of HQ staff. But by October 10 Lancelot was too far away from the guns to hear them any more and was billeted in a village only captured two days before. He was given the D.S.O.

STEWART, ALEXANDER
A Very Unimportant Officer
My Grandfather's Great War
Cameron Stewart
Hodder & Stoughton, 2008

In 1927 and 1928 Alexander Stewart came back to the brief diary he had written during the war and expanded it (also using his letters and postcards) into the memoir 'The Experience of a Very Unimportant Officer in France and Flanders during 1916–1917'. Stewart produced three typed copies of this memoir. He noted in his introduction that he had written it for his family and for 'his own amusement'.

One of his sons (Cameron Stewart's uncle) tried unsuccessfully to get the memoir published in the 1960s. So it gathered dust until Cameron produced the present volume 80 years after his grandfather had written it (he also presented stage and radio versions).

He joined the 3rd Battalion of the Cameronians (Scottish Rifles) in 1915 and went to France in March 1916. His diary started on March 21. The memoir expands many of these entries. He freely admitted that his memory may have failed him over many facts.

The battalion went to trenches near Béthune. His venture into no man's land to repair wire was nearly a disaster as the rookie soldiers made so much noise, inviting a hail of bullets, bombs and shells (April 3). On the next night he lost his way out there. There followed almost nightly wiring parties and searches for enemy patrols. He remembered how 'exciting' it was. On the 24th a whizz bang shell landed at his feet but he was unhurt (soldiers potentially faced much greater danger from shells which exploded some distance away and sprayed deadly splinters).

The Globe café in Béthune was much favoured by officers for its champagne cocktails. Stewart had a spell teaching a Royal Warwickshire

Battalion about trench procedures. For instance, he pointed out that if they all kept their heads down during shelling no one would be able to see what was happening in no man's land. He also taught them that if enemy shells were overshooting the trench it was quite safe to walk about in front of it. Not every body agreed with him.

The Cameronians took their place on the Somme. Alexander tried to recall what made the biggest impact on him: it was probably seeing how lethal the battle was for officers, who had to lead and show no fear. Accordingly their casualty rates were horrible. His favourite memory was of the rum ration. Discussing fear in general he thought that the best antidote was a drink. Less favourable memories were the lice and the stench of rotting bodies.

The battalion took over newly-captured trenches on July 15 beyond Mametz Wood (Maps 2 & 3), greeted by painful tear gas. In the assaults on High Wood (Map 3) they began to suffer a heavy rate of losses, especially amongst officers, from constant shelling and machine gun fire. It was hardly possible to move without attracting an enemy response. They then realised they were well in front of the British battalions on either side of them.

On the big attack on High Wood on July 20 Alexander described in great detail the plan of attack, and remembered how the actual event was so disastrously different. The planners took no account of the pitch darkness, deep empty trenches, strewn wire, corpses and shell holes. The only way that Stewart could let HQ know how they were doing was to have two reliable, panic-free runners who could take back messages and usually get them delivered.

The din was deafening and the troops could not hear officers' orders. By the time they reached near High Wood it was getting light and the Germans could pick them off in swathes with machine gun and rifle. The Highlanders had no option but to try and shelter in shell holes. Stewart sat in one all day, drank, smoked and wrote his diary! They managed to get through the day without being shelled or counter attacked.

Another battalion appeared to storm the wood but they were also mown down. No other officer in Stewart's company had survived. At night he brought back the remnants of his men. Only he and one other officer in the whole battalion survived on July 20!

In August they were back at Bazentin-le-Grand (Map 3). There were no more frontal attacks but they suffered from constant shelling and machine gunning. At the end of the month he was ill with hay fever and dysentery and he was in hospital for a week. Then there were a few weeks in which he had jobs behind the front line and rested on the French coast, enjoying concerts and other diversions. He loved football and boxing. He had leave in England in October.

He was back on the Somme as company commander on October 27, at Le Transloy (north-east of Albert – Map 2), a scene of devastation overlain by mud and water. As before he led a failed attack – same plans, same outcome. In the rest period he gave rather bloodthirsty instruction on bayonet fighting. Siegfried Sassoon recalled one of his lectures, describing Stewart as 'a massive, sandy-haired Highland Major'.

But he was very sick again (the strain of periodic front line leadership took its toll on the toughest men) in the spring of 1917 and had a long spell in England suffering from fever and rheumatism. Returning later in April he wandered for days around France searching for his battalion, in action somewhere on the Arras (Map 1) battle front. When he re-joined it this campaign was dwindling fast, settling into attritional struggles around the Hindenburg Line. He led his company in a large raid on May 27 but it was a failure like all rest of them: the German fortifications and fire power remained impregnable.

He had a miraculous escape in this action because a German rifleman missed him from point blank range. Stewart did not miss him.

In September the battalion was fighting on the Menin Road. Stewart was wounded in the neck on September 28. It was a Blighty One and he was in hospital and at rest in England for a long time before taking up light duties in an Officers' Cadet Battalion.

TALBOT KELLY, RICHARD (born 1896)
Memoir of the Great War 1915–1917
R. B. Talbot Kelly
Edited by R. G. Loosmore
William Kimber, 1980

Richard Talbot Kelly was commissioned as a 2nd Lieutenant in April, 1915 and joined the Royal Horse Artillery, 52nd Brigade in May in France in May. He wrote this Memoir 30 years 'or more' after the war. It is based on his war diaries and letters, which are still in existence. He was a gifted artist and some of his Western Front sketches are reproduced in the book. Members of his family typed up his work, and his sister, Miss Margaret Talbot Kelly, was instrumental in getting it published. The Editor added historical notes.

Richard first saw action at Festubert (Map 4) and immediately went into the artillery line and the observation post (OP) as machine gun fire, mortar bombs and the bullets of snipers swept past him and Very lights lit up the night sky. More lethal sniping the next day blew out the brains of the soldier standing next to him.

The British shell shortage was acute at this stage of the war and a German onslaught was expected at any time in the Ypres Salient. But Richard found relief on a pleasant Festubert farm with evenings spent shooting at rats in the cellars of the brewery. He also enjoyed drawing panoramas for brigade military use.

Longer rest came in August at Robecq, caring for the horses, swimming, cricket and nice meals in Béthune (Maps 1 & 4). But the Battle of Loos was looming. The brigade was in the Vermelles sector (south-east of Béthune) and did a lot of forward observing right in front of the Hohenzollern Redoubt. Shell supply was much improved and a big British bombardment opened up on September 21. But a 'Chinese attack' of the 23rd, planned to test German defence capability, was a hair-raising experience for the 2nd Lieutenant out in the forward observation post – 'we were certain of a fire-blasted death'. But they escaped; their poor signallers waiting outside were not not so lucky. They lay 'bleeding and unconscious'.

Everyone was 'still sure of success' as the brigade galloped up to their firing positions. But very soon hundreds of walking wounded Highlanders came stumbling past them in the opposite direction, soaked to the skin, covered in mud and blood –'glassy-eyed' – these had been proud Scottish warriors.

Talbot Kelly's battery came up to the 'shambles of battle' but soon retired themselves, away from the corpses of the Highlanders in front of the Redoubt. Last desperate attempts to hold the line there failed and the battle was lost by the end of the month.

The brigade moved up to the Salient firing on the front between Sanctuary Wood and Hill 60 ('a little hump'). Prolonged periods in forward observation left Richard utterly shaken and exhausted. In November he became the brigade signals officer in charge of 9 miles of telephone wire which had to be maintained if the Germans attacked once more. But as the year came to a close the prospect of this began to fade. In fact, he recorded that an unusual number of enemy deserters were getting away across no man's land.

After leave he remembered above all the dreadful new German poison gas – phosgene. Early in 1916 the brigade was in the Ploegsteert Wood to Armentières sector (Maps 1 & 4), fighting now alongside South Africans infantry. It was a pleasant springtime – much quieter and more fun in the billets (they found the C.O. trying to conceal 'immodest' French books).

Steel helmets arrived, worn over a cap comforter – 'utterly British in shape'. Richard trained battery runners at Hazebrouck (Map 1) and there were joyous evening sing-songs. A team of camouflagers arrived to paint the guns in lurid shapes.

The brigade moved down to the chalk downs of Picardy – Méricourt (west of Albert – Map 2) , alongside the French. Tons upon tons of shells were now pouring in – so many they had to be brought in during daylight hours, not a healthy situation. But the supply serviced the massive bombardment preceding the assaults of July 1; Richard fired his guns for

5 days – until the rain held them up. On July 1 he saw 'the glint of our bayonets'.

On that day, however, even the battery suffered casualties – two sergeants killed. Yet the assault at Montauban (Map 3) was the only relatively successful operation of July 1. Richard's most vivid memory of that day was having to pass badly wounded men without being able to help them. 'The dead were my most usual companions'. Corpses under the yellow clay heaved under his feet as Richard went up to forward observation in Bernefray and Trones Woods (west of Guillemont – Map 3) – 'days of intense terror', lingering gas everywhere. Just in front of him brave Bavarians fought valiantly to hold their line.

The British artillery had to fire almost without pause to support the hard-pressed infantry: Richard's guns fired for many hours on July 14 and 15 as the fighting raged around Delville Wood (Map 3). On the 16th he was hidden in a house in Longueval (Maps 2 & 3) across the road from the Germans correcting howitzer fire. To get away from this was the greatest relief of his war; there was fun in the river as a highly shaggy Australian swum naked.

There was a more peaceful existence in the countryside of the Arras area, not hit yet with the scars of battle. Snipers were the main danger here. But late in October they were back on the Somme – the Butte de Warlencourt (Map 3). Failure here created more low morale than ever: men spoke of getting their 'Blighty' wound as never before.

For Richard Talbot Kelly his diary entries for the end of 1916 and the beginning of 1917 were 'faint ghosts' in his memory. Some very brief entries for this period are shown in the book. Returning from leave on December 14 he reached his division on the Arras front (Map 1) – Martencourt. Although it was very cold the men were in a better frame of mind because they liked the town of Arras.

They covered the battle front at Roclincourt (north of Arras – Map 1). What stands out in Richard's memory here was the swing to the Germans of supremacy in the air. The British artillery caused a lot of damage to the German defences on Vimy Ridge (Map 1) and this was a big factor in the early successes of the infantry. But it had to keep firing day after day as the battle dragged on towards the usual stagnation.

Richard awoke one morning in what he thought was a safe dugout to find himself covered in chalk rubble: a shell had struck the dugout and not exploded. During the assault on Messines (Map 4) in June he was in hospital with impetigo. In the Third Battle of Ypres he was at St. Eloi (south of Ypres – Maps 1 & 4) in July. A few days into August a shell burst at his feet and he was dragged to the bottom of the crater, his 'insides' concussed. There was not a scratch on his skin but he was in great pain and this was his very nasty 'Blighty' one.

TENNANT, NORMAN (born 1896)
A Saturday Night's Soldier's War 1913–1918
Norman Tennant
Kylin Press, 1983

Norman only started a diary in 1916; for the years before for this memoir he relied on memory and photographs and press cuttings. He attended Ilkley Grammar School and his diary and the book are well-written. He was also a gifted artist and the account is decorated with numerous sketches he drew whilst serving as a signalman to a howitzer battery.

He joined the 11th Howitzer Battery, part of a Territorial ('Saturday Night Soldier') Division along with friends in 1913. Signalmen were particularly brave soldiers who maintained communication between guns and observation posts (OPs). The wire could not only be cut by enemy action but also by accidental damage to their own trenches and by traffic on the roads.

Norman arrived at Havre with his battery in April, 1915, billeting at St. Venant (north-west of Béthune – Map 1). A lot of time was spent on grooming and feeding the horses which pulled the huge guns. They also had to fill up thousands of sandbags because the ground was marshy in this area and breastwork 'trenches' were necessary.

The battery took part in the Aubers Ridge (Map 4) campaign, where Norman was cut in the face and needed a dressing. It taught him to be more careful: a Blighty one was the best sort of wound but something even less serious had its uses. Soon they moved north to Brielen just north of Ypres (Maps 1 & 4), where they stayed for six months. Most fondly remembered here was the Herburg de Kroone estaminet. Firing the big guns at Brielen was kept to a minimum because of the severe shortage of shells and the fact that the weapons they had were antiquated (they badly needed the new 4.5 inch howitzers).

The shell situation improved in December. The resulting bombardment brought a similar response from the Germans and the gunners must have preferred being short of ammunition.

Norman's diary begins on January 4, 1916 (comrades persuaded him to start it to accompany his drawings). There were entries for most days. They were now at Arneke (near Dunkirk) and were glad to be in an area where enemy shelling was less severe (but there was also the danger of being shot by a sniper whilst working on the wire or observing from a forward position). Now the new, up-to-date guns arrived as they shifted to near Amiens (Warloy – Map 2). Norman remembered the Expeditionary Force Canteen here.

They were then in Canaples (also near Amiens) from March to May, training for a much more substantial offensive. One of Norman's drawings was featured in 'The Buzz', the divisional magazine. There was much hard work getting ready to take part in an enormous bombardment, the largest in military history. Moreover, stables and horses meant much hard labour, not to mention parades: the artillery tried to match the infantry in military pride.

So, the move to the Somme came in June. By this time more new guns had arrived: there was a lot to do but time for swimming in the Ancre (Norman was a very keen swimmer) and also fishing in it (some men were adept at hitting fish on the head with a stick).

The bombardment commenced and Norman spent much time in forward positions. The wires were blown to bits daily. One advantage of being in an OP for hours was that it provided time to sketch.

It took his mind off the fact that he was right in front of the enemy unarmed.

But he contracted trench fever in July and finished up in Number 44 casualty clearing station at Wimereux (French coast). Returning to the battery on August 27 he became ill again (trench fever was always likely to strike twice especially if the soldier tried to continue working normally). One doctor told him there was nothing wrong with him but another one sent him straight to hospital and thence to Z Convalescence Camp at Havre.

It was late in September before he was returned to the Somme battle – in front of Mailly-Maillet. The period in early October proved very dangerous as the German artillery concentrated on trying to damage the capability of the British big guns, which had been prominent in the support of what success the infantry had achieved. Norman had several close escapes. On October 31 two high explosive shells landed a few yards away from him.

The rain was so persistent that dugout walls were in danger of collapsing and sending sheets of water down on gunners trying to sleep. He spent a month with an anti-aircraft battery in December, but did much more time building wooden platforms than firing at enemy planes. To cap his frustration a horse trod on his knee on the 28th .

On to 1917: on February 15 the cook refused to cook breakfast because they had stolen his coal to keep warm on a freezing night. During March the battery moved to Laventie (Map 4). Even though the Somme battle was over the front, there had more artillery fire than the new front. But the peace did not last long as they were called to support the assault on Vimy Ridge (Map 1) in April. Before the bombardment Norman paid a visit to 'Tottenham Tunnels' below the Ridge, a mile-long maze with dressing stations and dormitories for hundreds of men. Water and electricity was supplied.

There was also another tunnel ('Cavalier Tube') which provided even more accommodation. The successful advance took the howitzers as far as Souchez (west of Givenchy – Map 4) by April 14. But to Norman this had become 'a haunted and horrible place', smothered with dead Canadians and Germans – utterly devastated by artillery fire. Not long before the area had featured pretty, rolling hills.

It was thus good to get back to Laventie, not so good was the fact that so many horses and mules had been lost at Vimy that the battery had to borrow some to get its guns moving. But there was the best coffee in the land at Marie's cottage. Norman was also able to do plenty of swimming and play chess. Not so welcome was 'endless stabling' – cleaning, shining etc., and, even worse, 'spit and polish' parades.

They travelled north not to Ypres but to Nieuport (Map 1) on the Belgian coast, where the Allies hoped to open a new front to the north of Ypres. The artillery was busy trying to soften German defences but their resistance was massive, and Norman and his comrades were in serious trouble once more for six weeks from July to September. Norman's journeys along his wires to the OP were hectic and hazardous. Only the Y.M.C.A. canteen brought relief.

His senior officer thought a lot of Norman's efficiency, hard work and courage and had rewarded him with a stripe (not that he worried about commendation – he just got on with his job). But at this time he was persuaded to apply for a commission.

On September 9 they were at Messines (Map 4). The C.O. was trying to give Norman more amenable work and he spent some time here driving G.S. wagons with supplies. But he was soon back in front of the guns again in the Salient in October. But there were visits to Poperinghe (Maps 1 & 4) and leave in Paris.

November saw him back in the thick of the action but the Third Battle of Ypres had subsided and he was doing more grooming and cleaning than fighting in December, and there was some football, wrestling on horses and horse racing to enjoy. But in 1918 there was still dangerous work to be done and March brought new hazards as the Germans launched their new offensive. On April 8 a piece of shrapnel went right through his nose and lodged behind an eye. It was a Blighty one.

TYNDALE-BISCOE, JULIAN
Gunner Subalterns
Julian Tyndale-Biscoe
Leo Cooper, 1971

Julian Tyndale-Biscoe converted his diary and his war letters to his father into this narrative. He was commissioned into the Royal Horse Artillery on September 12, 1914. After artillery training in England he was posted to the Ypres Salient.

He copied extracts from his diary for July 18 to July 21, 1915 when he was near Zillebeke south-east of Ypres (Maps 1 & 4). This diary was in note form. He never included any more direct copy from the diary.

On July 19 he was desperately trying to find the ends of broken telephone wires – an 'awful sweat' because the Germans sent over 300 shells in less than 30 minutes. On the 20th a piece of shrapnel knocked over Gunner Lazzard's tea. 'Badly whizz-banged at dawn, then high explosives. 90% over-shooting'.

Near Sanctuary Wood Julian spent many hours ensuring that telephone lines were kept open to report enemy positions and on the accuracy of the shooting of his battery whilst 6 enemy batteries were delivering a 'hurricane' of fire. As his own guns responded Julian was 'dazed by the concussion and noise'. He could fry bacon on the scalding hot gun flanges.

He returned to his dug-out to rest and found his sleeping bag ripped to shreds by a hunk of shell casing and the Major was buried up to his neck in his dug-out, still fast asleep. Another shell blew Julian on to his back across the gun tail, but, like the Major, he was not hurt, apart from being smothered in grime and sweat. He had also gone temporarily deaf.

It was difficult to keep all the guns firing all the time because the oil in the hydraulic mechanism over-heated. A young fitter worked valiantly to keep them working aided by teams of gunners with buckets of water. Returning to their dug-outs they found all of them wrecked. They had fired over 1,000 rounds a gun. Getting up ammunition from the dump ten miles away had been achieved by a sergeant major because his Captain was away in Poperinghe (Maps 1 & 4) without permission. The NCO was promoted to Acting Captain and the real Captain was court-martialed.

The battery supported the assault at Loos (September 1915 – Lens sector – Map 1) with its own subsidiary bombardment in the salient across the Comines Canal (Maps 1 & 4). Julian was promoted to Lieutenant and he promptly invented a home-made flashpoint to improve observation of German artillery from OPs. While he was working on this rats ate the biscuits and raisins in his pocket.

Towards the end of 1915 there was a period of 7 days in his diary recorded by only one word in capital letters – 'MUD'. Leave in London in January was jolly good fun – the lights of Piccadilly and boxes in gorgeous theatres (the best show was 'Tonight's the Night'), meeting all his cousins and aunts and his friends. There were also 'scrumptuous' dinners.

He had to get back to Elverdinghe (Map 4) but managed a night at Talbot House on the way. He was asked whether he wanted to apply for a regular commission in the RHA. He got it but only as a 2nd Lieutenant.

They moved south to Arras (Map 1) in March 1916 and were there for 4 months. When they arrived it was snowing and the horses had great difficulty in keeping their feet on the icy ground. When they did fall the gunners had to use blankets to get them aloft once more. Julian proved to be very inventive: for instance, he rigged up a speaking tube from the OP in the roof of a house to the telephone in the cellar, using old drainpipes and water pipes, bits of curtain to tie them, a disused paraffin tin and an old tin bucket. No wonder they called him 'Hot Stuff'. He also loved practical jokes such as exploding oidine and ammonia tablets. There were more jolly japes on April 1.

'You know, the trouble out here is that I am having too good a time', he recorded. A visitor (on a 'Cook's Tour' of the front) complained about the singing of the nightingales which kept him awake.

Early in August Julian was in action near High Wood on the Somme (Map 3) trying to establish OPs in craters with blackened corpses and swarms of bloated flies. He directed fire from 32 guns of the battery, and he found this 'rather thrilling'. The range he established was perfect and he saw lines of panic-stricken German infantry fleeing from the trenches. He grabbed a rifle and started firing at them and he thought he hit some of them. But the German machine guns opened up with a hail of fire and Julian was hit in the back.

The bullet lodged between his heart and the base of the right lung, a Blighty One. It was a year before he was back on active service and he was posted to Egypt.

UNKNOWN SOLDIER Number 1
A Month at the Front-line
The Diary of an Unknown Soldier
Bodleian Library, 2006

This small black notebook came to the Bodleain Library as part of some donated material. Its author and origin are not known. However, this soldier was known to belong to D Company of the 12th Battalion of the East Surrey Regiment (Bermondsey Pals) and he was one of at least 14 men in the company wounded on April, 5 1917 in the Ypres Salient. These soldiers are listed in the this published version of the diary. They were fighting just to the south-west of the Ypres–Comines Canal (Maps 1 & 4).

The battalion were ordered into this front line 'as near as I can remember, about the middle of July'. In fact, no precise dates are given for any of these events. Also, no place names appear, just the names of woods or buildings. The account is understated, somewhat dispassionate, but nonetheless a vivid picture of an intense battle lasting around a month.

It was written after the soldier was wounded but not too long after because it has a wealth of detail which would have been forgotten if much time had elapsed. 'I find my memory had led me on too fast as I have omitted one or two details'.

The diarist had obviously received a good elementary education as the writing is clearly expressed and grammatical, with very few errors. But it does have rather quaint usages, such as the use of capital letters where they are not required; e.g. 'ENEMY', 'CANAL'. Also, some geographical features or statements are underlined; e.g. 'Battle Wood', 'but it never exploded'. This reminded me very strongly of my own father's writing style (see 'Weeks, George'). He came from the Isle of Dogs, the diarist from Bermondsey. Perhaps it was the East Ender's way of trying to be stylish. My dad liked phrases such as 'made the acquaintance of' and 'partake of' and words like 'repast' (rather than 'grub').

What is striking about the unknown soldier, in common with all other ordinary 'cannon fodder' or 'poor bloody infantry', is his utter ignorance of how a battle was faring apart from what he could see or hear. These soldiers did not have a clue about what was happening – a general picture of success or failure. 'It was something awful and no words will ever describe my feelings accurately'.

However, a quite amazing event was recorded by this soldier when he was caught out in no man's land at the mercy of surrounding enemy soldiers. He had managed to crawl into a very shallow shell hole which just about hid him from view. The Germans were tossing grenades at him. One hit him low on the back but 'did me no harm'. But another one struck him higher up and exploded 'but it did me no harm except gave me a shock'. At this point he surrendered.

'I was a P.O.W. But I never intended going to Germany, not me, there would be some rough work before I reached that notorious country'. But he was led off by a group of enemy soldiers.

At this juncture a rifle was poked through a hedge and the leading German was shot down. However, in the same volley our man was hit in the leg. In the confusion which followed he managed to fall into another shell hole out of sight. He started smothering himself with mud in order to provide camouflage. He was in terrible pain and shells were falling all around him. 'No words will ever describe the horror of it all. I never expected to get out of that hole alive and many other thoughts crossed my mind'. Here, the diary ended.

UNKNOWN SOLDIER Number 2
Line of Fire (August–September 1914)
Translated by Sarah Ardizzone from Barroux
Phoenix Yard Books, 2014

The French illustrator, M. Barroux, was walking down a Paris street when he saw this diary in a rubbish container and rescued it. It was written by an unknown soldier called up for this war. 'Line of Fire' has also been adapted for the stage, with music. Barroux illustrated the poilou's words.

August 4. He was in barracks in Paris. The official news confirmed that war had been declared. 'The women weep'.

August 5. 'Where are we going? Who knows?'

August 6. Our soldier and a comrade visit another unit in Saint-Mihel (south-east of Verdun), where there are 'ladies of questionable morals'. Our man is 'disgusted' by this.

August 7. At Buissieres they dig trenches in a storm.

August 8. 'We're beginning to hear the sound of artillery fire in the distance… my heart grows heavy'.

August 9. They march towards the fighting front. Mulhouse has fallen to the Germans. It is sweltering hot. 'My feet are bleeding. My legs can no longer hold me up'.

August 10. They billet in Ancremont.

August 11. This is a rest day – our man's feet must be very pleased.

August 12. He finds a 'decent' rabbit and cooks it. In the evening they are entertained by a café-concert singer as they sit around a fire in the garden. 'We wouldn't think we were at war'.

August 13. It has been a pleasant break in Ancremont; they spend the evening telling each other jokes.

August 14. They move around Verdun, marching in very hot weather.

August 15. He searches for a duck for dinner.

August 16. The company get a pig to eat. But the wine has ran out.

August 18. They occupy the village of Gremilly; the Prussians are only 14 kilometres away.

August 20. The Prussians destroy Pillon (near Verdun), 10 kilometres away.

August 21. The regiment moves past places where battles have raged. They have now marched 40 kilometres. White crosses by the roadside mark the graves of French soldiers. They reach Beaumont where a hospitable villager gives them coffee and brandy. After dark they are surrounded by the fires from neighbouring villages.

August 22. Walking-wounded French soldiers pass our unknown soldier as his unit goes into the reserve front line. They move even further forward, towards the Belgian village of Saint-Remy as enemy shrapnel flies around them. They are called upon to advance to the enemy barbed wire defences. They get through to the village, miraculously with no casualties. German bullets continue to whizz past them but they carry on up the slope beyond the village and down the other side and now the enemy fire is beginning to take its toll. 'This is a rout'. Our soldier is exhausted and can hardly stand on his feet.

August 23. They dig trenches in their new position but finally the intensity of German shelling forces them to retreat once more. Refugees crowd past them. They dig new trenches as an artillery duel opens up. They finally retreat to Marville.

August 24. There is a further withdrawal under heavy shelling.

August 25. The rout continues: 'We're very lucky… to survive.' He is totally worn out.

August 26. They have now gone back 30 kilometres to the banks of the River Meuse. Our man's battalion is ordered to remain on the northern side to protect the rest of the army as it crosses the river. At Vilosnes they finally get across and blow up the last remaining bridge and march on to Nantillois.

August 27. They reach Cunel.

August 28. The village has been reduced to rubble by the enemy bombardments. They dig trenches amongst it.

August 29. But they have to abandon this position as German reconnaissance planes circle overhead. They retreat to Aincreville.

August 30. Now the German artillery moves even closer and they decide that the position at Cunel is safer.

August 31. They move again towards Dun-sur- Meuse and continue to battle from new positions. But our soldier is hit in the left arm blood pours from the wound. A comrade bravely stays with him and dresses the wound. He can only crawl on his belly as shells explode around him. He is panic-stricken but another comrade carries his bag and helps him along and attaches splints to the wounded arm made from the branches of a tree (the arm is broken or fractured). At Bantheville he got into an ambulance. This took him to Clermont-en-Argonne and to hospital, where the medics confirm he has a fractured arm. It is properly dressed and he is taken to the train station.

September 1. He is in great pain and has a fever. He reaches hospital in Auxerre. Rumours flying around suggest that the Germans are encircling Paris.

(The diary's last entry is for September 12. 'I am bored to death and my heart is heavy…')

VAUGHAN, EDWIN (1897–1931)
Some Desperate Glory
The Diary of a Young Officer 1917
Pen and Sword, 2010

Vaughan was indeed young, just 19 in 1917, so if we hear that his record is of feelings of injustice, good and bad food, pretty girls, horseplay and practical jokes – as well as fear and fatigue – it is not surprising.

Vaughan was educated at the Jesuit College of St. Ignatius in Stamford Hill, north London. Then he joined the Artists' Rifles OTC in 1915. He was commissioned in June 1916 and travelled to France in January 1917. His diary runs from January 4 and ends suddenly on August 27. In January war was an 'exciting venture'. He wangled himself into the 8th Battalion of the Royal Warwickshire Regiment.

In Rouen he enjoyed himself chatting to foreign soldiers, civilians etc., a very cheery fellow. No one seemed particularly concerned about the war, he wrote. His diary is equally verbose – he had something to say about most things – good and bad, and some of the entries are very long.

The reader gets the feeling that this rather loud youngster could get up the noses of his seniors. His first C.O. even took a pip off him and he became 2nd Lieutenant after being Lieutenant. In Arraines-sur-Somme he rode a horse for the first time and enjoyed the company of Madeleine. He found it difficult to handle sloppy NCOs.

In the front line near Herbécourt (Map 2), with the Germans a stone's throw away in Peronne, Vaughan felt fear and wandered about confused as to where he was or what he had to do. He felt completely useless as everybody seemed to know what they were doing. He drank plenty of whisky, good preparation for four 42-inch mortar shells ('Minnies') falling in the trench by him. A sniper also just missed him as he went for a stroll.

But there was a pleasant interlude in Amiens (Map 2), where the food was good. Not so welcome were 'grenatenwerfer' which hit the trench by him followed by machine gun fire at point blank range. He buried a ghastly corpse and was then visited by a corporal who looked just like the corpse (March 12). A shell exploded in his dug-out but no one was hurt. His servant brought him a nice steak.

This was around the time when the Germans began their steady and planned retreat to the Hindenburg Line, leaving their deadly booby traps and strongpoints. They set fire to Peronne and blocked roads with mine holes and fallen trees. Another shell just missed him (March 25).

The Warwicks moved forward slowly with other units to try and occupy the blighted, snow-laden terrain with its hidden terrors, towards Villers Faucon (near Peronne – Map 2). Vaughan received the first of many fierce and rather unjust rebukes from his C.O. for allegedly becoming detached from a platoon.

It was dangerous work trying to repair communications in the open with the German artillery bombarding them. Locating the enemy became very difficult and Vaughan, under directions from a fellow officer, unwittingly took his men behind an enemy front (April 8): only mist and the slope of the land saved them. He was glad to get back to his saucy pictures and hopefully some sleep. Rest in shattered Peronne was a blessing later in April.

Vaughan continued to annoy senior officers, for instance, missing parade to get his teeth done.

Acting C.O., Major Gell, gave him hell, and Vaughan became very resentful and depressed. He consoled himself in a garden he was reconstructing and some wild evenings, like the one on May 3 when 'an enormous and disgusting' padre offered to fight six subalterns'. He gave them a hard time but was eventually subdued, debagged and spanked. Vaughan loved fooling about like a child. But he was a very decent cook.

The battalion moved north to Bullecourt (south-west of Arras – Map 1) – much quieter and with a much more inviting no man's land to patrol and have fun. Edwin was a real prankster – dropping defused enemy stick bombs in the officer's dug-out (June 4). But he did begin to get praise from above for his successful patrols locating enemy positions.

In the fine weather the grass was growing, so they could stick their heads above the parapet to get a good look-around with field glasses and

Edwin led a productive raid on June 17. There was time for football and cricket.

In July there was two weeks' rest in Berles-au-Bois (south-west of Arras – Map 1), where the French hospitality was as good as that enjoyed there by Dick Read , and the girls were pretty. But at the end of the month it was, back to the Ypres Salient. At least Edwin had time to go to La Poupée cafe in a very busy Poperinghe (Maps 1 & 4), where he was served by the ravishing 'Gingair'.

But on August 16 Vaughan became part of the Third Battle of Ypres as they arrived at Bridge 2A on the Yser Canal, in the thick of the action. The situation became terrifying as the Germans met the offensive to the east of the Canal with a furious and continuous bombardment. Near St. Julien Edwin was caught in the storm of shells, surrounded by corpses, some of officers and men he knew. He had to go out again on the 25th, across the Steenbeke stream as the enemy bombardment maintained its message of death or maiming on the ghastly terrain. The last entry of his diary – an extremely long one for August 27th ended, 'I gazed into a black and empty future'.

We do know that Edwin won the Military Cross in 1918 and finished the war with the rank of Captain.

WATSON, W. H. L.
Adventures of a Despatch Rider
William Blackwood and Sons, 1915
(Dunda Book Classic)

W. H. L. Watson was a despatch rider on the Western Front from August, 1914 to February, 1915. He constructed this narrative from letters to his mother and to 2nd Lieutenant R. B. Whyte of the Black Watch. It was written in 1915. It commences with a letter to Whyte telling him about the book (dated October 1, 1915).

Watson (a linguist student at Oxford University) joined the Signal Company of the 5th Division of the BEF at the outset of war. After brief training as an army despatch rider he was soon in France (at Hecq), moving to Dour in Belgium on August 21. His job here was to maintain contact between his division and the brigade. In Dour he 'ran down a civvy' and just missed a major. His machine took a battering, too – a belt-slip and a bent footstep, as 'nightmare' roads and uneven cobbles interspersed with big holes took their toll. At night his front lamp gave out only a feeble glimmer.

In the dire confusion of the retreat from Mons Watson spent time searching for generals, even whole units. He directed men who were lost. When columns of troops moved, some of them in a wrecked condition, such as the 2nd Cavalry Brigade which had made the courageous charge at Mons, the despatch riders guided them from the front.

However, Watson, and even the entire Signals Company, lost their bearings on occasions. Some of their bikes became damaged beyond repair and had to be abandoned as the Germans were in hot pursuit. The riders were always in danger of being shot at by their own troops or getting behind the enemy front line

He got to Le Cateau – 'about the battle itself you know as much as I do', a costly disaster. On August 27 he 'draggled' into St. Quentin almost asleep in the saddle. There was always the chance of being hit by a stray shell. Another 'wind-up' was being shot at by trigger-happy British sentries. A mechanic filled his tank with water. At least the cafés were dispensing good coffee, omelettes and bread. He slept where he could, sometimes by the roadside, in barns or attics in chateaux. By September 3 he was only 15 miles from Paris. The despatch riders had slaved away day and nearly all night for two weeks ('heroic days').

At this stage he was sent to look out for Germans; he had no need to worry as they got no nearer Paris. Watson finished up south-east of Paris at Tournan (September 4). The order now was to advance and to catch a turkey for The captain – 'an elusive bird with a perfectly Poultonian swerve'. But the cyclists caught a German in Mouroux (about 12 miles east of Paris) having a bath. Watson acquired a new motor bike as the Germans were struggling to get back over the River Marne (September 8).

Had they been lured into a clever trap by the French? The Battle of the Aisne got under way. 'Strategy in the ranks was elementary stuff pieced vaguely together'.

But shifting the enemy from the slopes north of the Aisne was not going to be easy. Watson spent a lot of time trying to locate the general or the unit to whom or which he had to deliver a message, all the time keeping a wary eye out for snipers or sentries. He couldn't drive fast because the noise of the engine drowned out that of an incoming shell.

But on the whole this was a better time for despatch riders – 'a couple of day messages and one each night'. But they experienced a strange nostalgia for the 'strenuous first days'. The capture of an enemy staff car was a new thrill.

There was going to be movement north, perhaps as far as Ostend. Eventually, it was no further than La Bassée (Maps 1 & 4), where the roads were really bad but the cafés were still good, and even better in Béthune (Maps 1 & 4).

To the north the struggle to hold on to Ypres was taking shape later in October but further south where Watson was there were serious dangers from the German artillery. Villages such as Festubert (Map 4) were systematically 'searched' by the enemy gunners each night. Watson did have several duties in Ypres, where the roads were 'greasy' (later 'icy').

Higher Command thought that despatch riders should learn to ride a horse and they also volunteered to learn about laying and repairing telephone cables. They were glad to get back to their bikes.

According to Watson, the Christmas 'truce' of 1914 was 'explained by our treatment of prisoners'. He also recorded that British soldiers got on very well with Flemish and French citizens. A burgher in Ypres forecast that 'after the war all England will flock to Ypres… a monstrous cemetery'.

Life for the despatch riders was distinctly less exciting as they turned into nothing more than postmen, bringing the mail to the units. The main enemy was the weather. It was not surprising that Watson left the Signals Company to take a commission in an infantry regiment (probably the Black Watch). By the time he published his book later in 1915 he was a Captain.

WEEKS, GEORGE (1898–1982)
Dangerous Work
The Memoir of Private George Weeks of the Labour Corps
1917–1919
Edited by Alan Weeks
Spellmount, 2014

My dad was never reluctant to talk about his war experiences; most of the events in his memoir are well-known to me, especially the comical ones – a military No. 1 military haircut on his beautiful curly locks, football and cricket injuries etc. There were not so funny ones, too, such as being covered in the blood of a blown-up horse.

But what made George want to write it all down when he was retired (in Liphook, Hampshire) and in his seventies. The answer lay in the box file in which he deposited his 78 sheets of cut-up wallpaper. In with these was a copy of the 1930 edition of Alfred McLelland Burrage's 'War is War' (he used the pseudonym 'Ex- Private X'). My dad had discovered this in a book sale in Liphook

"If he can do it," (ignoring the fact that Burrage was a professional writer) "why not me? I had adventures like that." And so he did – hours and hours of patient writing it up in his very neat handwriting (he was taught calligraphy at his elementary school – Glengall Grove on the Isle of Dogs). The only major ingredient of the memoir which needed correcting was the punctuation, apparently left out of his curriculum.

After more than 50 years George's memory played a few tricks. For instance, he said that the formation of the Labour Corps was in 1918 (it was 1917). This may have been partly due to the fact that he had proudly joined the Queen's Royal West Surrey Regiment ('Queen's') and he probably wanted to ignore the fact that his Labour Battalion was transferred to the new Labour Corps almost immediately following his mobilisation.

George in Cologne in 1919

At the beginning of March 1917 I was approaching My ninteenth Birthday which was the tenth of April. Little did I know that I was to celebrate this event on the Somme. I was employed as a Docker in the South West India Docks mostly discharging Sugar from Cuba this was extremely heavy labour being tall I was a back lifter in a piling squad consisting of five men, although I was a near six footer my wright was gone to 9 stone 2 lbs. I gradually realised that I was being dehydrated through excessive hard Work and lack of Nourishment so the time had arrived when I decided to alter these circumstances —

On the first Monday of March a brief consignment of Sugar got through the Salmarine Blockade. the Squad was busily engaged piling the heavy bags. after lunch which was not a lot. I envoyed the largest lout of the four at least twice my weight. He was under the mistaken impression that he could misname me with impunity. I answered this character so effectively,

Sundays, the weeks passed by and the old members of the Queens original Rank were being demobilised in increasing numbers and early in November my turn to go arrived on the third I journeyed down the Rhine to Rotterdam on the very vessel I had been employed on for quite a time earlier in the year, the next day survived an extremely rough passage across the North Sea to Harwich and arrived at Crystal Palace where I spent the night and was granted Demobilisation Leave the next morning November the fifth, 1919 — with the princely sum of nineteen pounds in my pocket —

George's Diary

288

Captain Albert Ball by his SES, on the day my father saw him, April 1917

On the other hand, he quite amazingly remembered most of the many places where he fought and some of the dates when he was in these places. For instance, he accurately recalled he was at Candas airfield (Map 2) on Monday, April 9, 1917, when he met a pilot whom he thought might be the famous Captain Albert Ball. He was right about this, too. It was Albert Ball.

'Dangerous Work', according to Lieutenant Colonel John Starling's introduction to the book, is the only known account by an other rank of the Labour Corps experience. All other known memoirs were written by officers.

George volunteered for service in March 1917 because he believed he would get more food in the army (Britain was suffering from the U-boat blockade) than working as a docker. Also, because of his C2 medical grading (he suffered from chronic migraine) he believed that he would not be sent to the Western Front. But he very quickly found himself in Boulogne because the BEF was desperately short of manpower for labouring purposes.

Indeed, George and his comrades worked very hard for very long hours – clearing the way for light railways into the Somme region deserted by the Germans, feverishly constructing desperately needed airfields (they could build a new one within a fortnight), clearing Contay Forest (north-east of Albert – Map 2) for front line timber and repairing crucial roads.

Later in 1917 he was in the Ypres Salient digging ditches for cables in deep mud beside the Yser Canal (resulting in trench foot and more migraine – he had his fair share of wounds and illnesses), being shot at by the Red Baron, digging more ditches for water pipes, trying to excavate liquid mud at Kitchener Wood for a foundation to support a super long-range gun.

During the great German offensive of Spring 1918 Labour Companies were extensively used to dig miles of new trenches. They were also armed to meet this critical situation. George then had his bout of Spanish flu.

When he got home leave in August 1918 he became inadvertently mixed up (along with hundreds of other soldiers waiting to get home) in a mutiny in Calais. George was eventually part of the Army of Occupation (B.A.O.R) in Cologne until December 1919. He had quite a few adventures here, too, including trips to and from Rotterdam on a paddle steamer. It is easy to understand that the First World War for men of my father's generation was the outstanding event of their lives.

WEIR, NEIL (1895–1967)
Mud and Bodies
The War Diaries & Letters of Captain N. A. C. Weir
1914–1920
Edited by Saul David
Frontline Books, 2013

Neil Weir's grandson, Mike Burns, discovered these documents in ten trunks left by Neil. There was a red book, slightly smaller than A4 size, entitled 'War Diary, 1914–1920. Personal recollections. Please do not destroy but use can be made of notices for the purpose of record, Neil Weir'. There were also a lot of letters, photographs and a kilted uniform.

Mike had no idea that his grandfather had fought in the Great War, indeed, had commanded a company of a Scottish Regiment. A friend of Mike's mentioned the trunks to a military historian, Saul David. He has edited this book, combining diary, letters and photographs, correcting a few errors and adding historical commentaries.

The diary is made up of period (often monthly) entries, with some important dates. It was probably written whilst Neil was in hospital in late 1916, and is thus more of a memoir than a diary.

Neil was educated at Oxford University and commissioned into the 10th (Service) Battalion of The Argyll and Sutherland Highlanders on August 26, 1914. It went to France on May 11, 1915. Soon after this Neil was promoted to the rank of Lieutenant and put in command of B Company (he was only 19 years old). He was also appointed Battalion Bombing Officer, in charge of the supply and deposition of grenades, mainly used to clear enemy dug-outs after offensives or raids.

The battalion was sent to the Armentières (Maps 1 & 4) sector, mainly constructing new trenches. It moved to the front line near Festubert (Map 4) in June. Here again the defences needed considerable attention. Neil's first battle action was the disappointing failure at Loos (Lens sector – Map 1) in late September. He was highly critical of the lack of direction by senior staff, and shortages of ammunition, bombs, artillery support, food and care of the numerous wounded. His Company came under severe shelling on September 26 (he was dazed by one explosion). On the 27th the Germans drove them back to their original front line.

In October the battalion moved north to the Ypres trenches at The Bluff. It suffered a lot of casualties when the Germans exploded a huge mine under their trenches. In November and December they were in Sanctuary Wood, enduring daily bombardment from shells and mortar and gas – with the trenches continuously damaged and requiring repair.

In the New Year 1916 the battalion moved to Ploegsteert Wood (Map 4 – Neil had Christmas at home). He remembered that the village had not been shelled; he thought this was because of the large number of spies living there. The British trench defences were again far inferior to those of the enemy, almost completely lacking in communication and support lines, which made the movement of troops to and from the front line a hazardous business. Nonetheless, British senior command demanded positive action in the front line – raids on the enemy. They appeared to be able to hear British telephone messages and know in advance about the raids. The German response was always heavy shelling and machine gun fire, making life very difficult for the battalion.

He was in this area for many months – well into June. Neil was now a very young Captain. They then came out of this line for 'rest', which in fact entailed a long journey south and training for the coming battle in the Somme region. They were not part of the initial assaults on July 1 but came up to Montauban (Map 3) a few days later, again, to very poor trenches, being shelled continuously and in very wet weather.

They were in the next stage of the battle – on July 14, the assault on Longueval (Maps 2 & 3) and Delville Wood (Map 3). Weir led his Company over no man's land, first at walking pace and then at the double into an inferno of noise and yellow smoke. At one stage they went so quickly that they ran into the shelling of their own artillery. They captured the German front line and stopped the neighbouring Black Watch troops from murdering German prisoners.

Although the Argyll and Sutherland Highlanders were far forward units on their flanks were not so successful, so they were shelled heavily from each side. Their bombers were even further ahead and as they were returning were fired on by their own infantry, who thought they were Germans (July 15).

By the 17th, however, there was progress as Delville Wood was captured. But the enemy was fighting back hard. Delville Wood was lost again. The battalion came out of the line on the 19th.

It was below Vimy Ridge (Map 1) until September but plans to storm the Ridge were postponed till 1917. They came back to the Somme after the assault with tanks on Flers (Maps 2 & 3), more successful and less costly than July 1 (although on a smaller scale). The plan for October was to advance towards Bapaume (Map 2).

Captain Weir prepared to take part in the attempt to take the Butte de Warlencourt (Map 3) but he was badly burnt in the upper left leg by a German flare discharged by accident in his own trench (October 9). He arrived at a hospital in Oxford on October 17.

The first inclination of doctors here was to amputate but the ambrine wax treatment not only eased the terrible pain but also saved the leg. He left hospital in December but was found unfit for service. He spent the next 15 months working with officer cadets.

He applied for a permanent commission but was turned down apparently because there were too few vacancies and Neil was too young to be considered. He then took staff learning courses and became a company commander in the 3rd (Reserve) Battalion.

WEST, ARTHUR (1891–1917)
Diary of a Dead Officer
Being the Posthumous Papers of Arthur Graeme West
Greenhill Books, 2007

Arthur West enlisted enthusiastically for the Public Schools' Battalion in January 1915 after several earlier applications, which had been rejected on account of his poor eyesight.

Shortly after the war ended Arthur's friend, C. E. M. Joad, a militant pacifist, published this first edition of 'Diary of a Dead Officer' (1918 – 1919)'. This consisted of extracts from Arthur's diaries plus a selection of his poems.

Arthur recalled that the main motivation for him as he joined up was the desire for a commission. The battalion went to France in November 1915. He wrote about 'The First Time in France' on November 26. On this day he read the 'Odyssey' and tried to relate it to war.

On December 7 he marched with his comrades through flooded fields in the open because the communication trenches had too much water in them. His first trench consisted of broken sections of it with no parados (back wall). There were support troops behind but they were cut off by a swathe of barbed wire. In front, the Germans were 200 yards away, and they could reach Arthur and his pals much quicker than the British support. Luckily, they appeared to be content with sniping and having machine guns trained on the British trench.

Luckily, too, this was strictly temporary, hasty protection, and they were moved to somewhere with corrugated iron roofs. Soon after Arthur wrote on 'Thoughts about Death' and experienced overwhelming desires to stay alive. He sent a letter to the 'Lad' on February 12, 1916 to report the death of a friend as he stood next to Arthur. There was also a description of a ghastly night patrol in the stinking horrors and heaps in no man's land.

But he was more 'interested' than afraid. Anyway, 'spring was manifest'. He had never developed a hatred of anybody and he regarded the Hun in 'a spirit of amicable fraternity'.

Late in March 1916 Arthur went to Scotland to train for a commission. Part two of this book is a series of diary extracts about his time there, especially about a thoroughly horrid Sergeant Major. He wrote that he was making progress in his aspiration for stoicism – as opposed to depression.

But stoicism did not work. Although commissioned in the Oxford and Buckingham Light Infantry and posted back to the Western Front on August 8, 1916, he 'now found himself disbelieving utterly in Christianity…', and wrote later, 'what right has anybody to demand of me that I should give up my chance of obtaining happiness?' – notes written at Box Hill Station on August,19, 1916.

He became determined to desert and even kill himself. He wrote to the adjutant of his battalion to say he would not be coming back. He either did not send this or retrieved it in some way.

He returned to France; on the 17th, in a foetid trench full of corpses drifting into a comatose state of mind. The smell of rum made him feel even sicker. It was worse at night and daylight made them all feel a little better. But this came at the expense of a gigantic German high explosives bombardment (it lasted for 5 hours). The only way he could deal with these terrified men around him was to stay quiet. They jibbered quietly in fear – trembling and shaking as one group after another was buried beneath heaps of wet soil. Arthur led the survivors to try and dig them out – mostly dead, muddy, grey masses. They sat like animals going to market in a cage, staring into distance, silent, shaking, incoherent with terror.

Arthur remained 'cool and useful'. He found himself not afraid of being hit because death or wounding would bring an end to his war. He did fear the actual initial impact of mutilation.

They were at 'G…' (probably Guillemont – Map 3) and near the 'River A' (Ancre?) on September 25. 'T… Wood' on September 29 would be Trones Wood (he was in the thick of some of the worst fighting during the battle of the Somme). 'Seven men killed by a shell as soon as we got to the trench: beastly sight!'

On October 1, 1916 he received information about a forthcoming series of lectures by Bertrand Russell (being harshly treated by the War

Office at that time). 'It showed the strength of the conscientious objector and pacifist movements'.

'But people will not lift a finger to even mould their own lives outside the rules of the majority' (October 5). He was in 'C…' on the 7th, probably Corbie (Map 2) – a nice patisserie, a large painted hall, cages of canaries and great dogs… song of girls.' He said he was happy (November 3).

He attended an officers' course in January 1917. Course members could not understand what he was saying. They were narrow-minded and racist. The ones who could shout the loudest won arguments. 'How I loved them all'.

Arthur West was killed by a sniper's bullet at Stand-To on April 3, 1917.

WHITTAKER, WILLIAM (1897–1983)
Somewhere in France
A Tommy's Guide to Life on the Western Front
William and Geoffrey Whittaker
The History Press (Stroud), 2014

This publication is based on the very large number of letters written by William Whittaker to his parents – 270 in all have survived.

In pristine condition, these came into the possession of William's grandson, Geoffrey, after William's death. He has edited this book, adding explanatory sections and more detail about his grandfather's life.

William was educated at Burnley Grammar School and was working as a clerk at the county court when the war began. He joined the Royal Army Medical Corps early in 1915, lying about his age. He served for the remainder of the war. He arrived in Havre on September 2 and travelled on by train to Beaunainville.

William was working with an RAMC sanitary section (41st). These men took care of waste disposal and general cleanliness, especially of water – in very unhygienic conditions. Their world was one of latrines, de-lousing, battles against insects etc. etc. Some of it was highly skilled: William worked for a time in a huge filtering system dealing with water from baths and laundries. A lot of it was not safe work: sanitary men were often required to be in the front line trenches. William's Section had lost 20 casualties by April 1916. Sir Douglas Haig strongly praised the work of the RAMC sanitary sections: front line health would have completely broken down without them. The comradeship of these men was as strong as amongst infantrymen. And there were the characters, too – Woolfe the Timid, Bradley the Orator, Mills the Pessimist etc.

Diaries by soldiers were forbidden in case important information fell into enemy hands; perhaps that was why many of them set down their experiences and reactions in letters, as in William's case. But the other pitfall here was censorship: letters could just as easily go astray. So there was likely to be friction between censoring officers and keen letter-writers, and this is what clearly happened in William's case and may have prevented his promotion (he only became a lance corporal) because he was obviously a skilled and hard-working member of his section.

On January 9, 1916 William (or 'Will' or 'Willie') complained how difficult it was 'to concoct a decent sized letter… considering that one is forbidden to mention the names of places or military detail'. He tried a code for a time but abandoned the idea because it was so risky. There was obviously constant friction with his C.O. For instance, he accused Will of writing a 'defeatist' letter in December 1916.

Indeed, censors were on a constant look-out for comments about lack of military progress or the terrible conditions troops had to endure. Anything optimistic, of course, was waved through with a flag. Will would obviously have had no trouble with 'A very popular feeling is that we should have peace before next autumn' (December 16 1916). The men, in general, in any case, did not want to alarm their folks at home.

Will was often under enemy shelling or bombing. 'Fritz has been shelling heavily all around us but good luck still favours us' (January 8, 1916). 'I know what it is like to be under bomb-dropping aeroplanes' (January 14, 1917).

Will also wrote about philosophy, politics, morality, and the news and journalists, as well as the more mundane topics of food, drink and tobacco. There was also material on entertainments, much etc., etc. What a letter-writer!

WILLIAMSON, FATHER BENEDICT
'Happy Days' in France & Flanders
With the 47th & 49th Divisions
The Naval & Military Press, 2009

Lieutenant Colonel Rowland Feilding wrote an introduction to this 1922 account. He revealed that Father Benedict was known to everyone as 'Happy Days' because of his 'unquenchable optimism: he lived 'in a world of sunshine' (amazing when you learn of the amount of rain which fell on him).

This is presented as a memoir but is squarely based on a daily diary. Thus the chronology is made very clear to the reader. Father Benedict left for France on May 22, 1917 and was posted to No. 10 Casualty Clearing Station. An assault on Messines Ridge (Map 4) was imminent and it was expected that the CCS would shortly start to receive many thousands of wounded men. His first daily duty, however, was with Captain Merriman, badly hit at Poperinghe. Father anointed him with Holy Oils.

Even before Messines the Ypres Salient was delivering thousands of wounded and Father was constantly on call giving the Holy Sacrament and Holy Communion. 'Our boys', he recorded, 'bore their agonies of pain as hope of a Blighty rested with them'. The nursing sisters were amazingly devoted and courageous (often enduring shelling). A constant duty for Father Benedict was to say Mass. As Messines got under way the average daily death rate at the CCS reached 70.

He moved to a field ambulance at Zelobes (west of Neuve Chapelle – Maps 1 & 4); he walked around to meet all the Catholics in their billets. But his major destination was Nieuport (Map 1), where an attempt to open a northern flank for the Battle of Ypres was being tried. But Nieuport was a real hell hole because the massed German artillery had the British force pinned down in the shattered town.

The British had thus turned the town into a fortress, with trenches in the streets and strongpoints in buildings. Father Benedict moved around in the midst of heavy shelling, passing 'Suicide Corner'. The advanced troops north of the river were pinned down in their position in the 'Redan' and to get across to them was perilous because the bridges were under constant fire. But he managed it. No Catholic was going to miss out if he could help it. In the CCS he witnessed the unsparing devotion to duty of the surgeon, Captain Weeks, working from the light of one candle!

Men came to Father Benedict all the time for confession and Holy Communion and so he was never really off duty and snatched a few hours sleep where and when he could. He even helped to rescue wounded men. It was a desperate situation and when he got away on August 17 he was a very relieved man to escape from the shells and the incessant rain.

There followed some 'quiet days' at La Panne (near Dunkirk), where there was a new danger from air raids. Father Gordon was killed in his billet. Father Benedict left with his division on September 23 to go to beyond St Omer but they were immediately recalled to Ypres, where the battle was also becoming a desperate struggle.

He said mass in the concrete pill boxes beyond St. Jean, where they crouched down under the light of one candle. The priests moved around all the time getting as near as possible to as many Catholics as possible. Father Benedict met a group of New Zealanders. "Any Catholics here?" he called. "Step aside and you can have Absolution and Holy Communion." Groups of soldiers came over. At the advanced dressing station nearby men poured in from the 'most terrible fighting of the war' (October).

It is interesting that he comments on the Labour Companies working on the roads without shelter. One of these men was my father (see George Weeks). Father Benedict walked up the lethal Menin Road to the advanced dressing station before dawn to miss the daily 'iron ration' from the German artillery. The next day he was at Hell Fire Corner: men were so pleased to see him. "God bless you, Father," they said. The following days he was amongst the shell holes at Zonnebeke. This brave man walked around in the midst of some of the most ferocious fighting in this war.

He had a little leave in England (even raining there!) then returned to the Menin Road in December. He moved with his division to near Albert (Map 2) to work from a field ambulance. The Battle of Cambrai (Map

1) had just ended and there were many, many wounded men to see. He went to the trenches at Ribecourt (south-east of Albert – Map 2). By this time he could hardly see a yard in front of him because of the effects of poison gas, but this not deter him. It was hard enough finding your way in this maze of trenches even if you could see well. Everywhere he went he would try to hold Holy Communion in trench dug-outs.

His work during the big German offensive took on new aspects as he needed to move around between as many advanced dressing stations as possible as the retreat gathered momentum. The French people were panicking and he tried to console them but they broke 'into such lamentation that conversation was impossible'. He tried to find machine gunners and artillery batteries so that Catholics amongst them would not miss out. The situation was very confused but he just carried on getting to as many as possible. It took a whole day to visit a battalion. He would even take Mass and Holy Communion for American troops. In the German retreat which followed Father Benedict came across more and more enemy men to give Holy Communion. He gave a moving account of a few hours with a young soldier sentenced to death because of his habit of wandering away from his duty station. This boy had an 'uncontrollable desire to wander'. He was not afraid of bullets and shells but he could not stop moving away. Father Benedict concluded 'It is indeed a great thing to have lived to see these days'.

WILLIAMSON, WALTER (born 1888)
A Tommy at Ypres
Walter's War: The Diary and Letters of Walter Williamson
Compiled by Doreen Priddy
Amberley Publishing, 2013

Walter Williamson arrived in Havre on December 2, 1916 (aged 34) with a draft of the 6th Battalion of the Cheshire Regiment. He wrote a long diary entry on many days until his demobilisation in February 1919. On other days there were just a few lines and some days were grouped together. There were gaps in the entries. It obviously depended on where Walter was and how busy he was. However, as a signaller he had more opportunity to write than the infantryman. His granddaughter, Doreen Priddy, also included many of the long letters Walter wrote to his wife.

Walter came from a middle class family in Oldham and had received a good secondary education and had worked for many years. He had a strong interest in music and the theatre. His long diary entries are quite amazingly protracted, with masses of detail about comrades, officers, his work and the travels of the battalion. He is often amusing and very perceptive, and like Alfred Burrage and other older soldiers, not averse to standing up for himself with officers.

Some idea of how much these battalions moved about is given by Doreen's list at the beginning of the book – 146 places in all (some, of course, visited more than once). Their first camp was near Poperinghe (Maps 1 & 4) but Williamson (largely because he could write his name and address quickly) was taken off for signals training at Vlamertinghe (Map 4). He passed his exams in February and was in the Ypres Salient trenches in March by Hill 60, housed in a deep signaller's communication tunnel.

A perennial task for the signals section was mending wires broken by shells. To do this Walter and fellow signallers had to crawl along the trenches trying to find the broken wire as enemy shells whistled overhead. Also, he got lice and sent home for Harrison's Pomade; Walter was short of hair and commented to his wife that the Pomade might not restore it.

In reserve in Ypres still entailed all-night trips to the front line armed with a pick and a shovel. 'Rest', too, still brought plenty of digging, carrying etc., as well as falling into very wet shell holes. 'Wagner at The Halle was only a tame affair' (March 25, 1917).

Rest further afield at Herzeele over the French border brought more relief, except for an old French woman who swore vividly at any Tommy she encountered. One of his mates lost his false teeth in the mud. Getting new ones was quite a job!

Like my dad (George Weeks), later in 1917, Walter helped to dig dugouts in the banks of the Yser ('Eyesore') Canal. They both did work on the roads, too, although Walter's efforts were in preparation for the Third Battle of Ypres whereas my dad repaired those damaged in the battle itself. It was clear to Walter from all this work that a big battle was in the pipeline.

The 6th Battalion was out near the French coast for training in fine weather in June (pretty villages of Coulomby and Moule – west of St Omer). Then it was back to the dangerous work by the Yser Canal (the Germans knew something was brewing and shelled the area intensely). Blessed training resumed.

The big battle duly opened up on July 30. The Cheshires moved forward after the massive Allied bombardment, behind waves of more advanced troops. Walter crossed the infamous Steenbeke stream by St. Julien. German machine gunners and snipers in shell holes were a menace. Signalling back to HQ became impossible and Walter's mate Pat had to scramble on foot in great danger.

The battalion's losses, in common with many other units, were very bad and Walter became totally isolated out in the wilderness. He ended August 1 in a narrow ex-German trench with its sides collapsing under heavy rain. Staying put risked being hit by a shell or being shot by a sniper so he was forced to make a dash for it over the shattered terrain pockmarked with deep holes and filled with water. Headlines in the English newspapers for August 1 read 'Day of Victory in Flanders'.

After getting new equipment Walter sat in a reserve trench for 4 days and then the Cheshires went into reserve with drafts of men to replace the heavy losses joining them. An officer complained to Walter about the enormous length of his letters home, which he had to read and censor, but Walter pointed out that there was no army regulation restricting the length of letters.

Walter was in and out of the Salient in September and October but not called upon for more heroics like those he suffered in the Battle of St. Julien. He enjoyed a fair amount of entertainment in Poperinghe (Maps 1 & 4): as a devotee of music and theatre he much appreciated these trips to the place which to Tommy was all that was left of civilized life.

Many of the incidents Walter recorded remind me of my father's war diary. They were in the same area, mention the same places. They both arrived in a new camp only for nearby enormous British guns to blast forth and give them the shakes.

At the end of 1917 Walter spent much time around and in Poperinghe. He had two stripes up by now. Like Dad, again, he was delayed in Calais going home for some Christmas leave and only managed to get away on the 24th. When he got back in January the battalion was largely suffering from trench feet and the C.O. and the MO were arguing fiercely about how many men should be allowed to go to hospital.

At the end of April they went down to a much quieter Somme front, glad to see the back of a dangerous and arduous Ypres Salient, despite the pleasures of Poperinghe. But then the shock of the German offensive arrived and everyone was on the run pursued by machine-gunning planes. They moved north to around St Omer in April and fought again in great danger. On November 11 Walter the signaller received the message he had been waiting for: 'Hostilities cease at 11.00 hours'.